Looking Back at the
Spanish Civil War

Looking Back at the Spanish Civil War

The International Brigade Memorial Trust's
Len Crome Memorial Lectures, 2002-2010

EDITED BY

Jim Jump

Lawrence & Wishart
LONDON 2010

Published in collaboration with the
Cañada Blanch Centre for Contemporary Spanish Studies
and the International Brigade Memorial Trust

Lawrence and Wishart Limited
99a Wallis Road
London
E9 5LN

Published in collaboration with the Cañada Blanch Centre for Contemporary
Spanish Studies and the International Brigade Memorial Trust.

First published 2010

British Library Cataloguing in Publication Data.
A catalogue record for this book is available from the British Library

ISBN 9781 907103 117

Text setting E-type, Liverpool
Printed and bound by ImprintDigital, Exeter

Contents

Introduction *Jim Jump*   7

1 *Helen Graham*   13
   The Return of Republican Memory

2 *Paul Preston*   31
   'No Soldier': The Courage and Comradeship of Dr Len Crome

3 *Francisco J Romero Salvadó*   45
   Killing the Dream: The Spanish Labyrinth Revisited, 1898-1939

4 *Richard Baxell*   65
   Three Months in Spain: The British Battalion at Madrigueras
   and Jarama from January to March 1937

5 *Enrique Moradiellos*   93
   Albion's Perfidy: The British Government and the Spanish
   Civil War

6 *Angela Jackson*   111
   Beyond the Battlefield: A Cave Hospital in the Spanish
   Civil War

7 *Ángel Viñas*   129
   September 1936: Stalin's Decision to Support the Spanish
   Republic

8 *Richard Baxell*   157
   Laurie Lee in the International Brigades: Writer or Fighter?

9 *Paul Preston*   177
   The Crimes of Franco

10 *Julián Casanova*   199
   The Spanish Civil War: History and Memory

Notes on contributors   209
Index   215

Introduction

Jim Jump

More than seventy years on, the Spanish Civil War still generates intense interest and controversy. We can begin to appreciate why by reading the contributions in this book. The range of the subject matter is vast and the topics always engaging: from the timing and motivation of Stalin's decision to become involved in the war – including the creation of the International Brigades – to the participation of the young writer and International Brigade volunteer Laurie Lee; from the bloodthirsty repression instigated by General Franco to the malevolent calculations of British foreign policy; from the heroic efforts of the International Brigade medical services to the complex factors in Spain's own history that sparked a conflict that was a prelude to the Second World War.

This collection of essays brings together the first nine Len Crome Memorial Lectures, which are given each year at the Imperial War Museum, London. Some have been published as individual booklets by the International Brigade Memorial Trust (IBMT), though not widely distributed. They are supplemented here by a tribute to the man who has given his name to the lecture series: the young doctor who, while working in Blackburn, decided in September 1936 to go to Spain, where he served with distinction in the medical services of the Spanish Republic for the next two years. The lectures began in 2002, the year after Len Crome died at the age of ninety-two, and the first three were organised by his younger son, Peter Crome, with help from the IBMT. Originally that was all that was planned. But such was their success – itself testimony to the continuing public interest in the Spanish Civil War – that the IBMT agreed to make the lectures an annual fixture and take on full responsibility for them.

What the written page cannot convey is the lively atmosphere of the lectures and the unique flavour of each occasion. The question-

Veterans at the International Brigades memorial, Jubilee Gardens, London, in 2006; from left: Bob Doyle, Lou Kenton, Sam Lesser, Paddy Cochrane, Penny Feiwel, Jack Jones and Jack Edwards. Courtesy Jess Hurd/reportdigital.co.uk.

and-answer or round-table sessions that follow the lecture are often as stimulating as the main talk itself. Speakers bring their own personal styles. Some perform forensic dissections of diplomatic policy, others deliver passionate denunciations of Francoism and its neo-revisionist adherents. On International Women's Day, Helen Graham spoke about the ghosts of the Republican dead against the haunting backdrop of a portrait of Amparo Barayón, murdered by the fascists in October 1936 for the crime of being an emancipated 'new woman'. In 2007 Julián Casanova showed newly restored footage of the Barcelona funeral of anarchist leader Buenaventura Durruti in November 1936 before making a plea for reconciliation through knowledge and a renunciation of violence – and in doing so he contributes a fitting epilogue to this book. Ángel Viñas lectured without any notes whatsoever – his chapter here was written afterwards, though it covers much of the same ground of his talk. Richard Baxell brought the International Brigade volunteers to life by playing clips of TV interviews with them and extracts of recordings from the Imperial War Museum's extensive Spanish Civil War sound archive. The popularity of the lecture has also meant that the venue has switched from a conference room in the museum to its much larger cinema auditorium. And what began as a stand-alone lecture has now become a full day of events, including book launches, film screenings and evening socials.

Most importantly of all, the proceedings have been animated by the presence of surviving International Brigade volunteers, though in sadly dwindling numbers with every year. In three memorable instances, veterans were there to hear talks on historical events in which they had participated: Penny Feiwel as a nurse who had worked with Dr Reggie Saxton and other medical staff who featured in Angela Jackson's description of the Battle of the Ebro cave hospital, and Bob Doyle as the volunteer who, as Richard Baxell recounted in his lecture on Laurie Lee, escorted the young writer to the International Brigade base at Albacete. Finally, in the audience for Baxell's second lecture, on the British Battalion's baptism of fire at Jarama in February 1937, were Jack Edwards, who was wounded during the battle, and Sam Lesser, who was in Spain at the time, though still recovering from wounds sustained in earlier fighting while serving in a French battalion. The first few lectures were chaired by the IBMT's president, the late Jack Jones, another veteran of the Battle of the Ebro; more recently the task has been carried out by Paul Preston, an IBMT patron who is widely regarded as the world's foremost historian of the Spanish Civil War.

These and the other International Brigaders had the moral clarity in the 1930s to see what their own government failed or refused to see: that fascism had to be defeated in Spain. They were proved right by subsequent international events, though their reward in the immediate post-war decades was in many cases to be vilified as communist dupes, while Franco was rehabilitated as an anti-communist ally of the US. Thankfully the work of historians such as Preston and others represented in this book has done much to put the record straight. Each in their own fields of inquiry has demonstrated the essential truths about the Spanish Civil War: that it was a conflict between the legally constituted and democratically elected Spanish Republic and a group of rebellious army officers – the so-called 'Nationalists' – who were supported by Hitler and Mussolini; that the Republic's defeat was sealed by the arms embargo enforced by Britain and the other Western democracies; and that the volunteers who came to the aid of the Republic did so with enormous idealism and self-sacrifice.

It is worth noting that the success of the lecture series has run in parallel to the emergence and remarkable growth of the IBMT, the association that keeps alive the memory and spirit of the 2,500 men and women from Britain and Ireland who served in the International Brigades during the civil war of 1936-39. More than 500 of them died in Spain, and there are now several memorials to the volunteers in the British Isles and Spain. These include the national memorial in Jubilee Gardens, London, where the IBMT holds an annual commemoration each July. The IBMT was formed in 2001 through a merger of the International Brigade Association, an organisation exclusively for veterans, and the Friends of the International Brigades. It now has its own website (www.international-brigades.org.uk), an electronic news service, a regular newsletter and an annual calendar of events – including the Len Crome Memorial Lecture.

Spain, meanwhile, has seen an even more extraordinary explosion of interest in the Spanish Civil War over the same period, specifically in those who sided with the Republic and in doing so paid with their lives. The process has come to be known as the *recuperación de la memoria histórica* and in 2007 was enshrined in law by the Ley de la Memoria Histórica which, among other things, conferred unconditional Spanish citizenship on surviving International Brigade veterans and provided public funds for the exhumation and reburial of the remains of victims of Franco's reign of terror that lie in unmarked graves. This phenomenon – which in differing ways is vividly described by several of the contributors to this book – is a belated but nonetheless welcome rejection of the *pacto de silencio* that accompanied the restoration of democracy in Spain following Franco's death in 1975.

My thanks for help in producing this book go to the Crome family, to Marlene Sidaway and the other officers of the IBMT, to Sally Davison at Lawrence & Wishart and Paul Preston at the Cañada Blanch Centre for Contemporary Spanish Studies and, above all, to the authors themselves. They are among the finest historians of the Spanish Civil War in Britain and Spain. The IBMT is justifiably proud too that, through the Len Crome Memorial Lecture and its other activities, it is playing its part in ensuring that this crucial chapter in twentieth century history continues to be remembered and studied and that the role of those who supported the Republic, not least Len Crome and the others who joined the International Brigades, is properly acknowledged.

The Return of Republican Memory

Helen Graham

In 1989, the North American-raised son of the Spanish Republican novelist Ramón Sender published an account of his own and his sister's search for the remains of their mother, Amparo Barayón, and for the truth about her imprisonment and extra-judicial murder. She was killed at the age of thirty-two, in rebel-held Zamora in north-west Spain, the Catholic heartland of Old Castile, in the early months of Spain's civil war. The book, called simply *A Death in Zamora*, charts an extraordinary odyssey in time, space and memory.[1] On his return to Spain in the 1980s, Amparo's son, also called Ramón, discovers he has a whole extended Spanish family, which emerges like a lost continent, bearing with it the history, the traces, the unquiet ghost of his mother. He meets Amparo's niece, Magdalena Maes, who in 1942 at the age of seventeen had, in an act of tremendous courage, with her own hands removed her beloved aunt's remains from the common grave where they lay, reburying them in the family tomb.

> *The bad thing [Magdalena tells Ramón] was that they [had] put quicklime in with her. There was no coffin or anything, just the body and the quicklime.*

For this act of temerity, even though Amparo's niece had sought and received the requisite official authorisation, she and her family received anonymous death threats.

A Death in Zamora is an extraordinary book that deserves to be much more widely known and read. It tells in microcosm almost every profound thing one could want to say about the civil war in Spain, as a *civil* war; its complex social and cultural causes and its tremendous costs in the long aftermath of uncivil peace, up to and well beyond the death of Franco in 1975. Above all, its narrative paves the way for the

13

Amparo Barayón.

long, slow and painful recuperation of Republican memory, the memory of the defeated, that is only now exploding in Spain: the most well-known examples of this phenomenon are probably the campaign to open common graves to identify the remains of those extra-judicially murdered by the Francoist forces both during and after the war; the campaign for recognition and compensation by those used as forced labour by the regime; and most recently the television documentary about the lost children of Francoism, most notoriously those who were taken from their mothers, Republican women prisoners, and forcibly adopted by Francoist families – which for us now immediately recalls the shades of later violations in Videla's Argentina or Pinochet's Chile.

In the title of this memoir, *A Death in Zamora*, one death stands for the many, just as in Michael Ondaatje's great novel of a different civil war, *Anil's Ghost*, Sri Lankan forensic scientist Anil has to identify her 'ghost' – the anonymous victim of a recent and violent death. The ghost has to be given a history because he is the representative of all those lost voices: 'to give him a name would name the rest'. And in an important sense that is also true for Amparo Barayón in the case of Spain. For the tens of thousands of people killed in the Francoist repression had one thing overwhelmingly in common with each other: they had benefited in some way from the redistribution of power under the Republic. Local studies of the repression demonstrate quite clearly that those targeted the length and breadth of rebel Spain were precisely those constituencies on whom the Republic's reforming legislation had conferred social and political rights for the first time in their lives. Conversely, the many who supported Spain's military rebels (whether we take this 'many' as individuals or as entire social constituencies) had in common a fear of where change was leading – whether their fears were of material or psychological loss: of wealth, professional status, established social and political hierarchies, religious or sexual (gendered) certainties or a mixture of these things.

And the assuaging of this overwhelming sense of fear was a very important element driving the Francoist repression. Horrifying acts of repression took place everywhere in rebel-held territory, including in many places – of which Zamora was one – where the military rebels were in control from the outset, and where there was no military or armed resistance, or even any political resistance to speak of – in short, where one would be hard-pressed to find a 'war-situation' at all (at least according to a conventional definition of 'war'). Nor is it feasible to argue that in these areas the initial violence stemmed, as it did in the Republican zone, from 'uncontrollable' groups. In Republican Spain the military coup provoked the total collapse of the state apparatus. But in the rebel-held zone there was no collapse of public order. It would have been possible at any time for fascist Falangist or clerical Carlist militia and other volunteers of the right to have been disciplined by the military authorities that from the beginning underwrote public order. But not only did this not happen: instead, as the research of the past decade has made clear, the military actively recruited thousands of civilian vigilantes to carry out a dirty war.[2] Thus military and civilian-instigated repression existed in a complementary relationship. This was the beginning of the 'fellowship of blood', of the complicity of whole sectors of Spanish society, 'ordinary Spaniards' who became enmeshed in the murder of their compatriots.

Who was targeted by this repression? As already suggested, it was all sorts of people, whether or not they were active combatants: the rural landless, but also many rural smallholders, above all lease-holding farmers who had achieved new tenancy rights under the Republic, urban workers, progressive teachers, trade unionists and 'the new woman'. The military rebels and their civilian supporters were redefining 'the enemy' as entire sectors of society that were perceived as 'out of control' because they were beyond the control of traditional forms of discipline and 'order'.

I mention 'the new woman' because a pathological fear and loathing of emancipated women was a very powerful motive force among the rebels. Amparo Barayón wasn't just killed in lieu of her husband, the famous Republican writer Ramón Sender, as many commentators have previously claimed. No, she was killed, as it were, in her own right. For Amparo was a modern woman. In 1930, as Spain's monarchy crumbled, Amparo had, aged twenty-six, left the conservative provincial backwater of Zamora and gone to Madrid, the 'big city', to become independent. She had found work as a telephone switchboard operator – a new employment opportunity which was itself an indicator of Spain's burgeoning modernity. In Madrid she supported herself, she lived independently, educating herself both politically and culturally, and she met Ramón and began living with him – which was quite something for those times, even in urban metropolitan Spain, for Madrid was not Berlin or Paris. Although back in Zamora they wouldn't have known about Sender, the very fact that Amparo had spread her wings would have inspired horror among the pillars of provincial society – and also among conservative members of her own family, who saw her as on the road to damnation. And it was the bigotry of some of these family members that would be responsible for denouncing Amparo to the military authorities in Zamora. This happened in the late summer of 1936, after she had fled back to her hometown with her two young children in the aftermath of the military rising. She did this in the mistaken assumption that home would mean safety – a mistake she shared with the poet Federico García Lorca, and with many thousands of anonymous victims of the repression.

As a result of the denunciation Amparo was imprisoned in late August 1936. What happened to her then takes us to the heart of what the rebel repression sought to achieve. She was interrogated with the express intention of making her 'recant'. In her case the objective was that she make a formal denunciation of her husband, Ramón Sender (her husband by a Republican civil marriage ceremony, though Amparo herself was a practising Catholic). She was subjected to extraordinary pressure – including from a priest, who directed a torrent of abuse at her, and, after she had made her final confession, refused her absolution. In other words Amparo Barayón was subjected to a form of sustained psychological torture, the object of which was to humiliate her and ultimately to break her. She had avoided the public forms of violent humiliation commonly visited upon Republican women the length and breadth of rebel-held Spain – the head shaving, the 'purging' with castor oil and public parading; and she was not tortured and raped, as many, many other female Republican prisoners were in the course of police interrogations. But the object was the same: to break her. Then one day her name featured on the list of those the death squads had come by night to 'take out' of gaol in the deadly *sacas*. On 11 October 1936, nearly three months after the military coup against the Republic, Amparo Barayón was taken from the town gaol to the cemetery. There, by lantern light, they shot her, burying her where she fell, in a common grave next to the cemetery wall.

We know of Amparo's fate from several specific sources – including from the priest in question, who gave an account to members of her family days after she had been killed. Most notable, however, is the testimony of two of the women who were in gaol with Amparo, who were tracked down in the 1980s by her son Ramón. One of them, Pilar Fidalgo, who was herself saved from execution by a prisoner exchange, wrote her own account of her imprisonment, which was published in 1939, outside Spain. Before the exchange could take place, however, her baby, who had been imprisoned with her, had succumbed to illness and died. Fidalgo was one of many Republican women to be imprisoned with their babies or young children – both during and after the war; and in these massively overcrowded and insanitary conditions such deaths were not an unusual occurrence (both inside the gaols and in the transportation to or between gaols). Indeed this seems to have been part of the punishment for their gender transgression. One prison official remarked to Fidalgo that 'red' women had forfeited their right to nourish their young, while there are many accounts of police interrogators remarking pointedly that 'red' women should have had more sense of responsibility than to have had children – because 'reds are without rights'. There were also cases of women being imprisoned in an advanced state of pregnancy, their executions being delayed until after their confinement. For children who survived, the price of nourishment (via Francoist social welfare organisations) often involved what Fidalgo herself described in her 1939 memoir as 'moral suffering': 'obliging orphans to sing the songs of the murderers of their father; to wear the uniform of those who have executed him; and to curse the dead and blaspheme his memory'.[3]

If we can think past the sheer horror of these events – as historians, eventually, always have to do – we must ask what was going on here, what did these things mean? To answer that question we clearly need to focus on the purpose of habitual physical and psychological torture. Why was there such a need to humiliate or to break the enemy, publicly or otherwise? All these forms of violence (in which I include the humiliation and 'moral suffering' inflicted on Republican children who came under the tutelage of the Francoist state) were functioning as rituals through which social and political control could be re-enacted. The manner in which the 'enemy' so often met his or her death at rebel hands is also of significance here: at the start of the civil war, there were mass public executions followed by the exhibition of corpses in the streets; mass burnings of bodies;[4] and in July 1936 the quasi *auto da fe* of a socialist deputy in the Plaza Mayor of Salamanca.[5] Executions in the centre-north of the rebel zone often took place on established saints and feast days; and there was frequently an uncanny mixture of terror and fiesta – executions followed by village fêtes and dances, both of which the local population was obliged to attend. This violence served to exorcise the underlying fear of loss of control that was the subconscious linkage uniting the military rebels with their various groups of civilian supporters. When they murder the 'enemy', they are murdering change, or the threat of change. And there was an assumption, uniting the various civilian and military components of the rising, that 'Spain' could only be reborn through a blood sacrifice.[6] The widespread complicity of priests throughout Spain in the mass process of denunciation, killing and torture of those deemed opponents has to be understood in these terms – as a reassertion of control, rather than solely as an avenging response to the phenomenon of popular anticlerical violence in Republican territory.

The Franco regime's imperative of 'cleansing' repression borrowed heavily from an apocalyptic, manichean brand of Catholicism, harking back to the Counter-Reformation. In its dialectic of fire and sword, the suffering of the 'heretic', his or her 'penitence', was a necessary part of the process.[7] It was not for nothing that the Francoist agency responsible for overseeing the labour battalions of Republican prisoners in the 1940s was called the committee for the redemption of prison sentences through work.[8] This meant that people could reduce their prison sentences through labour. But note that the term used is not remission, but redemption – it is laden with Catholic significance. The interior landscape of the rebels, and of Francoism later, also contained more 'modern' discourses of disease and impurity, whereby the Republicans' 'Marxist barbarism' was explained as a lethal virus, the germ of 'anti-nation', a form of 'degeneracy' which, if not 'cleansed' out to the last trace, would contaminate the healthy body of 'Spain'. Disease equalled disorder and, more significantly, disorder equalled disease. Hence the work of Francoist military psychiatrists who carried out psychological tests on both captured International Brigade prisoners and Republican women prisoners (they were particularly interested – not to say obsessed – with the women). This work, which has only relatively recently become the object of historians' attention, has often been billed spectacularly in the press as uncovering how Francoist doctors were hunting for the 'red gene'. Certainly their methodology was as crude as this suggests. But the genetic backdrop of Francoist social Darwinism remained necessarily muted because of the evident clash with regime Catholicism. The circle was squared, however, by an all-embracing appeal to 'purification'; this is an absolutely crucial word in Francoist Spain, as it usually is in all of the barbaric episodes – whether racial or political – that inhabit Europe's dark mid-twentieth century.

In the end, what the military, Falangists and other rightist volunteers did to Republican men and women responded to something other than tactical necessity in a military conflict. There was a startling uniformity in the degradation and objectification inflicted upon Republican prisoners during and after the military conflict – in particular in the remarkable need of their captors to break (as in the case of Amparo) not only their bodies but also their minds before killing them (and, even where they were not killed, to leave them psychologically 'reconfigured' by their experience of prison/repression). All this was servicing the underlying rebels' project: to build (or 'rebuild' as they saw it) a homogenous, monolithic and hierarchised society. And it is this that leads some historians, myself included, to think that the original Francoist project was fascist – not primarily because of Axis mimicry, nor the role of the Falange, nor any specific high political analysis, but rather because of what the regime did to the defeated. Alongside Nazi Germany, Francoist Spain was the other country in which *Volksgemeinschaft* came to be realised in Europe.

For the civil war did not end with the Francoist military victory of 1 April 1939. Indeed Francoism constitutes the most notable and certainly the most enduring Western example of the reconstruction through violence of European polities, societies and nations in the mid-twentieth century – through the large-scale execution and mass imprisonment of compatriots.[9] How did this happen? How was it legitimised? In Spain, as everywhere else, it happened through what we are now coming to call 'the politics of retribution': through the creation of categories of the anti-nation, of non-persons without civil rights – in short, through the creation of the 'other', whether Jews, *Untermenschen,* enemies of the people or, in the case of Francoism, the catch-all epithet of 'red'. All the rebels' wartime political opponents were described as 'red'. But the term was also applied indiscriminately to entire social constituencies, predominantly to urban and rural workers, but also to Republican-identified intellectual and liberal professional sectors, and to women who did not conform to the rigid gender norms deemed appropriate by Francoism. In sum, in post-war Spain 'red' came to mean whomever the rebel victors chose so to label as a means of removing either their lives or their civil rights.

When the military phase of Spain's civil war ended on 1 April 1939, the Franco regime sought to institutionalise its victory and establish control through the manichean division of Spaniards into victors and vanquished, including by the manipulation of public memory. Aside from the 'cleansing' executions of the 1940s, hundreds of thousands of men, women and children spent time in prisons, reformatories, concentration camps and forced labour battalions, where, ostensibly, they were 're-educated'. This was intended to allow the reconstruction of certain sorts of political and social hierarchy that had been challenged in Spain during the 1930s. This exclusion of the defeated was inscribed in all spheres – the law, employment, education and culture, including the very organisation of everyday life.[10]

The 'sins of the fathers', in regime-speak, went on being visited on the children in various forms of civil death. Amparo Barayón's niece Magdalena, the one who reburied her, was denied access to university in spite of her first-class grades, for she was the scion of a 'diseased' family. Not only her aunt Amparo, but also two of her uncles (Amparo's brothers) had been shot as 'reds'. The defeated cast no reflection. No public space was theirs. Above all, their dead could not be publicly mourned. This necessarily produced a devastating schism between public and private memory in post-civil war Spain.

The 1980s odyssey of Ramón Sender and his sister, told in *A Death in Zamora*, ends with knowledge of the dense web of reasons for their mother's death and, through it, of the complex dynamics of the civil war itself.[11] That knowledge could not expunge for them the enormous moral responsibility of those implicated. But worse, nor could it bring solace, because the conditions of Spain's transition to democracy after Franco's death in 1975 required that Amparo remain, in the words of her son Ramón, 'an unshriven ghost'. She was unshriven in both senses: denied absolution, by the priest in Zamora gaol, but also unrelieved of her burden of wrong – the wrong done to her – which made her a 'ghost', if we understand by that one who has been denied voice and memory and thus denied a space. Although Amparo had – extraordinarily – been reburied in the family tomb in 1942, her name was not inscribed on it until after the end of the dictatorship in 1975. It simply wasn't safe for anyone to do so before then.

No one could be brought to account for her murder. First, because Franco won not only the civil war but also, in the end, the Second

World War. Put briefly, in spite of Franco's close political identification with the Nazi new order in Europe, he did not align Spain militarily with the German-Italian Axis and thus never directly threatened Allied imperial interests. So, the Allied liberation of Europe stopped at the Pyrenees. And Franco's dictatorship was left in place by Western powers increasingly preoccupied with Cold War divisions, and prepared to turn a blind eye to mass killing and repression inside Spain in return for Franco's repeated affirmation of crusading anti-communism.

Given this scenario, there was no outside force powerful enough to query or challenge the Franco regime's highly tendentious view of the civil war as a war of liberation against those without ethics or value – a mythology on which Franco never ceased to stake his legitimacy. In 1964, as Spain's beaches began to fill up with mass Euro-tourism, the Franco regime – which was still executing people for 'war crimes' – celebrated its 'twenty-five years of peace'. In the public ceremonials and the millions of posters plastered over walls in towns and villages the length and breadth of the country, the war was still portrayed as a religious crusade or war of liberation (never a civil war, the words were never used) against the hordes of anti-Spain in thrall to the Judeo-Marxist-masonic conspiracy; a war for national unity against separatists, of morality against iniquity. So even in the mid-1960s what was being celebrated was not in fact 'peace', but 'victory'. And even ten years later, with the physical disappearance of Franco in 1975 and the beginnings of superstructural political change, in important respects the 'post-war' (that is to say, the 'war') was still not going to be over.

Why not? The most obvious reason was that the return of democracy (Spain's 'transition') had been agreed by the Francoist elites in return for a de facto political amnesty, based on the so-called 'pact of silence'. No one would be called to account judicially, nor would there be any equivalent of a Truth and Reconciliation Commission. This was the agreement and, for fear of the army and the considerable residual firepower of the civilian extreme right, it was accepted by the regime's democratic interlocutors as the lesser of the available evils. But the disadvantage was that those who had been obliged to be silent for nearly forty years were once again being told that there could be no public recognition of their past lives or memories.

Yet one of the most remarkable features of the 1980s in Spain was an explosion of detailed empirical works of history which have minutely reconstructed the repression on a province by province basis. By the end of the 1990s about 60 per cent had been researched to some degree.[12]

This ongoing work constitutes the necessary memorialisation of the civil war and its long aftermath. Most crucially it means the public recognition of all the stories that could not surface under the dictatorship, nor under the very special and precarious circumstances of the democratic transition in the late 1970s. This new history of the repression, told with real names, and counting the dead from municipal registers and cemetery lists, is, in a very real sense, the equivalent of war memorials for those who never had them, for those who were not liberated in 1945.[13] For only the Francoist dead had war memorials or their names carved on churches: 'caídos por Díos y por España' ('those who fell for God and Spain').

This empirical historical research and the ensuing publications are, then, an act of commemoration for whole groups of Spaniards who could never be mourned publicly when they died; a memorial for people whose lives and memories were traduced by a fascist state. In short they are an act of reparation, of democratic and constitutional citizenship. Similarly, the recent explosion of accounts (including in films and documentaries) of the guerrilla fighters of the 1940s in Spain, who saw themselves not in isolation, but as a component of the European wars of resistance against the Nazi new order, is also about restitution in the work of collective memory.[14]

This historical work, now an avalanche, is also looking at the myriad forms of judicial and economic repression at village level in the details of everyday social and economic life, and in particular here one should cite the work of Conxita Mir.[15] But this new work has revealed something even more overwhelming, if that is possible: that the 'pact of silence' was needed not only because of the Francoist elites, but also because of the widespread complicity of 'ordinary Spaniards' in the repression. Not only the civilian militia or local priests across Spain, but also hundreds of thousands of 'ordinary' people – for political reasons and many other sorts of reasons – had responded to the regime's enthusiastic encouragement to denounce their neighbours, acquaintances and often even family members – denunciations for which no corroboration was either sought or required. It is Mir's work – above all on the mechanics of civil justice – which has really opened up the magnitude of this complicity with the regime. It was widespread social fear that underlay the 'pact of silence' – the fears of those who were complicit, the fear and guilt of the families and heirs of those who denounced and murdered, as well as of those who were denounced and murdered. There was fear, in short, of the consequences of reopening old wounds that had been expressly and explicitly prevented from healing by the social and cultural policies of Francoism, decade on decade.

But while the democratic left in Spain had the civic humanitarianism to renounce claims to legal-political redress, and in so doing made the Spanish transition, in effect, the Spanish transition, this did not mean that it had relinquished its claim on the right to public remembrance. As Juan Marsé's epochal novel *The Return of the Hero* (published in 1982) concludes:

> ...*forgetting is a strategy that enables life to go on, although some of us keep our finger on the trigger of memory, just in case.*[16]

Marsé is alluding to the Francoist past, but also, perhaps much more clearly, to the future (onwards from 1982) and thus to the apparent tension between the need to remember, to achieve collective reparation – for reasons of living justly – and, on the other hand, the need to move on as a society, not to live shackled to the past. But this is, I think, only an apparent tension, because the importance of public remembrance is precisely that it permits, or liberates, the process of private forgetting. Once there has been public recognition, then there can be private forgetting, the necessary letting go. Moreover, public remembrance is important for all of Spanish society. That too is the profound message of Marsé's novel, which shows how the brutal binary that underpinned Francoism built a 'peace' that also diminished, and even in some cases destroyed, the 'victors'.

But, for remembrance to happen, fear had to be overcome and that has taken some time – effectively until the start of the new millennium.[17] In the past two years or so there has been an explosion of Republican memory. In particular we have seen the success of civil pressure groups who petitioned the Spanish government (with assistance from the UN's High Commissioner for Human Rights) to exhume from common graves the remains of those executed by Francoist forces, both during and after the war, so that they may be identified and reburied by family and friends.[18] Likewise, those who were forced labourers are now demanding that what happened to them be acknowledged publicly before they die – something which would potentially make some of them eligible for compensation as political prisoners.[19] And in 2002 the Spanish parliament voted, if somewhat contentiously, to rehabilitate the thousands of men who had fought in the guerrilla war during the 1940s, finally overturning the Francoist definition of them as criminals and brigands.

There has been an absolute flood of academic and journalistic books: on prisons, labour battalions, the guerrillas and most recently on the most emotive subject of all perhaps – the 'lost children' of Francoism.[20] Who were they? They were legion. They were the babies and children who died in the cattle-trucks transporting them and their mothers across Spain from 1939 onwards, either from concentration camp to prison or between prisons. They were the babies and young children who died in prison (many of whom were born and died there, like Pilar Fidalgo's child). They were the babies and young children whose names were changed so they could be illegally adopted by regime families. And they were the thousands and thousands who were sent to state institutions because the regime considered their own 'red' families to be unfit to raise them. They were also, though more unusually, refugee children kidnapped from France by the Falange's external 'repatriation' service, and placed not with their families but in Francoist state institutions.[21]

The Franco regime spoke of the 'protection of minors'. But this idea of protection was integrally linked to regime discourses of punishment and purification. In theory, the punishment was of the parents, the redemption or rehabilitation of the children. But the reality, as experienced by Republican children, was of an ingrained belief on the part of state personnel (religious in particular, but others too) that the children had actively to expiate the 'sins of the fathers'. Yet, at the same time, the children were repeatedly told that they too were 'irrecuperable'. They were frequently segregated from other classes of inmate in state institutions, and were mistreated in other ways, both physically and mentally. This desire to punish and control was probably also connected to a fear of the children as potential takers of revenge. Francoists were so fixated on retribution that here, as in other spheres, they projected their own obsessions onto the defeated and could only think of the 'enemy' in terms of the revenge that he or she might take. In short, as Marsé's novel intimates, victory also brutalised the victors.

The explosion of Republican memory now occurring constitutes an outpouring – before the generations who suffered what it remembers pass for good. And here, of course, the comparison to be made is with Holocaust memory in its broadest sense – in that one of the crucial triggers is the end of 'biological memory', and the tremendous sense of sadness, loss and danger that that engenders.[22] But the return of Republican memory is necessary not just for those who must tell their story, but for all living Spaniards of whatever generation. Because democracy in the end cannot anywhere be constructed on an unacknowledged hecatomb. With the current opening up, and the return of Republican memory, we can say that the transition to democracy in Spain is at last complete. Ramón Sender and his family can at last shrive Amparo, and not so much lay her ghost as bring it home, give it space, thus recuperating both voice and memory – in Spain, as in Michael Ondaatje's Sri Lanka, the one ghost and the many.

This lecture was delivered on 8 March 2003 at the Imperial War Museum, London.

NOTES

1. Ramón Sender Barayón, *A Death in Zamora* (Albuquerque: University of New Mexico Press, 1989).
2. Cf Ángela Cenarro, 'Matar, vigilar, delatar: la quiebra de la sociedad civil durante la guerra y la posguerra en España (1936-1948)', *Historia Social*, no.44, 2002.
3. Pilar Fidalgo, *A Young Mother in Franco's Prisons* (London: United Editorial, 1939).
4. The exhibition and burning of corpses took place most infamously at Badajoz, but both occurred in other places (north and south), and everywhere mass graves were to be found: Barayón, *A Death* (bodies at the roadside, p.137; common graves, pp.149-50, 155, 162-3); Carmen García García, 'Aproximación al estudio de la represión franquista en Asturias', *El Basilisco* (Oviedo), época 2, número 6, julio-agosto 1990, pp.69-82, includes information on different kinds of *paseo* (summary execution), on common graves, bodies on the streets and *razzias* (searches) of working-class areas.
5. Reported in *Heraldo de Aragón* (Zaragoza) and then by *El Socialista* (Madrid); Rafael Abella, *La vida cotidiana durante la guerra civil: la España republicana* (Barcelona: Editorial Planeta, 1986), p.38. There are many

accounts reporting the 'auto da fe' atmosphere which permeated rebel Spain: see Antonio Ruiz Vilaplana, *Doy fe ... un año de actuación en la España nacionalista* (Paris: Editions Imprimerie Coopérative Etoile, 1938).

6. Cenarro, 'Matar, vigilar', pp.73-5.
7. The expectation that the Republican population should suffer is repeatedly pronounced by rebel cadres and supporters of all kinds. For example, an intelligence officer in Burgos in 1937, in response to his Quaker interlocutors' concerns about the significantly greater material deprivation being endured by the Republican population, commented that 'just as soon as we can get things cleaned up in the North then there'll be more suffering there too...': Dan West, 'Needy Spain', Reports from the field, vol.II (report authored February 1938), Friends Service Council FSC/R/Sp/4. For an analysis of the political functions of 'suffering' and 'penitence', see Michael Richards, *A Time of Silence. Civil War and the Culture of Repression in Franco's Spain, 1936-1945* (Cambridge: Cambridge University Press, 1998).
8. Patronato central para la *redención* de penas por el trabajo.
9. For Greece, which in some important respects was comparable, see Mark Mazower (ed.) *After the War Was Over: Reconstructing the Family, Nation and State in Greece 1943-1960* (Princeton: Princeton University Press, 2000).
10. The law was a major instrument of war: especially the (retroactive) Law of Political Responsibilities (February 1939), and the Law against Communism and Freemasonry (March 1940). There was also a law (February 1939) to purge civil service/state employees.
11. The family members who denounced Amparo were also motivated by material greed in the matter of a disputed inheritance. But while that too should alert us to the sociological complexity of the murderousness unleashed by the apparently simple exhortation of the military rebels to 'denounce the enemies of Spain', it should not deflect our attention from the sheer hatred Amparo provoked for what she symbolised as a woman. For that too was a real and central cause of the denunciation. And whatever the poisoned nature of intra-family relations, it was what the military coup unleashed that made it possible for this to become literally murderous.
12. North-east Aragón and the south (excepting Badajoz) have been investigated exhaustively. The most telling gap is – unsurprisingly – the conservative heartland of the centre-north and north-west and Galicia. In central Spain, Cuenca and Guadalajara remain unstudied, and Madrid province and capital have only been researched partially to date.
13. Cemetery lists are invariably fuller and more accurate records because many people were too frightened to register deaths officially, lest they too become the object of police/state attention.

14. See the recent major historical study by Francisco Moreno Gómez, *La resistencia armada contra Franco: tragedia del maquis y la guerrilla* (Barcelona: Editorial Crítica, 2001); and Montxo Armendáriz's and Javier Corcuera's documentary film, *La guerrilla de la memoria* (2001).

15. Conxita Mir, *Vivir es sobrevivir: justicia, orden y marginación en la Cataluña rural de posguerra* (Lleida: Editorial Milenio, 2000); and also her work in Julián Casanova (ed.), *Morir, Matar, Sobrevivir: la violencia en la dictadura de Franco* (Barcelona: Editorial Crítica, 2002).

16. 'El olvido es una estrategia del vivir, si bien algunos, por si acaso, aún mantenemos el dedo en el gatillo de la memoria.' This novel, *Un día volveré*, remains, unfortunately, without an English translation.

17. Cf the retrospectively optimistic (and surprisingly political) voice-over at the end of Pedro Almodóvar's 1997 film, *Live Flesh* (*Carne Trémula*): 'Luckily for you my son, we stopped being afraid a long time ago in Spain.'

18. Notable among these groups was the Association for the Recovery of Historical Memory (Asociación para la Recuperación de la Memoria Histórica). For more on this see *The Volunteer*, vol.XXIV, no.3, September 2002 – for the El Bierzo and Babia regions of León.

19. In 1990-92 the central PSOE government of Spain passed enabling legislation for the over-65s who had spent more than three years in gaol under Franco. Legislation approved by some of Spain's regional governments since then has widened this scope, but in other regions legislative attempts have failed and no provision is available.

20. Televisió de Catalunya screened a documentary of the same name (*Els nens perduts del franquisme*) in March 2002, and there is an accompanying book: Ricard Vinyes, Montse Armengou and Ricard Belis, *Los niños perdidos del franquismo* (Barcelona: Plaza y Janés, 2002). See also R Vinyes, *Irredentas: las presas políticas y sus hijos en las cárceles franquistas* (Madrid: Temas de Hoy, 2002).

21. By the decree of 30 March 1940, women prisoners had the right to nurse their children until they were three years old. This measure made it possible for the authorities legally to remove three-year-olds from prison. But it did not of course legalise the subsequent 'disappearance' of those children. Children were not usually passed to prisoners' families but to state tutelage. Under the terms of the law of 4 December 1941, 'red' children who couldn't remember their names – for whatever reasons (repatriated refugees, orphans, children whose parents couldn't be located, etc) could be given new names. It was this law that facilitated the the 'disappearances'/illegal adoptions. The Servicio Exterior de Falange frequently 'retrieved' children from abroad against the wishes of their parents resident in Spain. An estimated 11,000 children were still listed as refugees in the 1940s (excluding those who were part of exiled families). By 1943, 12,042 children were under state tutelage. But there were many more thousands in state institutions.

22. Hence, I would argue, the remarkable and unexpected success of a novel like Javier Cercas's *Soldados de Salamina* (Barcelona: Tusquets, 2001), which sold hugely in Spain and went to a third edition in under two months.

'No Soldier': The Courage and Comradeship of Dr Len Crome

Paul Preston

A courageous and brilliant doctor, and veteran of the Spanish Civil War, Len Crome was born Lazar Krom on 14 April 1909 in the town of Dvinsk, also known as Daugavpils, in what is now Latvia, then part of Russia. He was later amused to discover that he therefore shared his birthday with the Spanish Second Republic, which was established in 1931 and for which he volunteered in 1936. He began his remarkable collection of languages as a child, speaking Russian with his father and at school, German with his mother, and also picking up the Yiddish that his parents used when they vainly wanted to keep secrets from the children. During the First World War, Dvinsk, as a fortress and garrison town, came under German attack. The front was close, and Len remembered seeing the first fatality: a peasant in a cart hit by shrapnel from a German bomb.

His early recollections included a visit to his school by Tsar Nicholas II and the later excitement of the revolutionary upheavals of 1917. He and his class-mates were thrilled by the tumult of frequent demonstrations, the flying of red banners and the sight of the double-headed Tsarist eagle being torn from the school building. Russian soldiers billeted in the Krom household let him ride their horses and, after the capture of Dvinsk, the German soldiers – welcomed by the Latvians as liberators – let him play with their rifles. In 1918, the Krom family moved to Libava on the west coast in independent Latvia. There Len attended the only Russian school in the town. Although by his own account a poor scholar and badly behaved, he graduated in 1926 having scored high marks for Russian and biology. Len's father was a relatively prosperous businessman, which meant that he could afford for his children to be taught English. He had connections in Scotland, from where he used to import barrels of herrings. These links facilitated Len's request to join a friend studying in Edinburgh. There he quickly

Len Crome, uncharacteristically in uniform in Spain.
Courtesy Peter Crome

perfected his English and completed a degree in economics. In his final year of economics, he did the first year of a degree in medicine, and qualified as a doctor in 1933. In the course of his time as a student he had incurred the wrath of the Latvian authorities by not returning home to do compulsory military service. They considered him to be a deserter, and he did not even regard himself as Latvian. Accordingly, in 1934, he took the opportunity provided by his eight years of uninterrupted residence to become a naturalised British citizen.

Len was working as a junior doctor in a hospital in Blackburn when the military uprising took place in Spain. Although not a member of any party, Nazi anti-semitism had pushed him to the left. He was an avid reader of Left Book Club publications and was alarmed by growing evidence of Nazi German and Fascist Italian intervention in Spain. Learning that many men and women were leaving their homes and families to risk death in the International Brigades because of a premonition of the consequences of victory for Franco and his Axis allies, he determined to do the same. Like them, he believed that, if fascism was not defeated in Spain, France and Britain would be next. Unsure as to how to be of most use, he wrote to Harry Pollitt, General Secretary of the Communist Party of Great Britain (CPGB). Pollitt suggested that he join the Scottish Ambulance Unit that was being organised by the Glasgow coal magnate and philanthropist, Sir Daniel Macaulay Stevenson. When the young doctor went for an interview to Stevenson's home, he arrived early, which was typical of his self-discipline. Stevenson's butler showed him into the great man's library to wait for the members of the committee who were to interview him. There he was shocked to see on the wall a dedicated photograph of Adolf Hitler. Despite this, the fruit perhaps of Stevenson's having campaigned against the harsh treatment of Germany in the Treaty of Versailles, it was clear that the Scottish magnate supported the Spanish Republic. The committee was delighted to secure the services of a doctor and suggested that he join the convoy about to go to Spain, with a group of drivers and other auxiliary staff taking trucks loaded with chocolate, condensed milk and medicines for the Republic. Len arranged with his brother, Jacob Krom (Jascha), who was by now studying in London, that his parents should be told that Lonya, as Len was called at home, was going on a prestigious medical expedition to central Africa and would be out of touch for several months.[1]

On 17 September 1936, the first convoy of the Scottish

Ambulance Unit had set off for Spain under the leadership of a feisty middle-aged woman, Fernanda Jacobsen. Priscilla Scott-Ellis, an English aristocrat who had served with Franco's Nationalist forces, was greatly amused when she met her in Madrid after the war: 'An incredible woman, small and square, with a huge bottom. She always dresses in a kilt, thick woollen stockings, brogues, a khaki jacket of military cut with thistles all over it, huge leather gauntlet gloves, a cape also with thistles, and, the crowning glory, a little black Scottish hat edged with tartan and with a large silver badge on it.'[2] As Len was to discover, the problem with the pugnacious Miss Jacobsen was not so much her bizarre appearance as her questionable politics. That she was still around and carrying out humanitarian work after the entry of the Francoists into Madrid was an indication of the ambiguity of her politics. Certainly, Len's experiences with the Scottish Ambulance Unit were to be the real beginning of his political education.

The Scottish Ambulance Unit set up headquarters at Aranjuez to the south of Madrid. It did valuable work and took considerable losses in the fight against Franco's advancing African columns, dealing with about 2,500 wounded and evacuating 1,000 refugees. However, when the much-depleted unit returned on leave for Christmas 1936, there was a shadow hanging over it. Four of its members were accused of robbing corpses on the battlefield. The unit was reorganised in mid-January 1937 and new volunteers were recruited, and one of these was Len Crome, who met the Scottish convoy at Dover. As soon as they reached the besieged Spanish capital they were thrown into action. Len was the medical manager of the unit. They had to cope with civilians hurt in the Francoist bombing raids on the city as well as with the unending flow of soldiers wounded in the frenetic fighting around Madrid. Working out of headquarters in an annexe of the British embassy building in the capital, the unit spent most of February in the thick of the Battle of Jarama, ferrying the casualties to improvised rearguard hospitals at Chinchón and in the Hotel Palace in Madrid. Despite their commitment to this valuable work, Len and others in the unit became uneasy about some of Miss Jacobsen's decisions. She was distributing food donated by Scottish workers for the Spanish Republic to right-wing madrileños who had taken refuge in the British embassy. Len and his second-in-command, Roderick MacFarquhar, were even more distressed to discover that the Scottish Ambulance Unit was being exploited, with Foreign Office collusion, by the famous 'Spanish Pimpernel', Captain Christopher Lance.

Bandaging Franco supporters as if they were Republican wounded, he was smuggling them to Valencia and thence out of Republican Spain. In a tense confrontation with Miss Jacobsen, Len, Roddy MacFarquhar, Maurice Linden and George Burleigh announced that they had decided to join the International Brigades. After various hysterical threats, she insisted that they meet the British consul. When he arrived, she told him to order them back to Britain. Not only did he refuse to do so but also thanked them emotionally for what they were doing for the Republic.[3]

In Madrid, the famous Canadian surgeon Dr Norman Bethune took Len and the other exiles from the Scottish unit to an International Brigade hospital on the Valencia road out of Madrid. At the time, Franco was trying to close the circle around Madrid. The bloody Battle of Jarama had just ended and that of Guadalajara was about to start. The British contingent was part of the 35th Division under the Soviet-trained General 'Walter', the Pole Karol Swierczewski – portrayed as Goltz in Hemingway's *For Whom the Bell Tolls*. In May Len was slightly wounded by shrapnel while in the Casa de Campo outside Madrid. Until the summer of 1937 he worked as assistant to the Chief Medical Officer of the 35th Division – another Pole, Dr Mieczyslaw Domanski (known as 'Dubois'). After the Battle of Jarama Len had been asked to produce a plan for the preventive health services of the division. Dubois had showed it to Walter, who was greatly impressed and asked to meet its author. The diminutive Walter was something of a military dandy, in a figure-hugging uniform, with smart breeches and highly polished boots in the manner of a Polish cavalry officer. When he first met Crome, Walter was anything but impressed with his scruffy and shambolic demeanour. When Crome asked Dubois why the general had treated him so coolly, he told him: 'You dress and behave like a civilian. That's why he hardly spoke to you. You must learn to be a soldier.' On the next day, an uncomfortable Len had to go to Madrid to be measured for a smart military uniform, which he very rarely wore.[4]

In early July, the Republicans attacked Brunete, fifteen miles west of Madrid, in a diversionary attempt to pull Franco's forces away from the north where they were threatening Santander. After early success, Franco poured troops into the sector, determined to recover lost territory, and Brunete developed into a bloodbath. Len was working as a field surgeon at the International Brigade hospital in El Escorial. Dubois asked Len to help in the collection and evacuation of the wounded. After air bombardments, he would go out searching the dug-outs for wounded. Aleksander Szurek, Walter's adjutant, wrote later:

> *Although Dr Len Crome was not a [Communist] Party member, he had excellent relations with the General. He worked hard. During an engagement, he worked day and night inspecting every medical post. If necessary, he did not sleep for several nights. Bullets did not frighten him.*[5]

With insufficient doctors to cope with the casualties, Len and some of his colleagues wondered if, in the process of triage, there might be a case for concentrating on helping the lightly wounded on the grounds that they had a better chance of recovery and subsequent return to action. Accordingly, Len went to discuss the question with General Walter at headquarters in an olive grove about one kilometre from the front. When he suggested that there might be a case for not spending too much time on hopeless cases, such as those with severe head injuries, Walter exploded:

> *I never knew you were such cannibals! Tell your doctors from me that if I ever hear such talk again they will be sent one and all to the front lines, and without rifles! You will be the first to go. And when you are wounded you may well wonder if your injury is light enough to warrant treatment.*[6]

Some days later, in the course of the Battle of Brunete, with the Republican front collapsing before the Francoist counter-attack, Dubois was badly hit. Len got him into an ambulance and then walked through the fields to Walter's headquarters. The general was deeply shocked by the news and now revealed a warmer and friendlier approach. Without hesitation, he told the twenty-eight-year-old Len to take the place of Dubois. He was given a field promotion to the rank of capitán-médico. When Dubois was killed one month later, at the Battle of Quinto in Aragón, Len became permanent chief of the divisional medical services for the XI Brigade (mainly German-speaking) and the XV Brigade (primarily English-speaking). On 13 September 1937, he was promoted to major.

Given the appalling state of the primitive roads, Len had to work in makeshift hospitals as near as possible to the front to avoid the wounded being bumped and jostled on route to treatment. Wards were set up in tents, barns, caves and even railway carriages; his brilliant improvisations saved many lives. His divisional medical reports were converted into statistical information by his assistant, Nan Green, which helped get the best out of the over-stretched Republican medical services.

However, although early reports on his service were extremely favourable, his efforts were not always appreciated.[7] On 6 June 1938 he wrote a letter to the head of health services for the Ebro, pointing out that most of the ambulances sent from abroad were inadequate and inappropriately equipped. Given that it cost time and money to make them functional, and thus undermined what he called 'the war being fought by the working class in Spain', Len suggested closer coordination between the Centrale Sanitaire Internationale and the foreigner donor organisations.[8] His well-intentioned letter provoked a witch-hunt. Within a month, Jacob Maurice 'Hans' Kalmanovitch, a French communist of Yugoslav origins and the Secretary General of the CSI, had complained about Crome's letter to André Marty, the ferocious Comintern delegate in charge of the International Brigades. 'Kalma', as Marty called him, had been a long-time member of the French Communist Party, had been one of the first French doctors to reach Spain and had taken part in the defence of Madrid. He was a man after the French Stalinist's own heart – hierarchical and authoritarian. For Marty, Crome's letter was 'une dénigration systématique de la CSI'. He immediately wrote to Enrique Sanmartí Falguera, the medical chief of 211 Brigada de Carabineros and of a section of the International Brigades medical services. In his letter, he denounced Crome's phrase 'the war being fought by the working class in Spain' as contrary to the party line that the Republic was fighting a war of independence and thus as 'on the same level as fascist claims'.[9]

Crome was summoned before officials of the International Brigades' medical service, the Ayuda Médica Extranjera, in Barcelona and accused of making enemy propaganda. After interrogation, he accepted his 'fault' and was obliged to make the humiliating plea that he was merely a bourgeois individual who understood little of political matters. A number of his colleagues, including Nan Green, came forward in support of Crome. In consequence, the matter was temporarily dropped.[10]

Nevertheless, revenge was taken by Enrique Sanmartí Falguera and another senior functionary of the International Brigades' medical services, Carlos G Díaz Fernández, a Stalinist who had been medical chief of the communist Fifth Regiment and subsequently of the Ejército del Este (Army of the East). They wrote a vicious assessment of Crome's time in Spain that was appended to his record of service. In this document, they accused him implausibly of fostering a disastrous disorganisation within the medical services by dint of laziness and inexperience.[11] Moreover, after Crome returned to England, Marty would take up the issue again.

In April 1938, the Francoists had reached the Mediterranean and split the Republican zone in two. The Republic's last fling, a surprise crossing of the River Ebro on 24 July, led to the longest and bloodiest battle of the war. Trapped in the hills near Gandesa, the Republicans, including the International Brigades, were subjected to fierce artillery and air bombardment for nearly four months. In sweltering heat, with little or no water, shelled from dawn to dusk, they held on. While the preparations for the Ebro crossing were under way, the headquarters of the 35th Division Medical Corps had been in an old farmhouse. However, shortly after the crossing of the river, on the night of 25 July, Len Crome's medical staff moved to an emergency hospital in a huge cave in the side of a hill near the village of La Bisbal de Falset near the River Ebro. Crome's administrative secretary, Nan Green, would analyse the day's casualties from lists compiled by the doctors in charge of the front-line dressing stations. She would classify them by category (head wounds, leg wounds, amputations and so on) and the weapons that had caused them (mortars, shells, bullets). She then produced water-coloured graphs which greatly assisted in identifying the crucial supplies most needed, ranging from steel helmets to medicaments, and also helped in the prioritisation of treatment. This system was taken over by the distinguished New Zealand surgeon, Douglas Jolly, who used it during the Second World War in North Africa and Italy.[12] The nurses who served in the cave hospital later commented on the untiring kindness with which Dr Crome encouraged their work throughout endless nights and days caring for the wounded in the Battle of the Ebro.[13] Despite the appalling conditions, it has been estimated that the men under his care got better treatment than they might have received in the best English teaching hospitals of the time.[14]

The Republic withdrew the International Brigades in September 1938 in a vain attempt to prompt international mediation. Len handed over the divisional medical services to a Spanish doctor and left for England on 26 September. He always remembered the comradeship and his participation in the fight against fascism as 'a gloriously happy time'. He had gone to Spain without party affiliation but what he saw had made him sympathise with the Communist Party: 'I saw that the communists did most of the fighting, were most steadfast and that without them it would have been impossible to continue resisting the fascists.' He asked Walter if he thought that he should join the party. To his surprise, Walter told him that even the most courageous cadres were inhibited by fear of losing their party card. The general did not want anxieties about denunciations distracting Dr Crome from his real work.[15]

There was considerable paranoia at the time, especially amongst the Germans. Presumably with the unpleasantness with Marty in mind, Len wrote later:

> ...one of the least pleasant features of life in the International Brigades was frequent denunciation. To be sure, not among the English, who were as far as I know quite innocent of this, partly no doubt, because they were unfamiliar with illegal dangerous political work underground. No officer could retreat a yard without risking denunciation of being a secret Gestapo agent, or Trotskyist, which at the time came to much the same thing. Some of the reports were honestly believed in by the people who made them, but I have no doubt that many were inspired by personal animosity or envy, by a wish to prove one's own virtue, and often came from malicious, incompetent persons. Not being a communist I was seldom shown any of these 'documents'. However, a day came when Walter handed me one. It was written by a Yugoslav or Bulgarian medical student called Petrovich about a Belgian surgeon, René Dumont, who worked with us and was an exceptionally able, inventive and attractive worker. This did not stop Petrovich from accusing him of being a secret fascist sent to Spain to kill as many wounded as he could. I had no idea what to do and decided that the best procedure was to confront Dumont with the letter and ask him to comment on it. Dumont was dumbfounded and stammered out that I ought to suspend him temporarily pending an investigation, whereupon I assured him of my full confidence in him.

Len's response, combining his characteristic practicality and sense of justice, won the approval of Walter, despite the fact that not to have handed the case to the security services involved considerable risk for both of them.[16]

It is unlikely that Len Crome ever saw the report sent to Moscow by Enrique Sanmartí Falguera and Carlos G Díaz, but his experience in being hauled over the coals for his remarks on inadequate ambulances would more than account for his tone of regret if not bitterness. In fact, he did not know the half of it. In December 1938, Marty wrote an even more hostile assessment. In it, he picked up on the report by Sanmartí and Díaz, writing that, through Crome's 'incapacité', the medical services had functioned badly during the Battle of the Ebro. This was all the more suspicious, to Marty's singularly paranoiac mind, because Crome had collected around him in the XV Brigade medical services 'les éléments internationaux les plus douteux' ('the most dubious foreign elements'). With Walter, he was accused of provoking disorder and total indiscipline. Crome's letter about the ambulances was now inflated to the point where 'Crome a mené une campagne violente contre la Centrale Sanitaire Internationale' ('Crome has waged a violent campaign against the Centrale Sanitaire Internationale'). As a result of these 'violent criticisms' (Marty used the word 'violent' three times within two sentences), he concluded: 'Ce Crome doit être suivi de très près dans toute son activité.' ('This Crome should be followed very closely in all his activities.') Given that Crome had still not joined the Communist Party, such remarks are deeply revealing of Marty's paranoia.[17]

In the immediate aftermath of the Spanish Civil War, any regrets that might have been occasioned by his treatment at the hands of Marty and his cronies were surely wiped out by a number of intensely moving letters that he received from French concentration camps sent by comrades from the International Brigades interned therein. In one such letter, Guillermo Rodríguez, a sergeant who had accompanied Len at the front both in Aragón and Catalonia, wrote that the 'virtudes y buen compañerismo' ('courage and comradeship') were a frequent topic of conversation among the Brigaders and commented: '...para mí no había otro camarada mejor que el Dr Croome [sic]' ('for me there was no finer colleague than Dr Crome').[18] Shortly after reaching England, he joined the CPGB, joining a group of doctors in London's Belsize Park. He was working as a GP in Camberwell and was soon using his experience of Spain to train first-aid ARP (air raid precautions) workers in Islington. He was advised that his experience in Spain would be invaluable to the British Army in the forthcoming struggle – which, for Len, was merely the continuation of the one that had been interrupted by Franco's victory. He applied for a commission and was turned down in June 1939 on the grounds that he failed to fulfil the conditions of the regulations for the Territorial Army 'that every candidate for a commission must be a British subject and son of British subjects'.[19] A second failed application led him to conclude that his communist affiliations were the problem. As it was, he had plenty of work with his medical practice. Moreover, he was working hard to secure the release of imprisoned Brigaders from camps in France. He also looked after refugees from Czechoslovakia, falling in love with one of them, Helen Hüttner, whom he soon married. He described meeting her as the luckiest thing that ever happened to him.

After the German invasion of the Soviet Union in June 1941, Len received a request from the wife of Ivan Maisky, the Russian ambassador, to help in purchasing medical equipment for the Red Army. However, in December 1942 conscription finally reached his age group and he was called up as a private. Given his medical qualifications and Spanish experience, he was quickly recognised as officer material, and became a captain in the Royal Army Medical Corps. After brief training he served as a medical officer in Norfolk. Then, in the spring of 1943, he was sent to North Africa. After the defeat of the Axis forces there, preparations began for the landing in Italy. Len was anxious, while in Algeria, to help eastern European veterans of the International Brigades who had escaped there from France. He was appalled later to discover that on landing on Soviet soil they were rounded up by the GPU and hurled into the gulag.

During the Allied advance through Italy, Len was the commanding officer of the 152nd Field Ambulance. For his achievement in clearing casualties under heavy fire during the battle for Monte Cassino, and to his astonishment, he was awarded an 'immediate' Military Cross. A few weeks later, he was presented to King George VI when he visited Italy. The citation for the award read:

During the battle for the crossing of the river Gari shortly after the bridge Amazon was established on 13 May 1944, this officer established an Advanced Dressing Station on the west side of the river, having worked there himself from the time the bridge was established until he decided it was safe to bring his section across. The section location was subjected to very heavy intermittent mortar fire for the next forty-eight hours, during which time an infantry ADS nearby was forced to withdraw. Captain

> *Crome, by his courage and example, was instrumental in keeping the*
> *medical chain of evacuation open as established and his conduct is*
> *worthy of the highest praise.*

After the end of the war, by now a lieutenant colonel, he supervised the military arrangements of German military hospitals in the British zone in Austria which were looking after some 30,000 patients. He was allowed to have his family with him and they lived for a while in Villach. At this time he learned of the deaths of his parents and his older sister, Sima. His father had been deported as a capitalist when the Russians invaded Latvia and sent to a labour camp where he had died of starvation. His mother and Sima had been killed by the Germans. Fortunately, his younger sister Helena (known as Hilda) had come to London before the war to study at Birkbeck College. Accordingly, she, like Jascha, escaped the Holocaust. In 1946 Len was posted to Italy, at first as chief medical officer in the district of Riccione near Rimini and later as commandant of the British military hospital, first in Naples and later in Caserta, where his second son Peter was born.

In the autumn of 1947 he was demobilised and the family returned to London. Len was now able to fulfil a long-term ambition to become a pathologist. He obtained a trainee post at St Mary's Hospital, working in the pathology department headed by Professor Newcomb and in the bacteriology department headed by Professor Alexander Fleming. Later, he trained in neuropathology at the Maudsley Hospital, headed by Professor Alfred Meyer, specialising in the neuropathology of learning difficulty. In 1956 he became pathologist at the Fountain Hospital in Tooting, considered something of a communist hospital, but also an internationally famous centre for the treatment of learning difficulty. At the time of the Soviet invasion of Hungary he wrote critical letters to the *Daily Worker*, which were not published. As secretary of the medical section of the Society for Cultural Relations with the USSR and subsequently as chairman from 1969 to 1976, he visited the USSR several times. He was later critical of Gorbachev, because he was concerned about the likely consequences of the break-up of the Soviet Union. His principal occupation was medicine. He wrote many papers and collaborated on several books in the field of pathology – most notably, with Jan Stern, *Pathology of Mental Retardation*. He also wrote a book on resistance in German concentration camps, *Unbroken*, largely about his brother-in-law, Jonny Hüttner. After retiring from the NHS at 65, a lifelong workaholic, he acted as a locum pathologist in many hospitals including spending three years at the University of Amsterdam, during which time he added Dutch to his remarkable array of languages. His wife Helen died in 1995. Until his death on 6 May 2001 he was chairman of the International Brigade Association, and was always proud of having helped the ordinary Spanish people in their struggle for democracy.

A shorter version of this tribute was delivered by the author on 12 March 2005 at the Imperial War Museum, London.

NOTES

1. Len Crome, 'Autobiographical Notes', kindly facilitated by Professor Peter Crome; Jim Fyrth, *The Signal Was Spain: The Aid Spain Movement in Britain 1936-39* (London: Lawrence & Wishart, 1986), p.185; Alexander Szurek, *The Shattered Dream* (Boulder: Eastern European Monographs, 1989), p.213.
2. Diaries of Priscilla Scott-Ellis (deposited at the University of Cardiff Library Archive; manuscript no.3/233), 3 April 1939.
3. Fyrth, *The Signal*, pp.181-4; Ian MacDougall (ed.), *Voices from the Spanish Civil War: Personal Recollections of Scottish Volunteers in Republican Spain 1936-39* (Edinburgh: Polygon Press, 1986), pp.78-82; CE Lucas Phillips, *The Spanish Pimpernel* (London: Heinemann, 1960), pp.85-8, 104-17.
4. Len Crome, 'Walter (1897-1947): A Soldier in Spain', *History Workshop Journal*, no.9, Spring 1980, p.117.
5. Szurek, *The Shattered Dream*, p.212.
6. Crome, 'Walter', pp.117-8.
7. 'Característica del camarada Crome, Leonard', 23 May 1938, Moscow Archives (MA), OPIS 6, 545/6/114 (International Brigade Memorial Trust).
8. 'Cuestión de las ambulancias', 6 June 1938; MA, OPIS 6, 545/6/114 (IBMT).
9. Marty to Kalmanovitch, 7 July 1938, Marty to Sanmartí, 8 July 1938, MA, OPIS 6, 545/6/114 (IBMT). On Kalmanovitch, see Andreu Castells, *Las Brigadas Internacionales de la guerra de España* (Barcelona: Ariel, 1974), pp.84, 452, 462-3; and Francisco Guerra, *La medicina en el exilio republicano* (Madrid: Universidad de Alcalá de Henares, 2003), p.219. On Sanmartí, see Guerra, *La medicina*, pp.313, 597.
10. 'Explicación sobre esta crítica en la AME entre Crome y la Dirección', 16 July 1938, MA, OPIS 6, 545/6/114 (IBMT).

11. 'Característica de Crome, Leonard', 16 October 1938; 'Apreciación del camarada Crome, Leonard', 5 December 1938, MA, OPIS 6, 545/6/114 (IBMT). On Díez Fernández, see Guerra, *La medicina*, pp.454-5.

12. Nan Green, *A Chronicle of Small Beer* (Nottingham: Nottingham Trent University, 2004), p.71; Fyrth, *The Signal*, pp.127-9. Jolly wrote an important book, *Field Surgery in Total War*, based on his Spanish experiences. On Green, see Paul Preston, *Palomas de guerra: cinco mujeres marcadas por el enfrentamiento bélico* (Barcelona: Plaza y Janés, 2001), pp.97-164.

13. Angela Jackson, 'Beyond the Battlefield: A Cave Hospital in the Spanish Civil War' (Len Crome Memorial Lecture, 2 March 2002, London: IBMT, 2002), p.1. The preamble containing a tribute to Len Crome is not included in Jackson's chapter in this book.

14. Crome, 'Walter', pp.116-28; Richard Baxell, 'Dr Len Crome', *The Independent*, 11 May 2001; Paul Preston, 'Len Crome', *The Guardian*, 12 May 2001; Fyrth, *The Signal*, pp.110, 149.

15. Crome, 'Walter', pp.126.

16. Crome, 'Autobiographical Notes' and 'Walter', p.120. This was possibly a reference to Grujo Petrovic, from Kosor in Montenegro. Petrovic served under Crome in a field hospital within the 35th Division (Guerra, *La medicina*, p.375)

17. Marty, 'Crome', 7 December 1938, MA, OPIS 6, 545/6/114 (IBMT).

18. Rodríguez (Gurs) to Crome, 24 June 1939.

19. DADMS (Deputy Assistant Director of Medical Services) 44th (HC) Division (signature illegible) to Crome, 23 June 1939.

Killing the Dream: The Spanish Labyrinth Revisited, 1898-1939

Francisco J Romero Salvadó

It has been a puzzling experience – and exasperating for scholars – to witness in the past decade or so the success in terms of popularity and sales of a number of so-called revisionist authors in Spain. The word 'revisionist' is misleading. Rather than revising, their objective is to counter the historical paradigms established in the flood of academic research that followed the demise of General Franco in 1975, and the subsequent rapid dismantling of the dictatorship, and to re-brand the old distorted myths.[1]

Hailed by an array of cultural and media institutions, these revisionists have fought a fairly successful battle in terms of influencing public opinion, and have even claimed to be victims of, and rebels against, 'la dictadura del pensamiento único' ('the tyranny of uniform thought') – for which a left-wing dominated academia is held to blame, with Professor Paul Preston being one of the key targets of their vitriolic attacks.[2] They have avoided the messianic rhetoric of the Francoist past, such as the references to the 'glorious crusade against the anti-Spain' and even here and there carefully planted some mild criticism of the Nationalists. However, the obvious clichés of Francoist discourse remain. For example, they portray the CEDA (Confederación Española de Derechas Autónomas), the largest right-wing force during the Second Republic, as a modern Christian democratic party. By contrast, the left in general is associated with political extremism and public disorder. According to them, it was the revolution in October 1934 which provided the starting-point of the civil war, and thus deprived the left of any moral high ground when the right did the same in July 1936. Furthermore, Franco's revolt was justified because the Popular Front, elected in February 1936, was unwilling or unable to implement law and order and had been overwhelmed by the Bolshevised forces of

'Victory: the whole world is awaiting the news', says this poster by J Huertas that was published by the PSOE socialist party.

the labour movement. Finally, they argue that the Nationalists emerged victorious because of the discipline of their troops and the wise command of their officers. According to the revisionists, foreign intervention did not play any relevant role. Hitler and Mussolini did help Franco but only in terms of responding to and matching the copious amount of equipment sent to the Republic first by France and then by the Soviet Union. Of course, they also stress that Stalin had in mind, right from the start, the transformation of Spain into a communist satellite precursor of the eastern European states that were established after the Second World War.[3]

In analysing aspects of this manipulation of history, which, unfortunately, still surrounds the study of the Spanish Civil War, it is necessary – without forgetting the broader European context – to explore what Gerald Brennan has described as the 'Spanish labyrinth'.

Contrary to the revisionists' claim that the civil war followed the left's inability to accept the ballot box results in November 1933, and its staging of a revolution one year later, the origins of this cruel conflict were much more deeply rooted in Spain's history. Its short-term seeds were clearly present a generation earlier. Indeed, political radicalism, social unrest and praetorian interventionism had already marked the previous regime, the Bourbon monarchy. Most of the leaders in both warring camps – Generals Franco and Mola and political leaders such as Gil Robles or Calvo Sotelo on the Nationalist side, and for the Republic Largo Caballero, Indalecio Prieto and Manuel Azaña – had not suddenly appeared on the political stage in 1936 but had been influenced by the twists and turns of the Spanish labyrinth.

The year 1898 is a good starting-point. This was the moment in which Spain lost her last overseas territories following a brief but fateful war against the United States. In an era of 'social Darwinism', in which the possession of colonies was seen as the hallmark of a vigorous nation, Spain emerged as a sick state. As the historian Manuel Tuñón de Lara concluded:

> … *not only was the nostalgic dream of imperial Spain sunk for ever but also the disaster brought into question the capacity of the existing governing classes to rule the country.*[4]

Following the calamity of 1898, calls for national regeneration or the thorough overhauling of Spain's social, economic and ideological foundations began in earnest. However, the pursuit of this regeneration included two opposite prescriptions: the progressive belief in mobilisation from below versus the authoritarian search for 'an iron surgeon', a strong leader capable of applying from above the necessary surgical measures to regain for Spain its past prestige and authority. Both these approaches constituted the two roads to modernity whose final clash would take place in 1936.[5]

It needs to be underlined that nobody foresaw, let alone planned, a long civil war. The conspirators who struck in July 1936 did not expect massive resistance. Spain was after all a country marked by constant praetorian take-overs; the most recent example, in September 1923, had immediately succeeded. In fact, the military insurgents' claim of having risen up to save the motherland from the reigning chaos was similar to that made by General Miguel Primo de Rivera, the leader of the 1923 coup and the self-proclaimed 'iron surgeon' that saved Spain.[6] The civil war was the consequence – a fact often forgotten – of the relative success of the Republic. Unlike what happened in 1923, when nobody was prepared to oppose the military insurrection, in 1936 the seditious officers had to contend with the resistance of workers and peasants, organised in trade unions, as well as that of significant sectors of the police and armed forces. Unlike so many other constitutional European orders that were overthrown by the forces of reaction in the interwar years with relative ease, the Republic fought back. It was thus the failure of the insurrection in two-thirds of the country that effectively led to the brutal fratricidal struggle.

It is not only misleading but also ridiculous to try to pass the onus of the conflict onto the left and in particular to single out the socialist-led revolution of October 1934.[7] Firstly, this contention deliberately ignores the structural issues which had divided Spaniards and determined the violent course of the Spanish labyrinth for decades, namely the unfair regime of land distribution, the lack of progressive social legislation, the demands for regional autonomy and the role of the Catholic Church and the armed forces in a modernising society.[8] Secondly, it also overlooks the crucial fact that the right's attempt to overthrow the Republic in 1936 merely followed the traditional pattern of interwar European politics. As in Italy in 1922 or Germany in 1933, there was not a real revolutionary threat in 1936 Spain, but in all of them the right used anti-revolutionary rhetoric to justify their bid for power, when in reality their aim was to crush the challenge to vested interests that genuine democracy entailed. As the leading Austrian socialist Otto Bauer wrote in reference to the authoritarian coup in his own country in 1934:

Fascism likes to justify itself to the bourgeoisie in terms of having saved it from proletarian revolution, from Bolshevism ... In fact, the capitalists and large landowners did not surrender power to fascism in order to protect themselves from the threats of proletarian revolution, but with the aim of depressing wage levels, reversing the social achievements of the working class and destroying the unions and their political power.[9]

Obsessed with the October Revolution of 1934, the revisionists also appear to ignore the failed coup to overthrow the Republic led by General José Sanjurjo as early as August 1932; and Sanjurjo was the very same officer who would lead the military rebellion of July 1936.

It is also ludicrous to suggest that the CEDA was a Christian Democratic force.[10] Paul Preston has analysed how all the right-wing political parties of the Republic (including, of course, the CEDA) acted as 'regiments of the same army'.[11] Along similar lines, Professor Ismael Saz has described how all of them underwent, in the 1930s, a process of 'fascistisation', sharing a rabidly anti-liberal programme and collaborating in the same goal: the destruction of the Republic.[12] The CEDA was a coalition of right-wing groups that included some social reformists as well as conservative hardliners. However, its ideological dependence on the Church and the overwhelming financial backing it received from agrarian associations meant that its overall leaning was towards the reactionary camp. Moreover, its refusal to declare its loyalty to the Republic, its bellicose rhetoric, full of admiration for Hitler and Mussolini, and its uniformed and violent youth wing, Juventudes de Acción Popular, made its professed willingness to participate in the democratic process sound extremely hollow.

Let us remember that in the early days of the Republic all right-wing forces had been part of a vast umbrella coalition known as Acción Nacional. The CEDA was only created in February 1933, following the failure of the Sanjurjo coup, due to the perception that the Republic was at that stage too strong to be overthrown by violent means. The idea was to embark upon a legalist strategy, play the democratic game, build a mass party with which to win elections and then destroy the Republic from within. But collaboration with more extreme right-wing forces at no point stopped. At the time of the birth of the CEDA, its leader, José María Gil Robles, confided to the monarchist leader Antonio Goicoechea that their incompatibility was not due to political differences but to reasons of tactics.[13]

Although Gil Robles never acknowledged his direct participation in the military conspiracy, he admitted in his memoirs that key members of his party were involved, and even that the crucial meeting of generals in March 1936, which effectively planted the seeds for the coup, took place in the house of the stockbroker José Delgado, a leader of the CEDA in Madrid.[14] Gil Robles also conceded that in early July 1936 he donated 500,000 pesetas from the party's electoral funds to General Mola; to give such a large amount of money to the director of the conspiracy was strange behaviour for someone innocent of collusion with the coup.[15] During the civil war Gil Robles served the Nationalist camp from Portugal, and, after Franco enforced the unification of all the right-wing forces in April 1937, he wrote a sycophantic letter to the Caudillo confirming the dissolution of his party and embracing whole-heartedly the 'Glorious National Movement'.[16]

It would be futile to deny that there was a breach of constitutional legality by the socialists when they led the October Revolution of 1934. However, we should remember that it was the entry into the government of the CEDA – a party that had never attempted to conceal its intentions to liquidate the Republic's basic foundations – that provoked that revolt. Furthermore, in the light of contemporary events on the continent, socialist misgivings were understandable. Both Mussolini and Hitler had accepted a minority of portfolios in coalition governments and then gone on to destroy democracy. This gave rise to widespread fear that Spain was heading a similar way. Even more recent and frightening was the Austrian example. There, in February 1934, Chancellor Engelbert Dollfuss, leader of a Catholic party ideologically similar to the CEDA, had staged a coup and established a dictatorship, after the brutal 'cleaning-up of Red Vienna'.

Another crucial point hammered to excess by the revisionists is the association of the left with political violence and public disorder.[17] One cannot deny that within the left, and in particular within the milieu of the anarchist movement, there were sectors that believed that their cause could be advanced by terror. Indeed, from the spectacular 'propaganda by the deed' of the late nineteenth century to the class wars of the post-First World War years, a subculture whereby the labour organisation lived side by side with small action groups committed to furthering revolution by violent acts remained an integral part of the tragic-romantic story of Spanish anarchism.[18] Under the lead of the revolutionary diehards of the Federación Anarquista Ibérica (FAI), the anarcho-syndicalists staged three massive uprisings against the Republic between 1931 and 1933. As the Republic's Prime Minister, Manuel Azaña, commented, it was difficult to find a modus vivendi with an organisation whose extremism rejected any reformist legislation with the argument that doing so would diminish the insurrectionary spirit of the militants.[19]

Political terrorism was far from being a monopoly of the left, however. The Spanish political arena was crowded by all sorts of forces that regarded a resort to violence as a valid means to impose their particular ideological agenda.[20] Indeed, it is difficult to find a movement with a longer tradition of bloodshed than Carlism.[21] Organised in their paramilitary militias (the so-called Requetés), some 60,000 Carlists played a crucial military role during the first months of the civil war, cleansing the rear of enemies and propping up the fledgling northern army led by General Mola with reliable troops. Nostalgic for an idealised golden age, the Carlists embodied conservative resistance and clerical intransigence to modernity. They had fought for God and the true king since the early 1830s. And during the class wars of the post-First World War years, working-class Carlists had constituted the backbone of the so-called Sindicatos Libres, who fought deadly battles with anarcho-syndicalists. They were part of the counter-revolutionary movement whose activities sparked a spiral of violence and paved the way for the military dictatorship of 1923.[22]

It was Spain's fascist party, the Falange, that played a vital role in the destabilisation of the country in the 1930s. Like its European counterparts, the Falange believed in what its leader José Antonio Primo de Rivera called 'the dialectic of fists and guns'.[23] But, given the existence of already strong 'fascistised' forces on the right, the Falange remained a tiny force until the outbreak of the civil war. The Falange was thus a less autonomous member of the counter-revolutionary movement than its counterparts in German or Italian fascism and was dependent on the monarchists for financial support. However, its terrorist activities meant that it fulfilled its part in pushing the country into a whirlpool of violence, generating through this the atmosphere of chaos which, magnified by rightist leaders and media, served to justify the military uprising.[24] Revisionist authors never wondered: *cui bono?* – for whose benefit was the atmosphere of public anarchy following the victory in the polls of the Popular Front in February 1936?

Given the weakness of the Spanish version of fascism,[25] Manuel Azaña was not wrong when he wrote in his memoirs that, leaving aside all the slogans and paraphernalia, 'swords and cassocks' were at the centre of the Nationalist coalition.[26] Indeed, the clergy and the armed forces – two institutions with a unique record of suppression of dissent – were the two key historic defenders of the eternal values of the motherland when it was threatened by the dangerous currents of modernity (the foundations of the 'anti-Spain').

By European standards, Spain's ecclesiastical establishment possessed an immense cultural, economic and political might, based upon its historic role, first during the epic 800-year struggle against the Moors ('la Reconquista'), and then at the centre of the Counter-Reformation during Spain's golden imperial age. As an integral part of the ancien régime, the Church constituted a reservoir of anti-liberal thought. After siding more or less openly with Carlism throughout the nineteenth century, the Catholic hierarchy had reconciled with the Bourbon dynasty by the turn of the century. In return for acquiring a paramount role in education and social services, the clergy constituted the 'organic intellectuals' of the monarchy, using its prestige to lend legitimacy to the crown. Its obvious support for vested interests identified the Church as the key symbol of wealth and power. In 1909, anger at the proletariat being called up to become the cannon folder of an imperialist adventure in Morocco degenerated into the so-called Tragic Week of Barcelona. Religious buildings became the target of popular anger, the 'Bastille of the Catalan working classes'.[27] The Catholic Church did not take a neutral stance following the advent of the Republic. On the contrary, it was the main ideological bulwark of counter-revolution and main unifying rod of all the anti-Republican forces.[28] At the outbreak of the civil war, religious properties and symbols became the primary objectives of mob fury and some 6,844 members of the clergy (including thirteen bishops) were killed.[29] Simultaneously, the Church's previous role as cheerleaders of the monarchy was now performed with gusto for the Nationalists. Using rhetoric reminiscent of medieval times, military sedition was legitimised as a crusade against the Moscow hordes. Franco, himself, was depicted as the 'Caudillo invicto' ('undefeated leader') who had led a new 'reconquista' to save the motherland. The Church never considered advocating forgiveness or reconciliation. Instead, the slaughter carried out by these modern crusaders was ignored when not greeted with enthusiasm. After all, courtesy of the new order, the clergy had regained its 'rightful' dominant position in society.[30]

If the Church was the ideological guardian of the throne, the armed forces were its praetorian guard. Indeed, during the monarchy outbursts of social unrest were frequently followed by the suspension of the constitution and the declaration of martial law, which granted the army final control over the maintenance of public order.[31] According to the Law of the Constitution of the Army of 1878, the military had as its primary function the defence of the nation from its internal enemies.[32] Therefore they were the guardians of the sacred values of the fatherland – national unity and social order. After 1898, embittered by the colonial defeat and extremely sensitive to any type of criticism, army officers began to question whether the existing constitutional practices were valid means to counter the pernicious effects of class conflict and peripheral nationalism. This feeling was confirmed in the aftermath of the First World War as the worsening economic dislocation and the example of the Bolshevik revolution led to unprecedented levels of industrial and rural strife. As in other European countries, existing liberal orders were no longer perceived as sufficient formulas of social control in a moment of escalating social warfare. The army emerged then as the central instrument of the subsequent social and political reaction, whose levels of ferocity were regarded by the Italian Marxist Antonio Gramsci as the precursor of fascism in his country.[33] This military-led counter-revolution initially acted behind the back of the impotent governments in Madrid, and eventually overthrew the regime in 1923.[34]

The army once again responded to right-wing apocalyptic messages to save the motherland in 1936. Nevertheless, the officer corps was not united in their seditious bid for power. If that had been the case it might have proved impossible to mount a successful resistance against the insurrection. In fact, the only major-general on active command in the mainland who revolted was Miguel Cabanellas in Zaragoza. The hard core of the rebellion – Generals Mola, Sanjurjo, Franco, Varela, etc – was made up of *africanistas*, or members of the elite colonial Army of Africa, who perceived themselves as untainted – unlike many of their peninsular counterparts – by the indolence of civilian life and the corruption of metropolitan politics. Already incensed by Azaña's freezing of promotions by war merits and aghast at the anticlerical and leftist character of the Republic, their political baptism of fire arrived with the outbreak of the October Revolution of 1934. Once martial law was declared, power passed into the hands of the War Minister and member of the

Radical Party Diego Hidalgo who swiftly appointed General Franco as his technical adviser, or the de facto person in charge of crushing the revolt. Franco did not hesitate then to order, for the first time, the use of colonial troops on the mainland. The success of this operation raised the status of both Franco and the Army of Africa within right-wing circles, and encouraged the Africanistas' own latent messianic mission to defend Spain's eternal values.[35] The victory in the polls of the Popular Front in February 1936 convinced them that the moment had arrived to take drastic measures to save the country from its godless and red government.

In order to achieve total victory, these Africanistas pursued war based on the strategy learnt in Morocco. Years of brutal military operations there had forged in them a particular ethos of cruelty and contempt for liberal values and human rights. They conducted their campaigns on mainland Spain as if it was a colonial struggle, with Spanish civilians playing the part of ignorant and ungodly natives. The enemy had thus to be exterminated and the potentially hostile population paralysed by sheer terror.[36] The savagery of the repression was therefore calculated, and pursued the ultimate goal of eradicating the cycle of reforms begun in 1931 and liquidating those who had dared to threaten Spain's true identity.[37] In Franco's own words: '… he was going to save Spain from Marxism at whatever cost'.[38]

When the entire course of the conflict is considered, the Nationalists can be seen to have found it much easier than the Republicans to co-ordinate their efforts and the resources at their disposal. Despite their different agendas, Spain's right-wing parties possessed a tradition of collaboration and were all prepared to subordinate their activities to the authority of the army. By contrast, the Republican camp never achieved a similar community of objectives. In fact, the great paradox of the insurrection was that it precipitated the very revolutionary process that the army claimed to be forestalling, and consequently produced the collapse of the Republican state. Although it would be gradually reconstructed, the Republican war effort was harmed by the competing aims of the central government with those of the Basque and Catalan administrations; the left's traditional aversion to militarism and centralisation; and the clashes between reformists and revolutionaries, Marxists and libertarians, among others.[39] However, to explain the Republic's ultimate implosion in terms of its own internal squabbling would be grossly misleading. The brutal conclusion of the Spanish labyrinth cannot be explained without its international context. The Republic's weariness and mounting defeatism was to a large extent produced by the decisive impact of external forces. This is something that the revisionists often play down since too much focus on foreign involvement would threaten the established cannon that the conflict was primarily decided by the Nationalists' superior strategy and Franco's inspirational command. Instead, they argue that international aid cancelled itself out, since both sides received roughly similar amounts of military supplies from abroad, and that Italo-German aid to the Nationalists was only a response to French and Soviet support for the Republic.[40]

Although Franco's apologists might well suggest that divine providence would have eventually guided the fulfilment of his holy crusade, there are sound reasons to speculate that without foreign intervention the rebellion might have been put down, or at the very least that the conflict would not have ended with the sort of unconditional victory that the Caudillo achieved in 1939. Indeed, based on demographic and economic resources, the Republic appeared to have the upper hand when the civil war broke out. After the first week, the Nationalist camp basically comprised that third of Spain that had historically voted for the right. By contrast, the government retained control of the most densely populated and urbanised part of the country. This included the main capitals, the vital industrial areas of northern and eastern Spain, practically the entire Mediterranean coast, nearly all the vast rural land of the south, most of the air force and the country's huge gold reserves. Also, crucially, the Army of Africa was unable to cross the Strait of Gibraltar after sailors overpowered their officers and retained control of the fleet. However, in a country lacking any significant armament industry, and whose forces were starved of modern weaponry, both sides turned abroad to acquire vital military supplies. Consequently, the crucial response of the Great Powers essentially determined the course and outcome of the war.

Ironically, the first hints of foreign reaction appeared to favour the Republic, which was, after all, according to international law, the legally established government of Spain. Both Italy, exhausted after the weary Abyssinian experience, and Germany, whose expansionist plans lay in central Europe, turned down the Nationalists' initial pleas for aid. At the same time, France, ruled by a Popular Front government headed by the socialist Léon Blum, appeared ready to help its Spanish counterparts.[41] However, the international context changed dramatically before the end of July. By then, a combination of opportunism and strategic considerations had led Hitler and Mussolini to reverse their previous stance. At that stage they believed that the reward for what they first assumed would be a secretive and small-scale operation could be huge: their sending of a few transport planes would enable the crack troops of the Army of Africa to be ferried across the Strait of Gibraltar. Once on the mainland and sustained by small but crucial air support and military equipment, Franco's troops, within a few weeks, would capture Madrid, the war would be over, and they would have acquired for a relatively cheap price a vital ideological ally in a strategically key area.[42]

Fascist involvement in Spain was consistent with their aggressive foreign policy of pushing and breaking the conditions of the Versailles Treaty. Their intervention not only rescued a botched coup d'état from potential oblivion but also tilted the balance decisively in favour of the Nationalists. However, their early expectations proved far too optimistic and they would find themselves dragged into a much longer campaign than initially anticipated. Nevertheless, the Republic soon discovered that it was not only under assault from the Axis powers but also from the attitude of the Western democracies.

The French Popular Front proved to be a frightened and paralysed friend. Despite obvious ideological and strategic reasons, and even existing commercial accords, its initial positive stance towards aiding the Spanish Republic was soon drastically altered. Following stormy cabinet meetings and abundant tears shed by Blum, the French administration, even after glaring evidence of Italian assistance to the Nationalists, settled for sending an appeal to the other European powers to subscribe to a non-intervention agreement in Spain. This policy was regarded by the French government as the best available solution for keeping the administration afloat in the face of massive internal and external pressures. In domestic terms, France was, like Spain, badly affected by economic dislocation and social polarisation. It was no secret that crucial sectors of the economic and diplomatic establishment, the armed forces and the Catholic Church, were thinking along the same lines as their Spanish counterparts, and believed that the French Third Republic under the Popular Front had fallen into subversive hands. French ministers thus feared that an open involvement in Spain could induce 'patriotic France' to emulate the Spanish rebels. Simultaneously, they were under huge pressure from Britain, France's key ally, to avoid any entanglement in favour of the Spanish Republic. This pressure included veiled threats that, if French intervention in Spain triggered a war in Europe, France would find herself alone.[43]

Professor Enrique Moradiellos, in his Len Crome Memorial Lecture, demonstrated eloquently how Britain pursued a game of deception during the Spanish Civil War, to conceal its malevolent neutrality towards the Republic.[44] And in his recent superb trilogy, the Spanish scholar Ángel Viñas has qualified that attitude, correctly in my opinion, to one of concealed hostility.[45] Let us also remember that the two highest authorities in the Republican camp, its President Manuel Azaña and its Prime Minister Juan Negrín, wrote that Britain's hypocrisy and deceitful stance had been their worst enemy.[46]

Due to class and upbringing, Britain's Conservative governing classes believed that a constructive understanding could be reached with the fascist powers, and regarded the Soviet Union as the obvious enemy. Their ideology, combined with huge British economic interests in Spain, led them to loathe all that the left-leaning Republic stood for.[47] This political bias was blatantly evident when, as early as 26 July 1936, Prime Minister Baldwin instructed his Foreign Secretary Anthony Eden: 'On no account, French or other, must [you] bring us into the fight on the side of the Russians.'[48] Notwithstanding that the Republic at this stage had not yet established proper diplomatic relations with the Soviet Union, it was viewed by Britain's diplomatic corps and government as a façade for Bolshevism. By contrast, General Franco was seen as a prudent officer fighting the spectre of social revolution, whose victory would lead to the establishment of 'a liberal dictatorship' very favourable to the interests of the United Kingdom.[49] The problem for British diplomacy was that the counter-revolution remained formally illegitimate, and thus, for reasons of public opinion, open intervention in favour of the rebellion was unthinkable.[50] Hence the proposal of a non-intervention agreement came as a gift sent from heaven.

The ill-named non-intervention strategy was evidence of retreat before British pressure; it reduced France to a subordinate role in the Western alliance, and doomed the Republic. The feeling of French impotence was clearly stated by André Blumel, Léon Blum's chef de cabinet: 'Non-intervention was essentially an attempt to prevent others from doing what France was incapable of accomplishing.'[51] Supervised by a committee based in London, non-intervention became the perfect instrument of British diplomacy. It turned into a surreal exercise of chicanery and window-dressing, which ensured the confinement of the Spanish conflict while formalising the legal anomaly of placing a democratically elected government on a par with a seditious military movement. Furthermore, it restrained the French from rushing to help the Republic, eliminated a potential confrontation with the fascist powers, and provided the perfect façade for the concealment of hostility towards the Republic, allowing the British government to maintain a semblance of impeccable neutrality for domestic public opinion.[52]

Revisionist authors dismiss non-intervention as an irrelevant factor that only confirmed the equilibrium of external forces in Spain.[53] In fact, under that charade, Franco was always able to obtain promptly and on credit crucial oil deliveries from the main Anglo-American companies, and weapons from the dictatorships, while the Spanish government, due to the international boycott, had to rely on the intrigues and inflated prices of the black market, for mostly obsolete equipment. And in contrast to the reliability of the Nationalist supplies, the long distance between the Soviet Union and Spain, and the dependence on contraband, meant irregular deliveries and constant shortages of vital military supplies.[54]

The Western powers' unwillingness to confront the dictators' blatant aggression in Spain only emboldened them. During the summer of 1937 Mussolini complied with Franco's request to strangle the lifeline provided to the Republic by the convoys of Soviet supplies in the Mediterranean.[55] Italian submarines, euphemistically described by the international media as 'pirates', attacked some thirty vessels – including French, British and other neutral ships. In fact, the Italians, informed by the Germans, were fully aware that British intelligence had broken their naval codes and knew them to be responsible for all the mayhem.[56] Indeed, following a conference held in Nyon in September, to discuss the existing crisis, the British government invited the Italians to participate in patrolling the Mediterranean. After boasting that the 'pirates had been turned into policemen', the Italian Foreign Minister, Count Galeazzo Ciano, described the surreal outcome of this episode as the decline of the Western democracies.[57]

Until the very end of the conflict, the British attitude hampered the Republic's hopes of survival. It is telling that, in the spring of 1938, the British government, while negotiating a new treaty with Mussolini which recognised formally the fascist conquest of Abyssinia, begged the Italians to halt the bombing of Spanish cities because the situation could be 'delicate' for Chamberlain.[58] It appeared to British statesmen that it was France's reckless behaviour, in allowing the entry of military equipment to Spain through her border, rather than the presence of Axis divisions that flouted the principles of non-intervention, that was leading Europe to the verge of war. At last, British diplomacy yielded a new success when, in the words of its ambassador in Paris, Sir Eric Phipps, the 'infernal frontier' was finally closed in June.[59] Of course, by then the Popular Front had collapsed in France. Its government was now presided over by the pusillanimous Edouard Daladier, and its foreign policy was in the 'safe hands' of Georges Bonnet, someone who did not need to be preached to about the usefulness of appeasing the fascist dictators.[60] The closing of the last and only safe channel of arms doomed the quickly fading hopes of the beleaguered Republic. The fact that against these daunting odds it still managed to resist for a further nine months is evidence enough of the incredible progress and determination of its forces under the spirited guidance of its last Prime Minister, Juan Negrín.

The fall of the monarchy in April 1931 gave way in Spain to a dream, that of the establishment of a new regime that could guarantee the creation of a more modern and egalitarian society. Supported by the traditional vested interests and blessed by the Catholic Church, Africanista officers rose in order to turn back the clock of history. During thirty-three months of cruel struggle, thousands of Spaniards died fighting for that dream. They were not alone. From more than fifty-three different countries, foreign volunteers were prepared to sacrifice their lives. They had perceived that fighting for Republican Spain was a last-ditch stand to tame the fascist beast. Their efforts were ultimately sabotaged by the attitude of the Anglo-French governing classes. Shielding their duplicity, cowardice and hypocrisy behind the safe cover of non-intervention, the Western leaders might have believed that by sacrificing a 'red Republic' they were ensuring peace on the continent. In fact, they not only delivered forty years of 'enlightened and benign dictatorship' to Spain under General Francisco Franco, but were also about to experience for themselves the consequences of appeasing, if not rewarding, aggression and tyranny.

This lecture was delivered on 14 March 2009 at the Imperial War Museum, London.

NOTES

1. As can be seen in the subsequent footnote, the book by Pío Moa (*Los Mitos de la Guerra Civil*) was already in its 35th edition in 2005. One cannot cease to be amazed by their use of flamboyant titles, including words such as mitos (myths), when, above all, the revisionists seek to update and re-package the old myths of the Francoist dictatorship. In general, most academics have chosen to ignore these authors. Welcome exception in terms of a sharp and thorough rebuttal of their arguments can be found in Alberto Reig Tapia, *Anti-Moa* (Barcelona: Ariel, 2006); and Enrique Moradiellos, 'Las razones de una crítica histórica: Pío Moa y la intervención extranjera en la Guerra Civil', *El Catoblepas, Revista Crítica del Presente*, no.15 (May 2003).

2. Pío Moa, *Los Mitos de la Guerra Civil* (35th ed.) (Madrid: La Esfera, 2005), pp.32, 186.

3. These clichés are repeated again and again in revisionist works. The two best known authors of this school are Pío Moa, with books such as *Los Orígenes de la Guerra Civil* (Madrid: Encuentros, 2007); *Los Mitos de la Guerra Civil* (op cit); and *Los Años de Hierro* (Madrid: La Esfera, 2007); and César Vidal with works such as *La Guerra que ganó Franco* (Barcelona: Editorial Planeta, 2006); and *Las Brigadas Internacionales* (Madrid: Espasa Calpe, 2006). This is a very succinct list from among their vast production. One of the still unexplained feats of these 'enlightened historical colossi' is the awesome amount of works they write. Vidal is supposed to have published 124 books since 1987, 27 of them in the years 2004-2005 alone (more than one per month!). A detailed list of clichés can be found in A Reig Tapia, *Franco: El César Superlativo* (Madrid: Tecnos, 2005), pp.344-6.

4. Manuel Tuñón de Lara, *España: La quiebra del 98* (Madrid: Sarpe, 1986), pp.13, 25.

5. Francisco J Romero Salvadó, *The Spanish Civil War: Origins, Course and Outcomes* (Basingstoke: Macmillan, 2005), p.2.

6. A summary in English of the manifesto published by Primo de Rivera at the time of the coup can be found in John Cowans, *Modern Spain: A Documentary Reader* (Philadelphia: University of Pennsylvania Press, 2003), pp.126-8.

7. Something done, for instance, in Moa, *Los Orígenes*, pp.9-10.

8. Eduardo González Calleja, 'La cultura de la guerra como propuesta historiográfica: una reflexión general desde el contemporaneísmo español', *Historia Social*, no.61 (2008), p.83.

9. Otto Bauer, 'Fascism', in David Beetham (ed.), *Marxists in Face of Fascism* (Manchester: Manchester University Press, 1983), pp.294-5.

10. For instance see Moa, *Los Orígenes*, pp.16, 221-3. In a more sophisticated manner, some mainstream conservative scholars such as Stanley Payne have stressed the CEDA's representative character (a large Catholic

constituency) and thus blamed the left for denying it its right to govern. See Payne's *Spain's First Democracy* (Madison: University of Wisconsin Press, 1993), pp.379-80; and 'Orígenes de la Guerra Civil', *Historia 16*, no.286 (February 2000), pp.59-61.

11. Paul Preston, *The Politics of Revenge: Fascism and the Military in 20th Century Spain* (London: Routledge, 1995), p.xiv.

12. See works by Ismael Saz, *Fascismo y Franquismo* (Valencia: Publicacions de la Universitat de València, 2004), p.61; and 'Paradojas de la historia. Paradojas de la historiografía. Las peripecias del Fascismo español', *Hispania* vol.LXI/1 (January-April 2001), pp.167-8.

13. José María Gil Robles, *No fue posible la paz* (Barcelona: Editorial Planeta, 1998), p.788.

14. Ibid, pp.697, 707-8.

15. Ibid, pp.774-5.

16. Ramón Serrano Suñer, *Memorias* (Barcelona: Editorial Planeta, 1977), p.184.

17. Moa, *Los Orígenes*, p.478.

18. The existence of these 'two faces' of the anarchist movement is analysed in Julián Casanova, 'La cara oscura del anarquismo', in Santos Juliá (ed.), *Violencia política en la España del Siglo XX* (Madrid: Taurus, 2000), p.67.

19. Manuel Azaña, *Obras Completas* (Madrid: Centro de Estudios Políticos y Constitucionales, 2007), vol.4, p.227.

20. S Juliá, 'Introducción: Violencia política en España. ¿Fin de una larga historia?', in Juliá (ed.), *Violencia política*, p.12.

21. For Carlism see Martin Blinkhorn, *Carlism and Crisis in Spain, 1931-39* (Cambridge: Cambridge University Press, 1975); and Jordi Canal, *Banderas blancas, boinas rojas: una historia política del Carlismo, 1876-1939* (Madrid: Marcial Pons, 2006).

22. For the political violence that led to the 1923 coup see Soledad Bengoechea and Fernando del Rey Reguillo, 'Militars, patrons i Sindicalistes Lliures', *L'Avenç*, 166 (January 1993); Eduardo González Calleja, *El Máuser y el sufragio: orden público, subversión y violencia política en la crisis de la Restauración, 1917-1931* (Madrid: CSIC, 1999); E González Calleja and F del Rey Reguillo, *La defensa armada contra la revolución* (Madrid: CSIC, 1995); and FJ Romero Salvadó, *The Foundations of Civil War: Revolution, Social Conflict and Reaction in Liberal Spain, 1916-1923* (London: Routledge/Cañada Blanch, 2008).

23. Cited in P Preston, *¡Comrades! Portraits from the Spanish Civil War* (London: HarperCollins, 1999), p.85.

24. Ibid, pp.78-9, 96; Saz, *Fascismo*, pp.71-2; Carlos Blanco Escolá, *Falacias de la Guerra Civil* (Barcelona: Editorial Planeta, 2005), pp.12-3, 65-9.

25. The Falange certainly exploded in numerical terms following the outbreak of the civil war. But unlike in Italy and Germany, one wonders how many 'genuine' fascists were amongst those converted in the last hour.

26. M Azaña, *Memorias Políticas y de Guerra*, 2nd ed. (Barcelona: Grijalbo, 1978), vol.2, p.313.

27. Joan Connelly Ullman, *The Tragic Week: Anticlericalism in Spain, 1875-1912* (Cambridge, Mass.: Harvard University Press, 1968), pp.169, 246-7.

28. J Casanova, *La Iglesia de Franco* (Madrid: Temas de Hoy, 2001), pp.38-9.

29. Julio de la Cueva Merino, 'Si los curas y frailes supieran', in Juliá (ed.), *Violencia política*, pp.221-3.

30. Casanova, *La Iglesia*, pp.16-7, 48, 303-4. Michael Richards, *A Time of Silence: Civil War and the Culture of Repression in Franco's Spain, 1936-1945* (Cambridge: Cambridge University Press, 1998), p.7.

31. Fundación Antonio Maura, *Antonio Maura's Papers*, Leg. 273, Carp. 4. Constitutional guarantees were suspended in all or part of the country twenty-five times between December 1875 and March 1919.

32. Manuel Ballbé, *Orden público y militarismo en la España constitucional, 1812-1983* (Madrid: Alianza, 1985), p.233.

33. Antonio Gramsci, 'On Fascism, 1921', in Beetham (ed.), op cit, pp.82-3.

34. For the army's central role in the subversion and destruction of the liberal regime see the works by S Bengoechea, *El Locaut de Barcelona* (Barcelona: Curial, 1998); and '1919: la Barcelona colpista; l'aliança de patrons i militars contra el sistema liberal', *Afers*, 23/24 (1996), p.311; González Calleja and del Rey, op cit; Carolyn P Boyd, *Praetorian Politics in Liberal Spain* (Chapel Hill: University of North Carolina Press, 1979); and Romero Salvadó, *The Foundations of Civil War*.

35. Sebastian Balfour, *Deadly Embrace: Morocco and the Road to the Spanish Civil War* (Oxford: Oxford University Press, 2002), p.256.

36. Herbert Southworth, *El mito de la cruzada de Franco* (Barcelona: Plaza y Janés, 1986), p.217; A Reig Tapia, *Violencia y terror* (Madrid: Akal, 1990), p.110.

37. Francisco Espinosa, 'Julio 1936', in J Casanova et al, *Morir, matar, sobrevivir* (Barcelona: Editorial Crítica, 2002), p.115.

38. In conversation with the American journalist Jay Allen, cited by P Preston, *Franco* (London: HarperCollins, 1993), p.153.

39. Romero Salvadó, *The Spanish Civil War*, p.xiv.

40. A melange of these arguments can be found in Moa, *Los Mitos*, pp.356-9, 474-81.

41. Jean Lacouture, *Leon Blum* (New York: Holmes & Meier, 1982), pp.306-7; Jules Moch, *Recontres avec Léon Blum* (Paris: Plon, 1970), pp.189-91; John E Dreifort, *Yvon Delbos at the Quai d'Orsay: French Foreign Policy During the Popular Front, 1936-1938* (Lawrence: University Press of Kansas, 1973), pp.32-3.

42. Ángel Viñas, *Franco, Hitler y el estallido de la Guerra Civil* (Madrid: Alianza, 2001), pp.344-75, 385-97, 430; Robert H Whealey, *Hitler and Spain* (Kentucky: Kentucky University Press, 1989), pp.5-7; I Saz, *Mussolini contra la II República: hostilidad, conspiraciones, intervención (1931-1936)*

(Valencia: Institució Valenciana d'Estudis i Investigació, 1986), pp.179-210; and P Preston, 'Mussolini's Spanish Adventure: From Limited Risk to War', in P Preston and Ann L Mackenzie (eds.), *The Republic Besieged* (Edinburgh: Edinburgh University Press, 1996), pp.21-45.

43. British pressure on the French to avoid aiding the Republic, including a tearful Blum explaining the situation to the Spanish socialist, Jiménez de Asúa, and the final settling for non-intervention, is in Lacouture, op cit, pp.308-29. See also Pierre Renouvin and René Rémond, *Léon Blum, chef de gouvernement, 1936-1937* (Paris: Presse de la Fondation Nationale des Sciences Politiques, 1967), pp.356-60; Moch, op cit, pp.214-5; Dreifort, op cit, pp.43-9; and A Viñas, *El Honor de la República: entre el acoso fascista, la hostilidad británica y la política de Stalin* (Barcelona: Editorial Crítica, 2008), pp.29, 36-8.

44. Enrique Moradiellos, *Albion's Perfidy: The British Government and the Spanish Civil War* (Len Crome Memorial Lecture, 8 March 2006, London: International Brigade Memorial Trust); reproduced as chapter 5 of this book.

45. A Viñas, *La soledad de la República: el abandono de las democracias y el viraje hacia la Unión Soviética*, 2ⁿᵈ ed. (Barcelona: Editorial Crítica, 2007), p.438. This analysis, with particular focus on the Chamberlain cabinet, is pursued further in Viñas, *El Honor*, pp.47-8, 58-9, 543-4.

46. Azaña, *Memorias*, vol.2, p.64. Negrín's view is quoted in E Moradiellos, *La perfidia de Albión: el gobierno británico y la guerra civil española* (Madrid: Siglo XXI, 1996), p.xiii.

47. These conclusions can be seen in works by Moradiellos such as *La perfidia*, pp.20-4, 32-47; and 'The Origins of British Non-Intervention in the Spanish Civil War: Anglo-Spanish Relations in Early 1936', *European History Quarterly*, vol.21, 3, (1991), pp.347-59; Viñas, *La Soledad*, pp.18-9, 74-7, 437-8. See also Douglas Little, 'Red Scare, 1936: Anti-Bolshevism and the Origins of British Non-Intervention in the Spanish Civil War', *Journal of Contemporary History*, vol.23 (1988), pp.292-302.

48. Thomas Jones, *A Diary with Letters 1931-1950* (Oxford: Oxford University Press, 1954), p.231.

49. Cited in E Moradiellos, 'The Gentle General: The Official British Perception of General Franco during the Spanish Civil War', Preston and Mackenzie (eds.), op cit, p.6.

50. Moradiellos, *La perfidia*, p.44.

51. Cited in Lacouture, op cit, pp.332-3. This feeling of decadence and decline is well illustrated in Jean-Baptiste Duroselle, *France and the Nazi Threat: The Collapse of French Diplomacy* (New York: Enigma, 2004).

52. Moradiellos, *La perfidia*, p.85

53. This idea is hammered in Moa, *Los Mitos*, pp.358-9, 367-8. It has been meticulously demolished in Moradiellos, 'Las razones de una crítica histórica'.

54. An excellent study of the effects of non-intervention and its harmful impact on the Republic is Gerald Howson, *Arms for Spain: The Untold Story of the Spanish Civil War* (London: John Murray, 1998).

55. 'Documents on German Foreign Policy 1918-1945', Series D, vol.3: 'Germany and the Spanish Civil War' (hereafter DGFP), (London: His Majesty's Stationery Office, 1951), doc. 408 (dispatch from the German ambassador in Italy, Ulrich von Hassel, 5 August 1937), p.433.

56. Ibid, doc. 418 (12 September 1937), p.443.

57. Galeazzo Ciano, *Diary, 1937-43* (London: Phoenix, 2002), pp.8, 14-5.

58. DGFP, doc.548 (21 March 1938), p.622.

59. Dispatch of Sir Eric Phipps to Lord Halifax (June 1938), cited in E Moradiellos, *El reñidero de Europa: las dimensiones internacionales de la Guerra Civil española* (Barcelona: Península, 2001), p.214.

60. Jean-François Berdah, *La democracia asesinada: la República española y las grandes potencias, 1931-1939* (Barcelona: Editorial Crítica, 2002), pp.371-6. See also Moradiellos, *El reñidero*, pp.209-10.

Three Months in Spain: The British Battalion at Madrigueras and Jarama from January to March 1937

Richard Baxell

This topic arises partly as a response to the many questions I have been asked by family members about the day-to-day experiences of their relatives in Spain. The politics and the military aspects of the volunteers' experiences have naturally received wide coverage, but what the volunteers ate, where they slept, how they spent their days in the line: these things have received less attention. However, they are important. As Helen Graham said recently in a typically forthright and lucid interview with ALBA, the American veterans' association: 'Telling big stories through individual human lives is a very powerful way of doing history'.[1]

This chapter therefore deals with the experiences of the volunteers during the first three months of 1937, from the formation of the British Battalion – through its baptism of fire at the Battle of Jarama in February, which saw its virtual annihilation – to the attempts to rebuild it in March and April. Crucial to this will be the words of the volunteers themselves, many drawn from the wealth of interview material held in the Imperial War Museum's sound archive. The material offers the opportunity to let the volunteers 'step out of the pages of history' and tell their own story.

The Battle of Jarama in February 1937 was, of course, not the first involvement of British volunteers in the Spanish Civil War. Since the military rising in July 1936, anti-fascists from around the world had been arriving in Spain to defend the Republic against the military rebels and their German and Italian backers. By the end of the year, almost thirty men – and women – from Britain and Ireland had already been killed.[2]

Established just after Christmas 1936, the 16th British Battalion

Officers of the British Battalion in Madrigueras (from left): Wilf Macartney, Dave Springhall, Peter Kerrigan, Tom Wintringham and Frank Ryan.

Courtesy Marx Memorial Library

of the XV International Brigade was formed mainly from volunteers from Britain and Ireland, though it also included those from a number of other countries, including Cyprus, South Africa and Australia. The battalion incorporated those already in Spain fighting in various militia units and with the mainly English-speaking company in the French XIV International Brigade, whose fighting reputation had already made them the heroes of the battalion.[3]

The majority of the new recruits arrived in the large influx during December 1936, travelling on a day return ticket to Paris, thus bypassing the necessity of owning a passport. From Paris, the volunteers travelled to Spain and mustered at Figueras, before being sent, via Barcelona and Valencia, to the main International Brigade base at Albacete, roughly half-way between Valencia and Madrid. Here the volunteers would be divided up into battalions based primarily on nationality and language. A training base was established for the British Battalion in a small village called Madrigueras, about 20 kilometres north of the main base at Albacete.

Two contrasting aspects of the village feature strongly in the volunteers' memoirs: the frightening levels of poverty and the imposing size of the village church.[4] As Bill Rust pithily described in his 1939 history, *Britons in Spain*, the village was 'not very lively ... like all Spanish villages it had a church – a very big one; and a school – a very small one'.[5] David Crook, a young volunteer from London, and one of many Jewish volunteers in the battalion, later wrote his impressions:

> *Madrigueras was a poor place with a population of 6,000, mainly families of hired labourers of absentee landlords. It was dominated by a large stone church, as much a fortress as a place of worship, with a few narrow slits of windows high above the ground, a massive, iron-studded wooden door and a tall tower overlooking the village square ... When we arrived, around the first week of 1937, the wall was pitted with holes. What were these? I asked. Bullet holes, I was told.[6]*

The church showed familiar signs of desecration, with the high altar, the pews and all signs of religious paintings having been removed, and it was being used as a communal eating place for the villagers and troops.[7]

A number of the volunteers also commented on the dreary winter climate of La Mancha. London sculptor Jason Gurney described Madrigueras in January as:

> *A very dull and depressing village ... Everywhere lay under a chill and drizzling rain, and in Madrigueras itself the unpaved streets had become churned up into a grey-green mud which got thicker and soupier with each passing day.*[8]

The volunteers were billeted around the village, some staying in the old theatre, others in villagers' houses. London taxi-driver Harry Stratton remembered being put up in a hay loft belonging to a Madrigueras peasant family.[9]

Whilst the billeting arrangements presented few problems – lack of decent sanitation aside – the food was a very different matter. Food was a constant issue in Spain. Nottingham volunteer Walter Gregory's feelings about the food were unambiguous: 'I think it could be accurately described as awful'.[10] Many of the problems were due to the dramatic change of diet, as Scottish volunteer Tommy Bloomfield later recounted: 'At first you all had queasy stomachs because of food in the oil. They fried rice. You had fried fish in the oil. Everything was in oil'.[11]

Londoner Fred Thomas had much the same impression:

> *The stew was unbelievably bad. I am quite certain that not once did its composition alter. It was, unfailingly, a dreadful concoction of bits of meat (donkey? mule?), rice and little scraps of potato, all boiled together in olive oil into a most unappetising mess. No one seemed to know what nationality the cooks were, though we were all quite clear that they had been born out of wedlock and were now fascist.*[12]

As Tony Gilbert, a veteran anti-Blackshirt fighter from London recounts, it was the quality of the food, not the quantity, that the volunteers took issue with:

> *Food wasn't plentiful, but I think the army was given whatever was available and I think the people gave it gladly. The meat we had was, of course, burro. You know what a burro is I suppose? A cross between a donkey and a mule, I think, but I don't know. I'm not sure.*[13]

The lack of drinkable water also caused problems for, as another volunteer described: 'You can't drink the water, except in coffee, and that's a problem, as the coffee is always awful'.[14] As Fred Thomas remembered, many turned to the only readily available liquid, wine:

> *Prior to Spain, most British volunteers were happy enough downing a pint of beer. Wines, had they been affordable, were considered somewhat sissyish. In Spain though, we took readily to the coarse red vino supplied liberally at meal times and usually available in the cafés. To some the question of its potency remained a constant challenge, too often unresolved until the questioner was beyond acknowledging defeat. Drunks were a damned nuisance.*[15]

The drinking culture presented serious discipline problems for the battalion leadership, who were working urgently in order to forge the volunteers into a cohesive military – and political – unit.

The military commander of the battalion was a Scottish journalist and World War One veteran, Wilf Macartney, who had previously served ten years in Parkhurst prison for spying for Russia.[16] The battalion political commissar, in charge of the political development and welfare of the volunteers, was Dave Springhall, the secretary of the London District of the Communist Party, who had studied at the Lenin School in Moscow, the finishing school for the party's elite.[17]

The battalion itself was divided up into four companies, one machine-gun company plus three of infantry. No.1 Company was led by Jock Cunningham, ex-Argyll and Sutherland Highlanders, and veteran of the battles in University City in Madrid and Lopera. No.2, the Machine-Gun Company, was led by Tom Wintringham, who had been in Spain for several months. An influential British Communist and the party's specialist in military matters, Wintringham also acted as second-in-command of the British Battalion. No.3 Company was led by Bill Briskey, an experienced trade union activist from London, and No.4 by Bert Overton, another British Army veteran.

Military training, such as it was, was put into practice. Fortunately, many of the volunteers had had some form of military training and 'the number who had never handled a rifle before was surprisingly small'.[18] There was 'a good proportion of ex-servicemen' and several others had served in the Territorial Army or some other form of military organisation. For example, Julius 'Jud' Colman was one of a group of six volunteers from Manchester who travelled to Spain together, arriving in late 1936. He described how all the members of his group had some form of military experience:

One of the British group, an artillery man from the Great War, was posted to a French unit. The rest of us had received some form of military training. I had fired a rifle at the Lancashire Fusilier barracks as a cadet in the Jewish Lads' Brigade. Some of the others were ex-servicemen.[19]

However, there was a sizeable number who had no such experience. At first, Tom Wintringham was rather horrified by the progress of the training:

The first days of training … were pitiable in the extreme. I did what I could to start training in tactics, but was dismayed to find that neither of the company commanders knew how to move men either on the parade-ground or the field. [One of the company commanders] … made his men string out and double forward at the sound of his whistle, exactly on the good old Boer War lines that I had learnt in the Officers' Training Corps at school. He loved blowing that whistle. I noted with real misery – standing ahead of the two companies and watching them move towards me in a formation intended to be that of attack – that this boy chose a nice hillock to stand on and waved his men forward with dramatic gestures. And I noted also that had I been an enemy machine-gunner I could have wiped out most of his company at ranges between six hundred and four hundred yards. He kept them bunched together, left them lying on skylines, was more concerned with the straightness of his line than with cover. This wouldn't do.[20]

George Leeson, previously a clerk working for the London Underground, here discusses the training he received:

Not effective. Not in the slightest. Not in the slightest. There was nothing. You see, it was just a case, really, of trying, what are you going to get the men to do? And so just keep them busy doing something so they don't get demoralised and keep them tough and strong as well, take them out on long route marches. About the only thing they really learned was how to take cover from aircraft. You know, they'd blow a whistle for aircraft and you scattered from the road and would lay face downwards. Even if you put your head in a load of mule manure you did that. And the other thing was forming artillery formation, which is arrowhead formation, which it turned out wasn't a very good formation for advancing in front of the enemy anyway.[21]

Tom Wintringham later claimed 'that in five weeks or so they had produced some very fair infantry';[22] but, in truth, as Vincent Brome quite rightly observed in his 1965 study of the International Brigades, five weeks of basic training was 'absurdly short'.[23]

Of course, many of the problems with training were a result of the well-documented limitations of quantity and quality of Republican arms and ammunition.[24] As Fred Copeman, a section leader at Jarama and later a commander of the battalion observed, the military training was 'of a very elementary standard because of the lack of equipment' – particularly weaponry and ammunition.[25] 'Guns and ammunition were scarce in the extreme';[26] and, in particular, 'the machine guns of the Second Republic's army were at this time, in February 1937, mostly a job lot of junk'.[27]

Volunteers were issued with a rough khaki uniform, boots and a French army tin hat. Brand new Russian rifles eventually arrived at the beginning of February, which came complete with a triangular bayonet that was designed to be in place when the rifle was fired. However, the bayonets were extremely cumbersome and most were either lost or discarded. A number ended up being used as tent pegs.

Dundee communist Tom Clarke was one of the more experienced volunteers, having served with the Cameron Highlanders from 1925 to 1933. He was given one of the new rifles supplied by the Soviet Union: 'I didn't like them. They were too long in the butt and they only held five bullets in the magazine. I preferred the Lee Enfield, but you [ha]d to make the best of what you could'.[28]

The infantrymen were given the opportunity to practice firing the rifles but, as many only got to fire five bullets, the value of this must be regarded as questionable at best. Jason Gurney's summary of the situation in early 1937 was biting: 'Many people writing on the International Brigades have described them as well-armed, highly disciplined and well-trained units. This we of the British Battalion were not'.[29] As Tony Gilbert discovered, the new volunteers had much to learn:

When the bombs began to fall, there were no air raid shelters, so we were told to run for the open fields. Less chance of casualties. We turned round and laughed at each other. There were two volunteers for Spain and there we were holding hands like, like two young kids. I suppose to help each other over our own feelings. We didn't realise it until we looked around at each other, but there it is. That's what we were. We weren't really soldiers. We really didn't know what we were letting ourselves in for.[30]

By the beginning of January 1937, there were approximately 450 volunteers based at Madrigueras.[31] However, the battalion suffered a major setback in mid January, when a number of the Irish volunteers, already unhappy with British officers' tendency not to make any distinction between British and Irish volunteers, discovered that two senior British figures in Spain – XV International Brigade staff officer George Nathan and the British Battalion commander himself, Wilf Macartney – had played a part in British covert activities in Ireland.[32]

That divisions had arisen between the British and Irish is not that surprising for, as James Hopkins described, 'most, if not all, of the Irish volunteers were members of the Irish Republican Army';[33] both the leading figures amongst the Irish contingent, Frank Ryan and Chris 'Kit' Conway, were experienced IRA fighters.[34] Not surprisingly, the ex-IRA activists found fighting alongside their old adversaries extremely difficult, no matter the internationalist rhetoric of the political commissars.[35] Likewise, many of the English seemed to find it difficult to overcome a rather ignorant and stereotypical view of the Irish as wastrels and drunkards.

A meeting was called on 12 January to attempt to resolve the simmering discontent, which was attended by approximately 45 Irish members of the battalion. During a stormy session, those wishing to remain with the British Battalion vehemently argued 'that distinctions must be made between anti-fascist working-class comrades from Britain and British imperialism'.[36] Nevertheless, the Irish group voted by a ratio of two to one to leave the British Battalion and instead join the American volunteers in the Abraham Lincoln Battalion.

Early February 1937 brought more problems, when there were two unsettling changes to the battalion leadership. The most significant was the replacement of Wilf Macartney as commander of the battalion in somewhat suspicious, or at the very least bizarre, circumstances. As part of his parole requirements following his release from Parkhurst prison for spying, Macartney had regularly to report to the authorities in Britain and he was due to return temporarily home.[37] Prior to his departure, a farewell supper was held in his honour at the International Brigade base at Albacete. At the end of the evening, Peter Kerrigan, the Scottish political commissar at the base, was exchanging pistols with Macartney, when the pistol went off, wounding Macartney in the arm and ensuring that his period of leave became rather more permanent.

Whilst many commentators have argued that the shooting was no accident, I think they are mistaken. It is certainly true that senior figures in the XV Brigade and the British Communist Party had become disenchanted with Macartney's leadership of the battalion, but the claim that Kerrigan shot Macartney in order to ensure his return to Britain makes no sense. Macartney was about to return home anyway. Had senior Communist Party figures decided that the battalion would be better served in Spain without Macartney, there seems little doubt that he could have been prevented from returning to Spain, as would be demonstrated later the same year when three senior British figures in Spain were recalled to Britain following heated infighting after the Battle of Brunete.[38]

Wilf Macartney was replaced as battalion commander by No.2 Company commander Tom Wintringham. Described as 'invariably pleasant, informal and unpretentious', Wintringham's popularity appears to have been widespread.[39] Volunteer Tony Hyndman, the boyfriend of the poet Stephen Spender, later wrote:

> *It took him only a few days to win the respect and loyalty of all under his command. He was cool, quick in deciding who did what, with a wry sense of humour.*[40]

However, Jason Gurney rather worryingly believed that 'I don't think he really knew any more about military affairs than I did'.

Wintringham was replaced as commander of the Machine-Gun Company by Harold Fry, an ex-sergeant from the British Army who had served in India and China.[41] The other change was the promotion of Dave Springhall to brigade commissar and his replacement by George Aitken, the full-time Communist Party organiser for the North-East of England.

A steady influx of new arrivals meant that the numbers in the battalion gradually increased to approximately 600 by February. Despite the earlier loss of the Irish group, the British Battalion was now considered to be of sufficient strength and readiness for front-line action. However, not everyone agreed:

> *We had built up to over 600 men. Something over fifty of them had been in action on the Cordova Front, and the remainder had received some sort of training in Madrigueras but had still not fired a shot from any of their weapons. Only one Company Commander had been in action, and that, only as the second in command of a platoon. We possessed an assort-*

*ment of automatic weapons of doubtful value as well as the Russian
rifles. The Commander of the Battalion was well intentioned but totally
inexperienced. The other three battalions which formed the Brigade were
not very much better off. It is quite certain that the Brigade was not the
well-armed, well-trained force that various people have pretended it to
have been. There was no lack of courage or firm intent amongst the rank
and file but events were to prove that this was not enough.*[42]

On 8 February, the battalion prepared to leave Madrigueras for the
front, which lay to the south-east of Madrid:

> *The next morning, the villagers got to know, somebody told them that we
> were leaving. The next day, we fell in on the parade ground, the entire
> village, again all their Sunday best clothes on. They were all dressed in
> their Sunday best. And as we left in these trucks, the entire village, as we
> went down the street, they all came running and running after us and
> my last memory of Madrigueras there is the entire village standing there
> weeping, weeping and waving to us as we rode away. We might have
> been their own sons going away there.*[43]

David Crook, a young volunteer from London who had recently been
an MP's private secretary, described his departure in similar fashion
and remembered the tears of Maria, a villager in whose house he had
been billeted:

> *The whole town was out, terrifically wrought up, lined up by the lorries,
> shouting, saluting, laughing and crying. Maria wept bitterly, which
> worried and puzzled me … I puzzled over Maria's tears for years.
> Finally I concluded that for all my education and her lack of it, she knew
> more about life and death than I did. She foresaw what I did not: that
> many of us would not come back.*[44]

The Battle of Jarama had begun two days earlier, on the morning of 6
February 1937. Following the failure of the attempts on the west of
Madrid in November and December 1936, Franco had prepared a
new offensive to the south of the capital, aiming to cut the vital road
that linked Madrid with Valencia, the seat of the Republican government.[45]

Colonel, later General Varela, Franco's field commander, had five
brigades of six battalions at his disposal, plus eleven reserve battalions,

totalling some 25,000 men, mostly elite Moroccan *regulares* and legionnaires, backed up by German armour.[46] The rebel offensive pressed forward quickly and by the evening of 6 February the Republicans had been pushed back to the Jarama river and rebel troops were within shelling distance of the Madrid-Valencia road.

Over the next three days Nationalists continued to force themselves forwards, despite the Republican commander, General Miaja, throwing the elite Spanish Lister, El Campesino and XI International Brigades into the defence. By 7 February, rebel forces had reached the junction of the Manzanares and Jarama rivers, and the following day they captured the bridge across the Manzanares and threatened to reach the Madrid-Valencia road. At the same time, despite herculean defensive efforts by the Republicans forces to the south, Nationalist troops managed to cross the Jarama river and prepared themselves for an assault on the ridge which overlooked them, the Pingarrón Heights. The XV International Brigade, of which the British Battalion was part, was now thrown into the defence.

The 600-odd members of the battalion made their way north by lorry to Chinchón, about 25 kilometres from Madrid and 15 kilometres south-east of the site of the rebel advance. Recent arrivals were given some hurried last-minute preparation. Harry Stratton described how newcomers such as he 'were issued with rifles and ammo on the way. I hadn't handled a rifle until then, but Jock McCrae taught me rifle drill with a walking stick on the way up'.[47]

Early in the morning of 12 February, the volunteers were moved up to the edge of the Pingarrón Heights and began climbing upwards to the plateau overlooking the Jarama river.[48] The battalion moved forward, but had no real idea of when they would meet the enemy. They advanced over a ridge, then, after crossing a narrow sunken road, began to descend into the valley of the Jarama, which lay in front of them. When the volunteers found themselves coming under enemy fire, they quickly pulled back to the top of the ridge and took up defensive positions. David Crook recounts what happened:

We were ordered to move. 'Get to the top of that bloody hill and don't leave it till you're told to.' Luckily I was with my pal Sam Wild. We took up a position at the right brow of the hill, threw ourselves down and I started firing light-heartedly at those puffs of white smoke. Not Sam. First he clawed the soil and reached for stones to build a parapet. Sam had been brought up in an orphanage, served on a merchant navy

*training ship, been unemployed. He knew how to fight for survival. My
life had been softer, more sheltered. Without his example I'd never have
survived the murderous fire on what came to be known as Suicide Hill.
Very few did.*[49]

The battalion was then subjected to a terrifying three-hour machine-
gun and artillery barrage. Tony Gilbert later described the horror of
experiencing an artillery bombardment:

> *The first time you hear a shell explode, the first time you hear it cutting
> the air, let alone the explosion, it's a, well, it was for me a tremendously
> frightening experience. Your stomach just turns to water. This happens to
> every soldier when he first hears metal tearing through the air and knows
> it's liable to be his finish.*[50]

When the barrage finally ended the battalion was attacked by 'at least
three battalions' of highly experienced Moroccan infantry, Franco's
crack troops, who were in their element advancing across the open
terrain of the Jarama valley.[51] Jason Gurney described the absolute
horror that the rapid advance of the North African troops had on the
poorly trained volunteers, and he effectively summarised the
inequality between the two opposing factions:

> *Nobody at Madrigueras had said anything about artillery fire or the
> genius of Moorish infantry to move across country without presenting a
> target for anyone but a highly-trained marksman – a category that
> included no one in our outfit … [The Moors] were professionals, backed
> by a mass of artillery and heavy machine-gun fire supplied by the
> German Condor legion. It was a formidable opposition to be faced by a
> collection of city-bred young men with no experience of war, no idea how
> to find cover on an open hillside, and no competence as marksmen.*[52]

The battalion's position worsened considerably when the members of
the Machine-Gun Company discovered that their Maxim machine-
guns had been given cartridge belts filled with the wrong
ammunition.[53] Under the ferocious Nationalist attack, the Franco-
Belge Battalion further to the north of the British was forced to pull
back, which brought the British companies under lethal enfilading
machine-gun fire that swept across them from their right. The British
tried desperately to hold their ground, but were cut to pieces.

As the day progressed, the rapidly mounting casualties put them in an increasingly untenable position. The surviving members of the battalion were left with little option but to retreat from Suicide Hill back to the battalion headquarters on the plateau, dragging their wounded comrades with them. But, as Oldham metal-finisher Albert Charlesworth noted: 'There weren't many to go back'.[54]

As the dispirited British pulled back, Moroccan soldiers rushed forward over the top of Suicide Hill in order to occupy the positions relinquished by the retreating British.

At this point, the battalion experienced perhaps its only moment of good fortune that day. After a terribly frustrating day spent without ammunition for the machine-guns, the correct calibre bullets had at last appeared. Quickly, the machine-guns were brought into operation and used with devastating effect on the Moroccan soldiers who, for once, were caught out in the open and totally unawares. The Moroccan troops either quickly dropped down out of sight and waited for the cover of darkness or, where they could, retreated out of range. This brought to an end the first day of the Battle of Jarama.

Like other Republican units, the British Battalion had endured seven hours of extremely heavy losses: 'Out of the 400 men in the rifle companies, only 125 were left. Altogether less than half the battalion remained'.[55] The remnants gathered at the headquarters on the sunken road, desperate for food and water.

During the night a number of stragglers were located by the political commissar George Aitken. He attempted to cajole them back to the line but, as he freely admits, some volunteers were pressed back to the front under the threat of his pistol.[56] Another group of men were found hiding in wine vaults in a farmhouse behind the lines. They were also marched back to the front. Coerced or not, the volunteers would be sorely needed on the front line over the next two days.

The following day was to be no less terrifying for the traumatised survivors. Just before daybreak, Wintringham prepared his depleted forces as best he could. When dawn broke, the members of Harold Fry's No.2 Machine-Gun Company were able to see a number of enemy soldiers who had moved up in the night between the ridge and Suicide Hill and quickly drove them back with concentrated machine-gun fire.[57] But as the day progressed the Nationalists pressed forwards and the battalion found itself once again surrounded on three sides. At this point the nervous commander of No.4 Company, Bert Overton, finally panicked and withdrew his company right back to the sunken road.[58] This left the Machine-Gun Company's flank totally unprotected and rebel forces quickly took advantage of the situation and surrounded them. As many as thirty members of the company, including its commander, Harold Fry, and his assistant, Ted Dickenson, were captured.

When Overton realised what he had done, he tried to make amends by leading a charge of 40 men in a desperate attempt to retake the trenches recently occupied by Fry's Machine-Gun Company. The Nationalist soldiers simply mowed them down with their own machine-guns. Only six of the 40 men made it back to the British positions. In the mêlée Tom Wintringham sustained a leg wound and was temporarily replaced as commander by the political commissar, George Aitken, until the well-respected Jock Cunningham opportunely returned from his sickbed in the evening. By nightfall only 160 men still remained in the line.[59]

The third day of the battle, 14 February, brought a new assault on the British Battalion's lines by a fresh Nationalist brigade, supported by tanks. Under severe crossfire and without any specialised equipment to combat the tanks, Jock Cunningham had little choice but to withdraw the battalion away from the sunken road. The Irish leader, Frank Ryan, later described their plight:

> *Dispirited by heavy casualties, by defeat, by lack of food, worn out by three days of gruelling fighting, our men appeared to have reached the end of their resistance.*
>
> *Some were still straggling down the slopes from what had been, up to an hour ago, the front line. And now, there was no line, nothing between the Madrid road and the Fascists but disorganised groups of weary, war-wrecked men. After three days of terrific struggle, the superior numbers, the superior armaments of the Fascists had routed them. All, as they came back, had similar stories to tell: of comrades dead, of conditions that were more than flesh and blood could stand, of weariness they found hard to resist.*[60]

With the British machine-guns crushed underneath the tanks, the weakened British line finally broke and the volunteers retreated in small groups back down the slope towards the Chinchón road.

But here they were stopped by 'Gal', the commander of the XV International Brigade, who explained to them that they were the only troops between the rebels and the Valencia road.[61] Despite their physical and mental exhaustion, 140 volunteers marched back with Jock Cunningham and Frank Ryan to try to recapture their lost positions. Under no illusions about the situation they were walking into, the volunteers marched, singing 'The Internationale' to bolster their spirits and picking up stragglers on the way. Londoner John 'Bosco' Jones relates the story of what became known as 'The Great Rally':

> *It was Cunningham who said, you've heard the story. 'Come on lads!' And we rallied. And I think maybe there was seventy-five of us or something and walked up this main road. I'll never forget it. And as we walked up this main road, there are things I can't believe but, you see, it happened. Someone burst out and started singing the Internationale. We were stone mad when I think about it. And as we moved up, troops from all around, Spaniards and all others, rallied. We found ourselves in a small army! Going forward, with Cunningham in front. And because Cunningham was that man, he said, 'Fix bayonets.' 'Fix bayonets?' He had seen and he's been told that the fascists were not so far in front. And singing that song and went charging across the fields. And the fascists fell back.*[62]

The Nationalist forces, fooled into believing that fresh reinforcements had been brought up to the front, retreated to their earlier positions. As Hugh Thomas admitted: 'It was a brave performance';[63] the volunteers held the line at a critical moment for the Republic. Tom Wintringham described how:

> *There were no Republican forces to the south of the British Battalion to their left. However, this weakness was disguised by the stubborn defence of Suicide Hill. This is the justification, the achievement, of the defence of Suicide Hill. We held our own half-mile or more; we masked the utter weakness, emptiness, of the three miles south of us.*[64]
> *... The biggest and best organized drive that Franco had so far made had been stopped – within a few miles of its starting place. Arganda Bridge was ours. The Madrid-Valencia Road was ours. Madrid lived.*[65]

During the night of 14-15 February, Spanish units were brought up and the gap in the line was finally plugged. Both sides dug defensive fortifications and a stalemate ensued, which neither side was able to overcome. The positions remained virtually static for the rest of the war.

However, it was not to be the end of the carnage, with men continuing to be killed, either by snipers or in futile attempts to break the deadlock. One of the most costly came shortly after the arrival on the front of the American Lincoln Battalion when, on 27 February, Colonel Gal launched an attack on the strongly held front between San Martín and Pingarrón. Facing well-directed Nationalist machine-gun fire, many volunteers refused to advance, and those who did were shot to pieces. This was the Americans' first experience of action and they suffered terribly, losing more than 120 volunteers.[66] Manchester volunteer Charles Morgan was involved in the disastrous attack:

We were all in trenches, we were told on the morning that there would be air cover, there would be a bombardment. There was neither. We were just rushed over the top to face crossfire and machine-guns. It was a slaughter. We didn't stand a cat in hell's chance! I saw lads, my comrades that I'd learnt to love, die and some of these boys never fired a bloody shot.[67]

As Jud Colman, a comrade of Morgan from the Manchester Young Communist League, explained: 'Most of the attacks were almost suicidal, because there's no way you can send men against machine-guns without losing some. It was just physically impossible'.[68]

Celebrated as a great victory over the fascist army, the Battle of Jarama was, like the earlier battles for Madrid in November and December 1936, really only successful in that it stemmed the rebels' advance on the capital. And at great cost: the Republicans lost somewhere in the region of 10,000 soldiers, to the Nationalists 6,000.[69] Of the 600 who had gone into battle with the British Battalion on 12 February, a conservative estimate would suggest that 136 were killed, a similar number wounded, with at least 50 leaving the front line (though some of these would return to the battalion), leaving less than half the battalion remaining.[70] As brigade commissar Peter Kerrigan later stated:

This battle has been reported on many occasions. Suffice it to say that it was the bloodiest of all the battles that the British Battalion was involved in, in Spain. There was none as deadly.[71]

The terrible losses at Jarama obviously had a dramatic effect on all those involved in the creation and running of the battalion, most significantly, of course, on the volunteers themselves and their families at home. But they also impacted greatly on those working as non-combatants in Spain, particularly those in medical units – first-aiders, stretcher-bearers, doctors, nurses – who, as British nurse Margaret Powell, who arrived in early 1937 described, were working flat-out to save lives and repair broken bodies and, with minimal resources stretched to breaking point, were being forced to make desperately hard decisions:

> *Men poured in as fast as the few ambulances and trucks that we had to bring them in. I was then in ward and the only nurse in the ward. And I had to decide who should be treated. And many died then because I couldn't divide myself into six. And this was, I think, the most terrible thing that happened to me in all my life.*[72]

She also quickly discovered the appalling conditions that the medics were operating under:

> *And we fairly frequently had to do amputations, for instance, without anaesthetics. But sometimes, I had one man, I can remember very well, who came in, who was brought in and said I don't, you can take it off, if it has to come off, without an anaesthetic, I can bear it. And, he did. And he didn't complain and nobody had to hold him down. The thing that seemed to grieve him most was that he wouldn't be able to fight anymore.*[73]

Morale sank further as the day to day experiences of life in the trenches took their toll. As Walter Gregory recounts, what he called 'the daily grind' led to a certain amount of disenchantment with the war:

> *I noted the change in the nature of the battle at Jarama. The all-out offensive and defensive warfare of the early days had been replaced by a far more static form of confrontation. Trenches had been dug and were protected by barbed wire, but the soil in this area was not suitable for trench-digging: it crumbled to dust, so that neat, military-style trenches were not to be seen. Attempts had also been made to build dug-outs as shelter from the sun and rain but, like the trenches, these collapsed at the first artillery bombardment.*[74]

As Frank Ryan acknowledged:

> *Trench warfare ... tested morale almost as severely as did the big battles of February. Monotony can often be as trying as heavy fighting. As the long vigil by the Jarama – the longest on record of any unit – dragged on, wall newspapers recorded less the enthusiasms of young recruits and more the cynicisms of 'old soldiers'.*[75]

As Jud Colman explained: 'The conditions for the volunteers in the trenches were extremely tough, with men ... [sleeping] ... rough in the trenches for over three months'.[76] The situation was exacerbated by the terrible weather.

> *We just sat in the trench and the rain poured in, you had this bit of plastic sheeting and you sat there and let the puddle form and gently eased it off and wait for another puddle to form – it was cold, it was damp.*[77]

The *Daily Worker* journalist, Claud Cockburn, describes how he felt the weather affected the volunteers:

> *It rained and it rained and it rained. They had all got the impression that they were going to sunny Spain. They'd all seen the posters. And the main source of discontent and grumbling and so on – all armies grumble – but the grumblings of these people were the feeling that somehow they had been swindled by the weather.*[78]

It certainly rained for long periods, making it virtually impossible to ever get warm and dry, and making any attempt at hygiene very difficult. A spate of orders from battalion headquarters warned of the importance of the digging and using of latrines;[79] but, as an official report states, 'there were times when, in spite of urgent need, there was a reluctance to let the pants down in the face of the icy wind, and one would try to wait for a least a momentary let-up in the rain'.[80] Paper shortages added to the discomfort, with one volunteer recalling 'one visit to the latrine when all I had was one cigarette paper'.[81]

The issue of the poor quality of food, which had caused much grumbling whilst the volunteers were training at Madrigueras, was raised once more. While Fred Copeman's claim that 'it was now usual to receive soup literally packed with maggots'[82] is probably an exaggeration, there is no doubt it was the cause of much unhappiness. According to Newcastle volunteer Frank Graham:

> *By March the Jarama front had settled down to humdrum trench warfare. The nights were bitterly cold and often wet with occasional warm sunny spells during the day. At least food was now regular, although always cold since we had no means of warming it in the trenches.*[83]

Waste food was also not disposed of, raising the risk of dysentery and typhoid.[84] In addition, the familiar scourge of soldiers in the trenches had appeared:

> *By this time everyone up in the line was infested with lice: translucent, yellow brutes which looked like sugar ants. They lived principally in the seams of any garment where they remained comparatively quiescent during the day, becoming violently active at night. Their bite produced large, raised weals that itched like hell. Up to now I had been able to avoid this particular form of misery. Down at Brigade HQ it was easy to keep clean and wash clothes regularly. But up in line it was a very different situation. Most of the men up there had not moved out of the trenches for more than sixty days. Their bodies and their clothes were filthy. Water was scarce as it had to be carried up over the hills and Gal had ordered that no fit man was to be allowed out of the trenches, even for an hour, owing to the shortage of man-power. There was no insecticide and the only effective method of dealing with the lice was to run all the seams of your clothing through a candle flame at regular intervals. The lice popped and hissed in a most disgusting way as they and their eggs hit the flame, but the treatment was partially effective. It was a most depressing business to see civilized men squatting around hunting through their clothes and persons in pursuit of vermin like a bunch of apes.*[85]

As February ran into March, attempts were made to restore morale and the volunteers were taken out of the line to be given a rousing pep talk at the nearby village of Morata by British Communist Party General Secretary Harry Pollitt (who had come out in order to settle differences that had arisen between a number of senior British figures in Spain).[86] Scottish volunteer Sid Quinn described how:

Not surprisingly, we got some deserters after that battle, and blokes who'd lost morale. There was a wee bit of agitation, and I remember Harry Pollitt came out and, man, were we naïve, but he moved us. What we really needed was guns, but he spoke to us, and what a speaker! The best I've bloody heard in my life. He'd bring tears to a glass eye.[87]

However, according to Walter Greenhalgh, the pep-talk's effect was somewhat transitory; 'the euphoria only lasted a very short time'.[88]

Other famous figures visited the battalion in Spain. The great American writer, Ernest Hemingway, came out to spend some time with the American volunteers, but also wanted to visit the British, as Fred Copeman recounts:

Hemingway turned up one day. Now Hemingway was the great American reporter [to] who[m] everybody bowed down. Well, he came up to visit the American Battalion and decided he would like to visit the British Battalion. He didn't ask, he just turned up. Big huge fella he was, with a funny greying beard. And I spied him. I said, 'Who the hell are you?' 'I'm Hemingway, from the New York Times or some such bloody paper, the Chicago News or something. I said, 'Well, you can piss off!'[89]

Another visitor was the brilliant scientist JBS Haldane, who gave lectures on the dangers of gas attacks and gave lessons in grenade throwing and spent nearly three months in Spain.[90]

And old Haldane was there. More bloody nuisance than it was worth. He was a big fat fella, who wore a little leather jacket with only one button on. I don't think he ever changed his bloody shirt in four months, you know. And the button used to meet on his big fat old belly, you know, and it kind of stuck out. And he had funny, dirty old trousers and yet he was a brilliant scientist. And he insisted on being on the front line when there was that and he had a little tiny revolver. I doubt if it would hit that bloody window if he tried. He would hop on the step and hold this bloody thing and I would go up and every time I would say, 'What bloody good do you think you are? First of all you're taking two blokes room, two blokes could sit where your fat arse is, so get down out and get back to bloody …' I'm being told politically that JBS Haldane must not get killed, he's too valuable. Keep him out of the line. He was all the time in the bloody line. After about three months of it, I had a long talk with him. I said, 'Look, you've done enough bloody talking old fat man.' I said, 'You've got to go home. You've got to go home.' [91]

Despite these clearly welcome visits, discipline remained an ongoing problem as the period spent in the front line continued to lengthen: As Copeman accurately put it: 'Lectures, rest periods, leave to Madrid, could not overcome the depressing feeling in many lads' minds that they would never return home'.[92] Much of the disillusionment developed from the realisation that promises of repatriation, following a fixed period of service in Spain, were unlikely to be fulfilled. It was soon realised that, in the words of the Scottish postman John Tunnah, 'while you could volunteer in, you couldn't volunteer out'.[93]

The response of a number of volunteers was to leave the line without permission. Frank Ryan related: 'Some grumbled and groused. Some begged for leave; some took it without asking'.[94] Many volunteers only left the line for a short time, but others attempted to return home to Britain. As Fred Copeman described:

> *By now the continuous time in the front line without relief was having its effect, in spite of the number of new recruits arriving from Madrigerus [sic]. Groups of men, led by some of the finest members of the battalion, were leaving the line without permission.*[95]

Opinion on how to respond to the spate of desertions varied. Copeman continues:

> *At Brigade headquarters the political side were demanding ruthless action. To me, a man did not become a traitor to the Republic simply because he found it impossible to overcome a desire to get to Madrid. The effect of heavy casualties, lack of sleep, bad food, living continuously in the front line, was in my opinion quite natural.*[96]

This might easily be written off as Copeman's attempt to shift the blame to the Brigade (in other words, Communist Party appointments) and to hold them responsible for the imposition of harsh discipline against his better judgement, were it not for the corroboration from political commissar George Aitken, who stated that he was approached at Jarama and later by higher officers 'and a[n unnamed] civilian' on the idea of trying, and possibly shooting, some of the deserters. Aitken was categorical in his claim that he remained 'totally opposed' to the shooting of men who were essentially volunteers, and he adds weight to Copeman's claim that there were bitter fights behind the scenes to resist this ruthless response to desertions.[97] Scottish volunteer John Tunnah agrees:

> *There was, from some sources in the British political scene, demands that a death penalty should be introduced for deserters or cowardice or … here, they were dealing with, what, over the whole time, at this time there were only about 600 there, but over the whole period maybe about 2,000 men, some young some old, who weren't soldiers, who didn't know what they were getting into and seemed to be a bit surprised when they found that the fascists were firing real bullets at them. And neither Copeman, nor Sam Wild would have any part of this and they argued very, very early on, they both argued, very violently against this … Against any death penalty for any reason.*[98]

That disillusionment set in during the long period in the line at Jarama is hardly surprising. The horrific levels of casualties in the battle itself and the conditions in the trenches in which they festered for nearly four months: these are things that would have sorely tested any army. The battalion was clearly in a state of crisis and it makes their return to the fight in July at Brunete – rebuilt, rearmed and with morale restored – an all the more astonishing achievement.

What the volunteers urgently needed was time spent out of the trenches, but the desperate conditions under which the Republican army was forced to operate made this extremely difficult. To add insult to injury, when the battalion was withdrawn from the front line at the end of April 1937, within 48 hours they found themselves back in their old positions. It was a bitter blow.

In response, Scottish volunteer Alec McDade penned the lyrics to a satirical song about the Jarama, sung to the tune of 'Red River Valley'.[99] It tells the tale of the filthy, hungry and exhausted volunteers waiting patiently, until on 17 June 1937, after 73 days in the line, they finally bid farewell to the Jarama valley, a place that they all knew rather too well.[100]

> There's a valley in Spain called Jarama
> It's a place that we all know so well,
> It was there that we gave of our manhood
> And most of our brave comrades fell.

We are proud of our British Battalion,
And the stand for Madrid that they made.
For they fought like true sons of the people,
As part of the XV Brigade.

With the rest of the international column,
In the fight for the freedom of Spain,
They swore in the valley of Jarama
That fascism would never reign.

We have left that dark valley for ever,
But its memory we ne'er shall forget,
So before we continue this meeting,
Let us stand for our glorious dead.

This lecture was delivered on 13 March 2010 at the Imperial War Museum, London.

NOTES

1. Online at: www.youtube.com/watch?v=3UcoZzWWQIk.
2. See Richard Baxell, *British Volunteers in the Spanish Civil War: The British Battalion in the International Brigades, 1936-1939* (London: Routledge/Cañada Blanch Studies on Contemporary Spain, 2004 and Pontypool: Warren & Pell, 2007).
3. Fred Copeman, *Reason in Revolt* (London: Blandford Press, 1948), p.82.
4. Jason Gurney, *Crusade in Spain* (London: Faber & Faber, 1974), p.58.
5. Bill Rust, *Britons in Spain* (London: Lawrence & Wishart, 1939), p.28.
6. David Crook, unpublished autobiography, chapter 3, p.6.
7. Interview with Tony Hyndman in Philip Toynbee, ed. *The Distant Drum: Reflections on the Spanish Civil War* (London: Sidgwick & Jackson, 1976), p.124.
8. Gurney, p.58.
9. Harry Stratton, *To Anti Fascism by Taxi* (West Glamorgan: Alun Books, 1984), p.33.
10. Walter Gregory, *The Shallow Grave: A Memoir of the Spanish Civil War* (London: Victor Gollancz, 1986), p.31.
11. Interview with Tommy Bloomfield in Iain MacDougall, ed. *Voices from the Spanish Civil War: Personal Recollections of Scottish Volunteers in Republican Spain, 1936-1939* (Edinburgh: Polygon, 1986), p.51.
12. Fred Thomas, *To Tilt at Windmills: A Memoir of the Spanish Civil War* (East Lansing: State University of Michigan Press, 1996), p.21.

13. Interview with David 'Tony' Gilbert from 'Yesterday's Witness: A Cause Worth Fighting For', BBC, 1972.
14. Bill Wright, 'Spanish Diary' (unpublished), p.18.
15. Fred Thomas, p.18.
16. Bill Alexander, *British Volunteers for Liberty* (London: Lawrence & Wishart, 1982), p.65.
17. John Halstead and Barry McLoughlin, 'British and Irish Students at the International Lenin School, Moscow, 1926-37', conference paper, Manchester, April 2001, p.3.
18. Tom Wintringham, *English Captain* (London: Faber & Faber, 1939), p.55.
19. Jud Colman, *Memories of Spain, 1936-1938* (Manchester, privately published, date unknown), p.3.
20. Wintringham, p.41.
21. Interview with George Leeson, Imperial War Museum Sound Archive (IWMSA) interview 803, reel 2.
22. Wintringham, p.51 & p.52.
23. Vincent Brome, *The International Brigades: Spain, 1936-1939* (London: Heinemann, 1965), p.106.
24. For a meticulous analysis of the shenanigans surrounding arms procurement for the Republic, which ensured they were equipped with sub-standard armaments, see Gerald Howson, *Arms for Spain: The Untold Story of the Spanish Civil War* (London: John Murray, 1998).
25. Copeman, p.80.
26. Interview with Eddie Brown, in MacDougall, p.110.
27. Wintringham, p.54.
28. Interview with Tom Clarke, in MacDougall, p.60.
29. Gurney, p.84.
30. Interview with Tony Gilbert, from 'A Cause...'
31. Marx Memorial Library, International Brigade Memorial Archive, Box C, File 8/5.
32. Nathan had served, probably as an auxiliary, with the Black and Tans in Ireland in the 1920s and strong rumours linked him to involvement in a hit squad that murdered two prominent members of Sinn Féin – George Clancy, the former Lord Mayor of Limerick and George O'Callaghan, the ex-mayor – in May 1921. See Richard Bennett, 'Portrait of a Killer', *New Statesman*, 24 March 1961, pp.471-472. Wilf Macartney was also rumoured to have served in the Black and Tans in Ireland. See Richard Bennett, *The Black and Tans* (London: Edward Hulton, 1959), p.147.
33. James K Hopkins, *Into the Heart of the Fire: The British in the Spanish Civil War* (Palo Alto: Stanford University Press, 1998), p.174.
34. Robert Stradling, *The Irish and the Spanish Civil War: Crusades in Conflict* (Manchester: Manchester University Press, 1999), p.131.
35. Joe Monks, a volunteer with a strong IRA background, felt that the volun-

teers were 'international' and should have been labelled as such. Interview with Joe Monks, IWMSA, 11303, reel 3.

36. Alexander, p.69.
37. See WFR Macartney, *Walls Have Mouths* (London: Victor Gollancz, 1936).
38. Fred Copeman and Walter Tapsell were also recalled, but allowed to return to Spain.
39. Gurney, p.63.
40. Interview with Tony Hyndman in Toynbee, p.124.
41. Rust, p.62.
42. Gurney, p.85.
43. Interview with George Leeson, IWMSA, 803, reel 2.
44. Crook, chapter 3, p.11.
45. The Republican government had 'divisively and controversially' moved itself to Valencia on 6 November 1936 when it looked at though the capital city might well fall to the rebels.
46. Anthony Beevor, *The Battle for Spain* (London: Weidenfield & Nicolson, 2006), p.209.
47. Stratton, p.35.
48. Gregory, p.44
49. Crook, chapter 3, p.13.
50. Interview with Tony Gilbert from 'A Cause…'
51. As battle-hardened crack soldiers, the Moroccan soldiers were used as shock troops by the rebels, just as the International Brigades were for the Republicans. Many other volunteers refer to the terror of coming up against the Moors. See, for example, interview with David Anderson, in MacDougall, p.94.
52. Gurney, pp.104, 108.
53. The problem was a symptom of the Republican army's forced dependence on antiquated military supplies. The belts were the correct type for Maxim machine-guns, and the bullets were also for Maxims, but for guns of a more modern design than the German Maxims that the British were equipped with. Wintringham, p.69.
54. As Charlesworth retreated he also joined the long list of casualties when he was blown into the air by an artillery shell. After a spell in hospital he rejoined the battalion and became its postman. Interview with Albert Charlesworth, IWMSA, 798, reel 1.
55. Alexander, p.97. Rust estimates that, including officers and members of the Machine-Gun Company, a total of 275 British were still in action by the end of the first day. Rust, p.46.
56. Interview with George Aitken, IWMSA, 10357, reel 1. However, Aitken never actually used it. Like most of the other senior figures in the battalion, he was vehemently opposed to the shooting of deserters.
57. Rust, p.47.

58. See written reports from members of the Machine-Gun Company captured that day; Harold Fry, Bert Levy, Donald Renton, Charles West and Basil Abrahams, undated, National Museum of Labour History, Manchester, CP/IND/POLL/2/5-6.

59. This total includes the remaining few remaining members of the Machine-Gun Company.

60. Account by Frank Ryan from Ryan et al, eds. *The Book of the XV Brigade: Records of British, American, Canadian and Irish Volunteers in the XV International Brigade in Spain 1936-1938* (Madrid: War Commissariat, 1938), p.58.

61. Fortunately for the British Battalion, and for the Spanish Republic, the rebel forces 'did not find this weak spot until February 14th or 15th, when it was no longer very weak'. Wintringham, p.82.

62. Interview with John 'Bosco' Jones, IWMSA, 9392, reel 3.

63. Hugh Thomas, *The Spanish Civil War* 3rd edition (London Penguin, 1990), p.592. Robert Stradling agrees: 'Although the British Battalion was neither significantly outnumbered nor outgunned by the forces actually facing it, its achievement was nonetheless an epic one. The assertion may ultimately be incapable of proof, but this writer is confident that its conduct – especially on 12 February – represents the greatest single contribution to the victory of Jarama, and thus to the survival of Madrid.' Stradling, p.166.

64. Wintringham, p.82.

65. Wintringham, p.117. As Wintringham notes, more significant than good fortune were the vigorous attacks of the Dimitrov Battalion to the north of the British, who eventually pushed the rebels back to the river valley gorge.

66. Peter Carroll, *The Odyssey of the Abraham Lincoln Brigade* (Palo Alto: Stanford University Press, 1994) p.102.

67. Interview with Charles Morgan, IWMSA, 10362, reel 1.

68. Interview with Jud Colman, IWMSA, 14575, reel 3.

69. Hugh Thomas, p.596.

70. If the Irish fighting with the Lincolns are included, the number killed could be as high as 166. A number of others working in medical units were also killed.

71. Interview with Peter Kerrigan, IWMSA, 810, reel 3.

72. Interview with Margaret Powell, from 'A Cause…'

73. Ibid.

74. Gregory, p.59.

75. Ryan, p.84.

76. Colman, p.8

77. Interview with James Brown, IWMSA, 824, reel 4.

78. Interview with Claud Cockburn, from 'A Cause…'

79. Moscow Archive (MA), (International Brigade Memorial Trust) 545/3/495, p.4.

80. MA 545/3/467, p.40.

81. Stratton, p.38.
82. Copeman, p.110.
83. Frank Graham, *The Battle of Jarama* (Newcastle: Frank Graham, 1987), p.71.
84. See battalion orders of 11 April and 15 May 1937, MA 545/3/495, p.6.
85. Gurney, pp.134-135.
86. The disgruntlement permeated right through to the upper ranks of the battalion; during his visit to the battalion Pollitt was forced to bring together Jock Cunningham and George Aitken, together with Fred Copeman and Bert Williams, in an attempt to resolve differences amongst the leaders in the battalion.
87. Interview with Sid Quinn, in Judith Cook, *Apprentices of Freedom* (London: Quartet Press, 1979), p.74.
88. Interview with Walter Greenhalgh, IWMSA, 11187, reel 5.
89. Interview with Fred Copeman, IWMSA, 794, reel 3.
90. Alexander, p.75.
91. Interview with Fred Copeman, IWMSA, 794, reel 3.
92. Copeman, p.109.
93. Interview with John Tunnah, IWMSA, 840, reel 1.
94. Ryan, p.84
95. Copeman, p.107.
96. Ibid.
97. Interview with George Aitken, IWMSA, 10357, reel 2.
98. Interview with John Tunnah, IWMSA, 840, reel 6.
99. The satirical version (below) has slightly different lyrics from the 'official' version, still sung at commemorations:

There's a valley in Spain called Jarama,
That's a place that we all know so well,
For 'tis there that we wasted our manhood,
And most of our old age as well.

From this valley they tell us we're leaving,
But don't hasten to bid us adieu,
For e'en though we make our departure,
We'll be back in an hour or two.

Oh, we're proud of our British Battalion,
And the marathon record it's made,
Please do us this little favour,
And take this last word to Brigade:

'You will never be happy with strangers,
They would not understand you as we,
So remember the Jarama Valley
And the old men who wait patiently.'

100. The lecture ended with film footage of volunteers Tony Gilbert and Bob
     Cooney discussing the value of songs on morale, concluding with
     Cooney giving an emotional rendition of 'Jarama':

> BC: *Sometimes, things got too much for you. But if you could laugh about
>   this and sing about this, then you didn't get demoralised about it.*
> TG: *Oh, we were great singers. We sang everybody else's songs and we
>   invented a hell of a lot of our own. The British sang the French songs,
>   the German songs and, of course, every single nationality sang the one
>   song which we all loved, which was 'The Battle of Jarama'.*
> BC: *Shall I sing it? There was a time, just after we had come home from
>   Spain that I couldn't even listen to this song you know, without
>   becoming very emotionally overcome. [Sings]*

Both interviews taken from 'A Cause…'

Albion's Perfidy:
The British Government and the Spanish Civil War

Enrique Moradiellos

The war which ravaged Spain for almost three years, between July 1936 and April 1939, was a foreign conflict which had an enormous impact on British political life and public opinion. This judgement was in fact already conveyed to General Franco by the Duke of Alba, his unofficial agent in London, during the course of the conflict: 'Our war has become the most passionate and divisive issue among politicians and public opinion in Great Britain'.[1] Twenty-five years later, the first academic study on the subject rightly reaffirmed the accuracy of that opinion: 'Probably not since the French Revolution had a 'foreign event' so bitterly divided the British people'.[2] And more recently, a comprehensive analysis of Britain and the Spanish Civil War opened its pages with these words:

> *The British have not always been as greatly moved by other people's wars as they were by the Spanish Civil War. Indeed, of all the foreign conflicts of the twentieth century in which Britain was not directly involved, the war in Spain made by far the greatest impact on British political, social, and cultural life.*[3]

No doubt, the main reason for the strange and passionate British interest in this foreign conflict lies in two different but interconnected factors:

1 the presence of a clear analogy between the pre-war crisis in Spain and the general European (and British) crisis during the so-called 'inter-war period' (1919-1939);
2 the existence of a chronological parallel between the course of the Spanish war and the course of the continental crisis which preceded the onset of the Second World War in September 1939.

Poster produced in 1937 by the Republic's Ministry of Propaganda in Valencia; there were also versions in Spanish and French.

As regards the first factor, the struggle in Spain between the reformist and revolutionary forces fighting for the Republic against an insurgent army of reactionary persuasion seemed to duplicate on a smaller scale the increasing triangular tension in Europe between the Western democracies (Britain and France), with or without the support of the Soviet Union, and the Axis of fascist powers (Germany and Italy). As regards the second factor, the timing of the outbreak of the struggle in Spain was of particular importance, occurring in parallel, and in close connection, with the final descent of Europe into World War Two. For that same reason, the policy followed by the Conservative-dominated British government towards the civil war has been and continues to be the subject of acute political and historiographical controversy.[4]

The starting point of any interpretation of British policy in the Spanish conflict would have to be the one fact on which all historians agree: British policy had a crucial influence on the course and final outcome of the Spanish Civil War. In particular, it was very favourable to the insurgent army led by General Francisco Franco in practical terms, and it was a serious obstacle to the war effort of the Republican government. Certainly, such was the effect of the policy of collective non-intervention promoted by the French and British governments from August 1936, and officially adopted by all European governments when they subscribed to the Non-Intervention Agreement and agreed to participate in its London committee of supervision.

Non-intervention worked against the Spanish Republic in two basic ways. In the first place, it meant the imposition of an embargo on arms and munitions to both sides without a parallel recognition of their belligerent rights, thus putting the legitimate Republican government and the military rebels on the same footing in this key respect of war supplies. Secondly, the embargo was applied mainly against the Republic, because Germany and Italy continued their vital support to the insurgents despite signing the pact, while Britain nevertheless upheld the embargo up to the end, and was followed under duress by France and other European governments. So a system of aids and inhibitions was created which was fatal for the Republic in the long term and could never be counteracted by Soviet help. To prove beyond reasonable doubt this essential point, it might be enough to quote the final words of a confidential report by the assistant British military attaché in Republican Spain. At the end of the conflict, Major EC Richards wrote to the War Office the following clever, confidential and impartial assessment:

> *It has become almost superfluous to recapitulate the reasons [for Franco's victory]. They are, firstly, the material superiority throughout the war of the Nationalist forces on land and in the air, and, secondly, the qualitative superiority of all their cadres up to nine months or possibly a year ago ... This material inferiority [of the Republican forces] is not only quantitative but qualitative as well, being also the result of multiplicity of types. However impartial and benevolent the aims of the Non-Intervention Agreement, its repercussions on the armament problem of the Republican forces have been, to say the least of it, unfortunate ... The material aid of Russia, Mexico and Czechoslovakia [to the Republic] has never equalled in quantity or quality that of Germany and Italy [to General Franco]. Other nations, whatever their sympathies, have been restrained by the attitude of Great Britain.*[5]

The crucial importance of the United Kingdom's attitude to the Spanish conflict derived from its large economic and strategic interests in Spain, and from its position as a leading European and imperial power in the 1930s.

As regards British interests in Spain, three basic points should be borne in mind:

1 The naval base in Gibraltar was crucial to British control of the Mediterranean and communications with India; its security was essential for imperial strategy and depended on Spanish goodwill.
2 Great Britain was Spain's most important trading partner, accounting for 25 per cent of Spanish exports and providing 10 per cent of its imports.
3 British capital accounted for 40 per cent of foreign investments in Spain, largely concentrated in the iron and pyrite mining industries.

Given the extent of those interests, the British Foreign Office followed with close attention the critical situation that developed in Spain from 1931, when the oligarchic monarchy was peacefully toppled by a democratic Republic bent on a programme of political and social reform at a time of deep economic recession. The consequent persistence of social and political upheavals, particularly after the narrow electoral victory of the Popular Front coalition in February 1936, convinced the British authorities that Spain had entered a process of revolutionary crisis, most probably fostered by the Comintern, which the Republican government was unable to resolve or to contain. In their view, 1936 Spain was experiencing a sort of re-enactment of 1917 Russia, with a Kerensky government clearing the way for an impending Bolshevik (or anarchist) take-over. So, by June 1936, the Foreign Office had all but given up any hope of a constitutional solution in Spain, and expected either a military intervention to restore order and avoid anarchy or some sort of leftist social revolution.[6]

The final crystallisation of this image of the Spanish crisis occurred in parallel to the beginning of the British policy of rapprochement towards Italy, as part of the so-called 'general policy of appeasement in Europe'. The British authorities were at the time confronting a difficult dilemma in their strategic and diplomatic planning. Since the start of the economic depression in 1929, an overextended British Empire was threatened at three different points by powers hostile to the status quo: Japan in the Far East, Nazi Germany in central Europe, and Fascist Italy in the Mediterranean. Britain had neither the economic nor the military resources, nor the political will, to confront the three dangers at the same time, either alone or with the help of its traditional French ally. This was mostly because, contrary to the experience of the First World War, the two European democracies could not now count on the vital help of the United States (which had withdrawn into complete isolationism), nor on the support of Russia (which had become a suspicious and threatening Soviet Union). Therefore, from June 1936, the main objective of British diplomacy was to restore harmonious relations with Italy (radically altered by the earlier Italian conquest of Abyssinia) in order to stabilise the Mediterranean situation and to avoid an Italian alignment with a potentially hostile Germany and Japan. Strategic considerations alone seemed to require such a course, but there was also the strong desire to prevent an arms race whose financial demands would endanger the economic recovery and the social and political stability of Britain and its empire. In addition to these two factors, there was also British suspicion of hidden Soviet intentions, and the conviction that any future war between capitalist powers would provide ample opportunities for the renewed expansion of communism. The Russian crisis of 1917 had proved beyond reasonable doubt that total war would again become the harbinger of social revolution.[7]

It is clear, then, that prior to the outbreak of the Spanish Civil War, anti-revolutionary preoccupations about Spain and the search for a Mediterranean entente with Italy were twin considerations at the Foreign Office and in the British cabinet. In fact, both factors were to establish the essential framework for the British reaction to the Spanish conflict, which began on 17 July 1936 with a large military insurrection against the Republican government.

Due to the internal divisions within the army and to the strong reaction of the working class, the military coup was doomed to failure in many important and populated areas, including Madrid and Barcelona. As a consequence, the coup was transformed overnight into a bloody civil war.[8] Since neither side had the means and equipment to wage a full-scale war, both were immediately obliged to look for foreign support to start military operations. From Spanish Morocco, General Franco, soon to be head of the insurgent army, asked Mussolini and Hitler for direct help, which secretly began to arrive by late July 1936. The Republican cabinet sought support from the newly elected Popular Front government in France. And both sides tried to gain the indirect help of the British government. These developments forced the British cabinet to respond urgently to the crisis; most of all because the whole policy of appeasement would be endangered if their French ally were to help the Spanish Republic while Italy and Germany were supporting General Franco.[9]

The British response was to adopt a policy of tacit neutrality (that is, never formally and publicly proclaimed), a neutrality which was nevertheless clearly benevolent towards the military insurgents. The essential aims of that policy were to avoid giving any direct or indirect help to a government side, whose legality concealed a repulsive revolutionary nature, and to avert any possibility of confrontation with rebel forces of mere counter-revolutionary persuasion. Not in vain had British diplomats in Spain warned the Foreign Office from the very beginning of the coup that 'no government existed today', and that 'there were military forces in operation on the one hand, opposed by a virtual Soviet on the other'. The extent of the anti-revolutionary feeling created by the Spanish crisis among the British authorities is clearly revealed by this private statement by Sir Maurice Hankey, the cabinet secretary: 'In the present state of Europe, with

France and Spain menaced by Bolshevism, it is not inconceivable that before long it might pay us to throw in our lot with Germany and Italy.'[10]

The British policy of tacit and benevolent neutrality was immediately implemented in four key aspects:

1 by the rejection of the Republican fleet in Gibraltar, which was neutralised for the rest of the war;
2 by the imposition of a secret embargo on arms to the Republic (the only side who could legally buy arms in the British market until the formal proclamation of neutrality);
3 by pressure on the French government in order to prevent it giving any help to the Republic;
4 by the avoidance of any confrontation with Germany and Italy over their military support for Franco.

Awareness of the British position and consequent fears contributed significantly to the French reluctance to support the Republic, and convinced Hitler and Mussolini that limited and covert aid to Franco would not provoke energetic opposition from Britain and might bring political and even strategic advantages to their respective expansionist foreign policies.[11]

In this context, the European non-intervention pact proposed by the British and French governments and signed in August 1936 by all the continental governments provided the necessary diplomatic cloak and shelter required by the British policy of tacit neutrality. Moreover, by its mere existence and apparent efficacy, the pact and its London committee of supervision were essential for the safeguarding of the diplomatic aims established by the Foreign Office: to confine the war within Spain, and at the same time to restrain the intervention of its French ally, while avoiding any alignment with the Soviet Union or any confrontation with Germany and Italy over their support for Franco. In this respect, Stanley Baldwin, the Prime Minister, had given a clear-cut directive to Anthony Eden, the Foreign Secretary: 'On no account, French or other, must [you] bring us into the fight on the side of the Russians.'[12]

Thus, for the British authorities, from the very beginning, the collective policy of non-intervention contained an element of fraudulence, in that its real aim was not the one declared (the prevention of foreign intervention) but rather the safeguarding of the political aims indicated above. It was perceived as the ideal means to carry out a policy clearly defined by Winston Churchill in a private letter to Eden:

> *It seems to me most important to make Blum [the French socialist premier] stay with us strictly neutral, even if Germany and Italy continue to back the rebels and Russia sends money to the government. If the French government takes sides against the rebels it will be a godsend to the Germans and pro-Germans.*[13]

The political strategy gradually formulated by the Foreign Office in late July and August 1936 was based on two conditioning factors, which mutually reinforced one another.[14]

The first factor was the clear preference for a victory of the military insurgents, who seemed to be less dangerous for British interests in Spain and Europe than the victory of a government perceived as presiding over a process of Bolshevisation. The following judgement by a Foreign Office official in a confidential memorandum encapsulated the general impression within official and Conservative circles:

> *Our reports [from Spain] show quite clearly that the alternative to Franco is communism tempered by anarchy; and I further believed that if this last regime is triumphant in Spain it will spread to other countries, and notably to France.*[15]

The second factor was the need to preserve a high degree of social and political consensus in Britain, where the trade union strength of Labour, along with growing popular and intellectual support for the Republic, precluded policies more favourable to the insurgents (such as immediate official neutrality or direct assistance). On 22 July, Salazar, who was already secretly supporting the military rebels, ordered the Portuguese representative in London to ask the Foreign Office what it would do to avoid 'the establishment of a communist regime in Spain'. The official reply received was this:

> *England would not intervene militarily in Spain, whatever the situation developed in that country. The British government would not have the support of public opinion.*[16]

That the Conservative cabinet had reason to be worried about popular attitudes towards the Spanish conflict is shown by the fact that public opinion polls systematically gave a significant majority of sympathy for the Republic: on average, 58 per cent of those questioned declared themselves in favour of the Republic, against 8 per cent in favour of Franco, and 34 per cent who did not answer.[17] The importance of both conditioning factors was summed up in the words of David Margesson, the Conservative Chief Whip. At the end of July 1936, he confessed in private to the Italian representative in London:

> *Our interests, our desire is that the [military] revolution should triumph and Communism be crushed, but on the other hand, we do not wish to emerge from our neutrality ... This is the only possible way of counteracting labour agitation.*[18]

Parallel to those conditioning factors, the British political strategy for Spain was constructed on two implicit assumptions.

The first assumption was the expectation that the war would be short, given that the inexpert and badly supplied workers' militias fighting for the Republic would not be able to contain the advance of an experienced regular army supplied by two European military powers. Therefore, the conquest of Madrid was thought to be a matter of weeks away, and a suitable political occasion for the public declaration of neutrality or the recognition of the new military government. British military intelligence had predicted by mid-August 1936 that 'prolonged resistance [in Madrid] is therefore unlikely', while the Foreign Office maintained 'the hope that the civil war would be of short duration'.[19]

The second assumption was that the 'diplomacy of pound sterling' would be enough to recover the goodwill of a future military regime, because such a regime would have to seek help in the City of London in order to finance the post-war economic reconstruction of Spain. An early report by the commercial secretary at the Madrid embassy confirmed this long-standing premise:

> *The natural tendency is to use up all available stocks of consumption goods in Spain such as oil, coal, motor cars etc, with the result that when the war is over Spain will be in need of imports considerably above her normal requirements. At the same time the war will have seriously dislocated the country's export trade. The result will be a strong tendency*

towards an unfavourable balance of trade. The country will be short of foreign exchange and there will be a grave need for extensive foreign credits ... In any case the obvious country in which to obtain such foreign credits will be Great Britain. The inference is that we shall, in the future, be in a very strong position for negotiating any commercial agreements with the new Spanish government, even though we may have offended them in the course of the war.[20]

Moreover, if the power of attraction of the 'diplomacy of pound sterling' should fail, there still remained in full operation the power of deterrence of gunboat diplomacy: the great superiority of the Royal Navy and its capacity to implement an economic blockade against a hostile or unfriendly Spain.

Only within the framework of the political strategy just outlined can a crucial and often overlooked aspect of British policy towards the Spanish Civil War be best appreciated: that it represented a specific and regional version of the general policy of appeasement in Europe. The fact is that British non-intervention conformed systematically to the parameters established by that policy.

Until December 1936, there was total agreement in the Foreign Office and the cabinet as regards the profile of British policy in Spain. Open criticism of non-intervention was confined to small sections of public opinion – to the vacillating Labour opposition and smaller left-wing parties (notably the active Communist Party). Towards the end of the year, however, the international and domestic situation began to change dramatically.

In the first place, the Republicans were able to hold on in Madrid in late November 1936, resisting the Nationalist military assault. Such an unexpected defensive victory was possible thanks mostly to substantial Soviet military aid, which began to arrive in early October, and to the entry into action of the first units of the International Brigades (whose numbers reached a total of 35,000 over the course of the war).

Secondly, to counteract this failure in Madrid, Hitler and Mussolini decided to intensify their material and diplomatic support for Franco. By the end of 1936, they had both concluded that Franco's victory could not be achieved merely by sending war materiel and a few technicians, but demanded full-scale army corps deployment. The result was the dispatch of the 5,000-strong German Condor Legion and the 40,000 men of the Italian Corpo di Truppe Volontarie. By the end of the war around 20,000 Germans and 80,000 Italians had fought in those two corps.

Thirdly, the blatant intervention by the Axis powers strengthened public sympathy in Britain for the Republic and forced Labour demands for strong action and cessation of the arms embargo on the Spanish government.[21]

These developments clearly implied the partial breakdown of the British political strategy, for they destroyed the assumption of a short war and undermined the confinement of the struggle that the non-intervention system had achieved to some extent. The British government was therefore obliged to readjust its Spanish policy to the new conditions of a long war and massive intervention by the Axis powers. It was in this process of analysis and reappraisal that the first splits appeared in the cabinet and the Foreign Office, giving rise to two distinct phases of British policy between 1937 and the end of the war in 1939.

The first phase lasted from January 1937 to February 1938. In this period, the Spanish policy of the British government reflected a precarious balance between the views of Anthony Eden, the Foreign Secretary, and the majority of the cabinet, led by the new Prime Minister (from May 1937) Neville Chamberlain.

Eden was increasingly worried by the growing expansionism of the Axis powers and their potential threat to British interests in Europe and the Mediterranean. He therefore favoured a firm policy of non-intervention in order to confine the Spanish war, and to foster international mediation which would prevent the establishment in Spain of a regime closely connected to the Axis and potentially hostile to Britain. He came to consider Spain as the touchstone of the policy of rapprochement with Italy. Consequently, he thought that any Anglo-Italian agreement would have to be conditional upon Italian proof of goodwill in Spain (by withdrawing Italian troops or by supporting mediation). Failing such proof, Eden thought that a prolongation of the conflict was in British interests in order to exhaust Italian resources and to debilitate Franco's military capabilities. In September 1937 (at the same time as Mussolini was in Berlin to sign with Hitler the final Italo-German alliance), Eden specifically gave the cabinet a strong warning in this respect:

The Secretary of State for Foreign Affairs said that until recently the Foreign Office had cherished the hope that the victory of one side or the other would be purely Spanish. That view was no longer held. With the duration of the civil war General Franco's dependence upon Italy had increased. It was felt that after the civil war ended Franco would be unable to control the situation without Italian assistance. Consequently that Italians were likely to stay for a year, or even longer. He did not believe that Signor Mussolini's motives were purely ideological, or for prestige. He agreed with what he understood to be the view of the French General Staff, that the Italians sought submarine bases in Spain to be used for bargaining purposes or pressure on other nations in case of war. British interests would therefore best be served by a stalemate leading to a compromise solution, and it would be against British interests that Franco should win in Spain so long as he was dependent on foreign aid. Above all, it was against our interests that he should win during the present year. Prolongation of the war for another six months would increase the strain on Italy, and if and when Franco should win, Italy would be less able to exploit his success and there would be slightly better prospects of Franco ridding himself of the Italians. On the other hand, an early victory would create a third Dictator State, this time in Spain, and this development, making for France a third frontier to be defended, would increase the likelihood of some early adventure elsewhere by the Dictator States.[22]

Contrary to Eden, the Prime Minister and the majority of the cabinet thought that there was a real possibility of splitting Italy from Germany due to their latent antagonism over Austria and the Balkans. And they considered that this strategic and diplomatic aim was (in Chamberlain's own words) 'so important to peace that it was worth running some risks' (for the sake of it in Spain). In Chamberlain's view, Italian help to Franco could be tacitly tolerated and condoned because Spain was a marginal affair in the European context, and there remained for Britain the lever of sterling diplomacy for post-war reconstruction (or, in the worst case, of gunboat diplomacy to secure Spanish goodwill by force). For this double reason, he thought that it was in British interests to help to shorten the civil war by a quick victory for Franco's forces. In a heated cabinet meeting of March 1937, the Prime Minister had already dismissed Eden's considerations and proposals with the following words:

It had to be remembered that we were dealing not only with the Spanish insurgents, but, behind them, with the Germans and Italians. General

Franco was not a free agent. No doubt he hoped to win, but hardly without assistance from the Germans and Italians. Consequently he was unlikely to agree to any undertaking which was unacceptable to the Germans and Italians unless we were able to do something disagreeable to him in return. The Germans and Italians would not allow him to do so. To insist up to the point proposed in the Secretary of State's Memorandum therefore, was not only useless but must lead to a very serious situation with Germany and Italy. If and when General Franco had won the civil war, however, the situation would be very different, and no doubt he would be looking round for help from other countries besides Germany and Italy. That would be the moment at which to put strong pressure upon him ... that would be the time for action.[23]

By February 1938, with the Nazi *Anschluss* of Austria on the horizon and Mussolini offering to negotiate an Anglo-Italian agreement, the difference of opinion between Eden and Chamberlain reached a climax. The result was the resignation of Eden, who was replaced by Lord Halifax at the Foreign Office. This crucial ministerial change opened the way for the second phase of British policy towards the Spanish Civil War, which lasted from February 1938 to the very end of the conflict in April 1939.

After Eden's resignation, any idea of mediation or effective non-intervention in Spain was abandoned in favour of quick reconciliation with Italy. Clear proof of this was given by the fact that there was only one plenary meeting of the Non-Intervention Committee during the whole year (against fifteen in 1937). In order to facilitate an agreement with Italy, the British cabinet actively promoted the end of the civil war with a victory for Franco, primarily by pressing the French government to close the Hispano-French frontier to the transit of Soviet war materiel for the Republic. As the private secretary of Lord Halifax stated in his diary on 5 June 1938: 'In Spain the government is praying for Franco's victory and bringing all the influence they can bear on France to stop the inflow of munitions to Barcelona [then capital of the Spanish Republic].'[24]

In fact, two days later, the British ambassador in Paris told the French Foreign Secretary that his government was:

... unable to appreciate why the French government are unable to carry out their undertakings under the non-intervention scheme and prevent the passage of munitions across the French frontier to Barcelona. It would

be most unfortunate if sympathy with France in this country were on that account to decline. On the other hand it will be most regrettable if we cannot reap the fruits of our agreement with Italy, and this cannot take place until some settlement has been achieved in Spain.[25]

Mostly as a result of this unrelenting pressure, by mid-June 1938 France closed its southern frontier with Republican Spain to the supply of Soviet arms. This signified the blockage of the last and only channel open for the importation of war supplies to the Republican army.

In late September 1938, after the settlement of the Czech crisis by the Munich agreement, the Anglo-French abandonment of the Spanish Republic was sealed. In particular, the offer of neutrality made by General Franco during that diplomatic crisis helped to calm any British and French anxieties regarding the future foreign policy of Spain. In fact, Franco's move had been a desperate attempt to separate the Spanish war from the Czech question and Nazi expansionism for obvious reasons:

It is enough to open an atlas to convince oneself of this. In a war against the Franco-English group one can say, without exaggerating at all, that we would be surrounded by enemies. From the first moment they would be surrounding us, on all our coasts and all our borders. We could contain them in the Pyrenees, but it would be nigh impossible to prevent an invasion across the Portuguese frontier ... Germany and Italy would only be able to offer insufficient aid to a weak Spain, and nothing they could offer us would make up for the risk of fighting on their side.[26]

At the beginning of October 1938, the Duke of Alba, General Franco's representative in London, telegraphed 'literally' the following declaration made by Lord Hailsham, Lord President of the Council: 'Offer of neutrality was received with great satisfaction ... Cabinet would love to see the earliest possible victory for General Franco, it would round off peace in Europe.'[27] In November, Lord Halifax implicitly recognised this in the House of Lords when he said:

It has never been true, and it is not true today, that the Anglo-Italian Agreement had the lever value that some think to make Italy desist from supporting General Franco and his fortunes. Signor Mussolini has always made it plain from the time of the first conversations between His

Majesty's Government and the Italian government that, for reasons known to us all – whether we approve of them or not – he was not prepared to see General Franco defeated.[28]

Against this background, the British cabinet approved the legal recognition of Franco's government on 27 February 1939, more than a month before the actual ending of the war by the total defeat of the besieged Republic. At that particular moment, Sir Robert Vansittart, chief diplomatic adviser to the Foreign Office, wrote a confidential assessment which may be regarded as more than appropriate:

... the whole course of our policy of non-intervention – which has effectively, as we all know, worked in an entirely one-sided manner – has been putting a premium on Franco's victory.[29]

It was a judgement clearly accepted within Francoist ruling circles, however strong the public animosity towards Britain and its so-called hypocritical position of non-intervention, wholly consonant with the traditional image of 'Perfidious Albion'. Pedro Sainz Rodríguez, a prominent monarchist and Catholic who was the Minister of Education in the first Franco government, wrote in his memoirs:

Many Spaniards, disorientated by the anti-English propaganda of the Franco regime, honestly believe that we gained our victory exclusively through Italian and German aid; I am convinced that, though this did contribute, the fundamental reason for our winning the war was the English diplomatic position opposing intervention in Spain.[30]

In conclusion, the evidence clearly suggests that long before the *Anschluss* of Austria and the Munich agreement, the Spanish Civil War had served as a crucial stage for the implementation of the policy of appeasement, and, by the same token, had developed into the main argument as to its viability. The only essential difference from their stance on the *Anschluss* and Munich was that an anti-revolutionary preoccupation remained part of the analysis and decisions of the British authorities. Were it not for this political-ideological element, carefully concealed in official circles, it would be impossible to understand the policy of inactivity in the face of the increasing strategic risks to the security of an area that was vital to the defence of the empire. It seems clear that the sacrifice of a so-called Red Spain was deemed a reasonable price to pay for Italian goodwill and the hope of preserving European peace; and as a result the British government washed its hands of the Spanish Civil War.

This lecture was delivered on 8 March 2006 at the Imperial War Museum, London.

NOTES

1. Dispatch, 3 May 1938. Archivo del Ministerio de Asuntos Exteriores, Madrid (hereafter AMAE), file R833, dossier 18.
2. Kenneth W Watkins, *Britain Divided: The Effects of the Spanish Civil War on British Political Opinion* (London: Thomas Nelson and Sons, 1963), p.viii.
3. Tom Buchanan, *Britain and the Spanish Civil War* (Cambridge: Cambridge University Press, 1997), p.1.
4. Enrique Moradiellos, *La perfidia de Albión: el gobierno británico y la guerra civil española* (Madrid: Siglo XXI Editores, 1996). By the same author: 'The British Image of Spain and the Civil War', *International Journal of Iberian Studies*, vol.14, no.1, pp.4-13.
5. 'Report on Offensive Strategy in the Spanish War', 25 November 1938. Foreign Office Records, Confidential Prints (FO 425), vol.415, doc.W16269. All British sources used are in The National Archives (Kew, Surrey).
6. On Anglo-Spanish relations before and during the civil war, besides the studies already mentioned, we should consider as well: Jill Edwards, *The British Government and the Spanish Civil War* (London: Macmillan, 1979); Douglas Little, *Malevolent Neutrality: The United States, Great Britain and the Origins of the Spanish Civil War* (Ithaca: Cornell University Press, 1985).
7. Gustav Schmidt, *The Policies and Economics of Appeasement: British Foreign Policy in the 1930s* (Leamington Spa: Berg, 1984); Paul Kennedy, *The Realities behind Diplomacy: Background Influences on British External Policy* (London: Fontana, 1981); Lawrence R Pratt, *East of Malta, West of Suez: Britain's Mediterranean Crisis, 1936-1939* (Cambridge: Cambridge University Press, 1975); RAC Parker, *Chamberlain and Appeasement: British Policy and the Coming of the Second World War* (London: Macmillan, 1993).
8. On the general course of the conflict, see: Hugh Thomas, *The Spanish Civil War* (Harmondsworth: Penguin, 1977); Paul Preston, *The Spanish Civil War: 1936-1939* (London: Weidenfeld & Nicolson, 1986); Sheelagh Ellwood, *The Spanish Civil War* (Oxford: Blackwell, 1991); Francisco J Romero Salvadó, *The Spanish Civil War: Origins, Course and Outcomes* (Basingstoke: Macmillan, 2005).

9. For a general and up-to-date survey of the international dimensions of the war, see Michael Alpert, *A New International History of the Spanish Civil War* (London: Macmillan, 1994) and E Moradiellos, *El reñidero de Europa: las dimensiones internacionales de la guerra civil española* (Barcelona: Península, 2001).

10. 'The future of the League of Nations', 20 July 1936. Foreign Office Records, General Correspondence (FO 371), vol.20475, doc.W11340. The previous quotation from a telegram sent by the commercial secretary at the Madrid embassy, 21 July 1936. FO 371/20523 W6575.

11. Pierre Renouvin, 'La politique extérieure du premier gouvernement Léon Blum', in *Léon Blum, chef de gouvernement, 1936-1937* (Paris: Fondation Nationale des Sciences Politiques, 1967), pp.329-53; John E Dreifort, *Yvon Delbos at the Quai d'Orsay: French Foreign Policy During the Popular Front, 1936-1939* (Lawrence: University Press of Kansas, 1973); Martin Thomas, *Britain, France and Appeasement: Anglo-French Relations in the Popular Front Era* (Oxford: Berg, 1996); John F Coverdale, *Italian Intervention in the Spanish Civil War* (Princeton: Princeton University Press, 1975); Robert H Whealey, *Hitler and Spain: The Nazi Role in the Spanish Civil War* (Lexington: University Press of Kentucky, 1989).

12. Quoted in Thomas Jones (ex cabinet secretary), *A Diary with Letters, 1931-1950* (Oxford: Oxford University Press, 1954), p.231.

13. Letter dated 7 August 1936. Foreign Office Records, Eden Papers (FO 954), vol.27.

14. E Moradiellos, 'British Political Strategy in the Face of the Military Rising of 1936 in Spain', *Contemporary European History*, vol.1, no.2, 1992, pp.123-37.

15. Minute by Gladwyn Jebb (Western Department), 25 November 1936. FO 371/20570 W15925.

16. *De Anos de Política Externa, 1936-1945: A Naçao Portuguesa e a Segunda Guerra Mundial* (Lisbon: Impresa Nacional, 1964), vol.3, documents 20 and 30.

17. Results of a survey conducted by the British Public Opinion Institute in October 1938. *News Chronicle*, 28 October 1938.

18. Dispatch from the London embassy to Rome, 29 July 1936. Quoted in Ismael Saz, *Mussolini contra la II República: hostilidad, conspiraciones, intervención (1931-1936)* (Valencia: Insitutució Valenciana d'Estudis i Investigació, 1986), pp.204-5.

19. Summary of Information, 14 August 1936. Records of the War Office, Directorate of Military Operations and Intelligence (WO 106), file 1576. Memorandum for the Secretary of State, 16 December 1936. FO 371/21383 W3018.

20. Minute by Mr Garran, 7 November 1936. FO 371/20519 W14919.

21. T Buchanan, *The Spanish Civil War and the British Labour Movement* (Cambridge: Cambridge University Press, 1991).

22. Cabinet minutes, 29 September 1937. Cabinet Office Records, Cabinet Minutes and Conclusions (CAB 23), file 89.

23. Cabinet minutes, 3 March 1937. CAB 23/87.

24. John Harvey (ed.), *The Diplomatic Diaries of Oliver Harvey, 1937-1940* (London: Collins, 1970), pp.148-9.

25. Telegram from the Foreign Office to the British ambassador in Paris and vice versa, 7 and 8 June 1938. FO 371/22659 W7332 and W7352.

26. Memorandum by Count of Torrellano, 'Consideraciones sobre la futura política internacional de España', 20 May 1938. AMAE R834/31.

27. Telegram from Alba to General Gómez-Jordana (Franco's Foreign Secretary), 7 October 1938. Archivo General de la Administración (Madrid), serie 'Asuntos Exteriores' (Records of the Spanish embassy in London), file 7.198.

28. Parliamentary Debates. House of Lords, 3 November 1938, col.1624.

29. Memorandum, 16 January 1939. FO 371/24115 W973.

30. Pedro Sainz Rodríguez, *Testimonios y recuerdos* (Barcelona: Editorial Planeta, 1978), pp.234-5.

Beyond the Battlefield: A Cave Hospital in the Spanish Civil War

Angela Jackson

The improvised hospital that is the subject of this chapter was one of those under Len Crome's command. It was set up in a large cave near the mountain village of La Bisbal de Falset, and played an important role during the Battle of the Ebro in 1938 – the last great Republican military campaign attempting to drive back Franco's forces. Amongst the wounded Republican soldiers in the cave were International Brigade volunteers from many different countries. Volunteers such as these had come to fight for the Republic in the belief that, if fascism could be defeated on Spanish soil, another world war would be averted.

Injured prisoners of war were also receiving treatment in the cave, in this instance mainly men from the Italian divisions sent by Mussolini to support Franco. In nearby beds were local civilians, victims of the bombing raids that were providing the German airforce with a welcome opportunity to gain experience in action. The medical staff in the cave, striving to save lives despite adverse conditions, included men and women sent out by the Spanish Medical Aid Committee in Britain. This had been one of the first groups to send aid to the Republic, within about three weeks of the outbreak of war in 1936. After up to two years of working close to the front lines, the staff in the cave were well practised in the treatment of battlefield injuries.

A study of this particular hospital is rewarding for two main reasons. Firstly, there are exceptionally vivid accounts of what happened in the cave during the war – the moving narratives of nurses such as Patience Edney, who had worked there, and of women such as the former Labour MP Leah Manning, who had written about her memorable visit. This period of the war, in the latter half of 1938, was

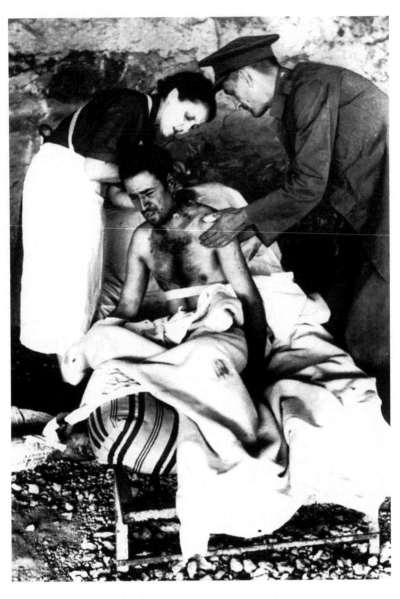

In the cave hospital: South African nurse Ada Hodson attends a
wounded prisoner during the Battle of the Ebro.
Courtesy Marx Memorial Library

heavily charged with emotion. There was for a short while the desperate hope that the tide could be turned and Franco's forces driven back, but this was soon followed by the anguish of defeat and the grim retreat of the Republicans. Such intense feelings helped to imprint experiences on the mind with a special clarity.

Secondly, the cave hospital and the nearby village are interesting because they represent what lies 'beyond the battlefield'. Hospitals such as these, although close to the front and directly linked to the area of combat by the presence of wounded men, are nevertheless distinct domains. As such, they have often been disregarded in historical studies of the Spanish Civil War. But they are part of the history of the war, and by studying them we can gain a different perspective from those of traditional histories that tend to focus on military campaigns and political factionalism.

The cave hospital and the events that occurred there are not only 'beyond the battlefield' in spatial or geographical terms. In temporal terms too, they are now quickly slipping beyond living memory. There is little time left for the work of collecting and preserving these memories. In the year 2000 I went to the village for the first time. Thanks to the warm welcome I received there, I have been able to write an account which combines the perspective of the villagers with that of the foreigners who went to the cave to work or to visit. Although the focus of this research has been on just one hospital, during only one battle in the war, it has allowed the exploration of much wider themes, such as the way in which we construct the narratives of our lives, the nature of memory and the functions of collective remembrance. I would like to look at just a few of the elements that relate to these larger themes.

Firstly, I would like to introduce the reader to a few of the key characters in this historical drama and look at a selection of their narratives. This, I hope, will illustrate some of the events that took place in the cave and the village during this period of the war. Secondly, I will explain briefly how these accounts were communicated to others after the war, and say a little bit about when and how they entered the public sphere. Lastly, I want to consider the public remembrance of these events, particularly the developments that are taking place today, especially in Catalonia, in the north-east of Spain.

Imagine for a moment the contrast in background between the villagers of La Bisbal de Falset and that of the foreigner volunteers they were to meet as a result of the war. In this remote and relatively isolated village, almost without exception, people worked for the local landowner cultivating and processing olives. Children spent little time at school and levels of illiteracy were high, especially amongst women. This was true of one of the women I interviewed, Teresina Masip. She had never been to school – with seven younger brothers to help care for, she had never had the chance. Even young children helped in the work of collecting olives, and the majority only stayed at school till aged nine or ten. Josep Perelló was more fortunate than most because his parents worked hard so he could stay at school till aged fourteen. He told me that, in those days in the village, people were accustomed to poverty. They knew that they had been born poor and that they had to die poor and they were resigned to that. He was a boy when the war began and was fascinated by the International Brigaders he talked to whenever they passed through the village or camped nearby. To him they seemed idealistic and adventurous, talking of their plans to go to revolutionary China after the war in Spain was won.

In general, the villagers supported the Republic – as Catalans, they knew a victory for Franco would mean the loss of any hope of independence for Catalonia. But they were not left-wing extremists. When war had broken out, groups of anarchists brandishing guns had come to the village in cars painted with skulls, demanding that the landowners and the local priest should be brought out and shot. The village committee of La Bisbal de Falset managed to resist these demands, and even helped the young priest to escape.

In the early summer of 1938, the cave was chosen as a suitable site for a hospital, a place where the wounded would be safe from aerial bombardment. As a result, many foreigners, women included, were sent to help with the work of setting up and running the hospital. Most of the British personnel, and those who visited to gather material for propaganda and fund-raising, were from urban backgrounds. Their education had continued till at least fourteen, and often beyond that. Some were politically aware, others much less so. For example, Patience Edney (Patience Darton as she was then) only had the most basic political awareness before volunteering to go to Spain as a nurse. She knew from her work as a midwife in the poorest areas of London that there was a need to 'do something', as she put it, to bring about social change. She heard that in Spain people actually had been trying to 'do something' and, when this aim was threatened by the outbreak of war, she wanted to go to help them. The political views she formed in Spain led her to join the Communist Party on her return. By contrast, Nan Green, who carried out administration work at the cave hospital, held firmly established socialist beliefs before the war began and was already a Communist Party member. Her husband was in the International Brigades. She is unusual in that she was one of the very few British women with children who volunteered to serve in Spain. This was a hard decision to make, and she only did so because a bene-factor offered to pay the fees for her two young children to go to a boarding school of her choice. She knew that this would give the children a chance to escape the poverty in which they were living. Both Nan and Patience had worked in many improvised front-line hospital units by the time they came to the cave.

From Nan Green's narratives we can learn about the early days of the cave hospital and a fiesta that was held in the village. The aim was to boost morale before the Republicans crossed the Ebro in the attempt to regain territory they had lost. The fiesta was to include speeches, a children's day and a sports day. Nan's account reveals something about attitudes to women at the time. 'La Pasionaria', the most famous Spanish woman politician of her day, was not regarded by the mayor of the village as a suitable role model for other women. Nan wrote:

> *I was given the task of organising the village women, whom I met every day at the one fountain, exchanging news and gossiping while our jugs filled from the slow trickle of water. I began by calling on the Mayor who was not at all forthcoming. This is not a job for women, he told me. Women haven't anything to do with politics, we shan't have a woman speaker. But what about Pasionaria? I asked. Ah, (he said) she's different.*[1]

Nan did manage to find a group of local mothers to help organise the children's events but, for her, the most important event was the sports day. She explained:

> *The Sports Day was remarkable. There was only one flat road in the whole village, the main road which passed at the end of the main street. This became the race-track, the athletic ground and the football field. Our lot (the medical people) played a group of Fortifications who were stationed there too. The whole event was intermittently interrupted by convoys of huge lorries coming down the main road towards the river, laden with arms and ammunition. Everyone knew where they were going, and what for, but nobody said a word. (The crossing of the Ebro,*

a day or two later, took the enemy completely by surprise. There were no Quislings in Bisbal).[2]

Nan goes on to stress again that the importance of her story lies in the maintenance of secrecy regarding this imminent Ebro crossing, despite the obvious transportation of pontoons and armaments along the road. She only refers in passing to the children's picnic and gives no details. For the younger children in the village, however, the picnic was the most enduring memory of the fiesta. During my visits there I was often told that this picnic, held by the hospital staff at the cave, had included the best food some of the little ones had ever tasted: dried cod and, most memorably, chocolate.

From the recorded interviews made with Patience Darton, we can learn more about the working conditions in the cave. She tells us how the patients were off-loaded in lorries in the valley below the cave, then sorted out in 'triage', a new system at the time. Some less seriously injured men were sent on to the rearguard, the others were carried in stretchers up to the cave for surgery and treatment. The 100 or so low camp beds were all higgledy-piggledy she says, because of the uneven rock floor and walls. In the gloom of the cave, with only one or two light bulbs run from a little generator, the nurses were continually banging their shins on the bed legs. She had to wage a constant war against scabies, scrubbing her arms with Lysol to keep them at bay. When the battle intensified, the casualties piled in.

> *We tended to get people in at night because the shelling was so enormous they couldn't move in the day. So for the first time, we got people rather long after the battle, we got them sometimes hours after they'd been wounded and some of course, we couldn't save because of that – they were already too bad.*[3]

She talked about the difficulties she faced when a patient died. She recalled:

> *I had terrible arguments there with the stretcher bearers who wanted to take my blankets to wrap the people in to bury them, and I said no, I must have the blankets to keep people alive with – had to pull the blankets off them which was very difficult … I mean, I felt the Spaniards were probably right, but I wasn't going to have the blankets gone because I really had to have them.*[4]

When talking of all this tragic loss of life, Patience was always careful also to mention the medical improvements made during the war that helped to increase the number of lives saved. In addition to new approaches to the treatment of wounds that prevented gas gangrene, recovery rates were also increased by developments in technology for the preservation and transfusion of blood. The blood transfusion unit stationed at the cave was run by a British doctor, Reginald Saxton, 'our dear Reggie', as Patience called him affectionately. Dr Saxton's transfusion laboratory was in a converted lorry in the valley below. Photographs show him giving one of the patients a blood transfusion in the cave. These photographs are amongst those taken by Winifred Bates. Thanks in great part to her, we have a better visual record of some of the medical units in Spain. Bates worked for the Spanish Medical Aid Committee, travelling round the units to check on the welfare of the English-speaking nursing staff. The cave hospital was imprinted vividly in her mind. In her short memoir she portrays the dying men she saw at the cave in a heroic light:

> *Men died as I stood beside them. It was summer time and they had been in long training before they crossed the Ebro. Their bodies were brown and beautiful. We would bend over to take their last whispers and the message was always the same; 'We are doing well. Tell them to fight on till the final victory.' It is so hard to make a man, and so easy to blast him to death. I shall never forget the Ebro. If one went for a walk away from the cave there was the smell of death.*[5]

Part of her job was to write articles about the medical units, which were vital in the work of raising funds. They often named particular nurses and gave details of the work that each nurse was doing. Writing in this way helped people in Britain to identify with the 'girl next door' image of someone who was nursing in Spain, and must have helped to bring in more contributions. The photographs she took were often used alongside the articles, and they still help to illustrate some of the fascinating stories associated with the cave hospital.

One photograph shows a young boy being cared for by a Spanish nurse, Aurora Fernández. During the bombing of a nearby village he had taken shelter under a water tower, which was then bombed and collapsed on top of him. Badly injured, he was nearly drowning in the gallons of water that carried him along with torrential force. He was rescued from almost certain death by a Canadian Brigader, who scooped him up out of the water. The Brigader could speak very little Spanish, and as he carried him along he could only say: 'Yo canadiense' ('I'm Canadian'). The boy, Manuel Álvarez, was taken to the cave hospital and eventually recovered. For years he searched for the unknown man who had rescued him, eventually even going to live in Canada. After almost forty years he found him and was able to say 'thank you' in person. He wrote a book about his experiences in this search called *The Tall Soldier*.

In another photograph we see Leah Manning during a visit to the cave, sitting beside a wounded man. In the previous year, she had been largely responsible for the evacuation of nearly 4,000 Basque children to England to escape the heavy bombing of Bilbao. She was involved in a great deal of committee work in the 'Aid Spain' campaigns and would speak at many public meetings, using her visits to Spain to give first-hand accounts of what was happening there. She wrote in her memoirs of how, in the cave hospital, she had recognised one of the gravely wounded patients as a young man she had met at a political meeting in Wales. He had been fascinated to hear her talk about Spain and the International Brigades, and even invited her back for tea with his 'Mam'. Soon afterwards he had managed to get to Spain as a volunteer. Leah sat by his side all night, in the cave, until he died.

Winifred Bates, Nan Green and Patience Darton all give accounts of this vigil. None of them give his name in their narratives, and so he fulfils a role as the 'unknown soldier', a volunteer like so many others who died in Spain. We know, however, from letters that Leah wrote to his mother on her return to England, that the man was Harry Dobson, and that he was buried in the cemetery of La Bisbal de Falset.

Another of Winifred's photographs shows Ada Hodson, a South African nurse, with a patient. But also noted in the caption for the photo is that in the top corner there is an injured woman civilian. This is Teresina Masip. Her tragic story could doubtless be echoed by many other mothers in this Spanish war, where civilian bombing was taking place on a large scale for the first time. On the morning of 4 August 1938, Teresina was at home with her two small children, Dolores and Pilar. Dolores, aged seven, was in bed with measles. Pilar, eighteen months old, was in her cradle. Neither survived when the bombardment of the village began at 9am and a bomb dropped directly on their house. Soldiers pulled Teresina from the rubble, burned black and seriously wounded by flying shrapnel. Her cries for her daughters could be heard across the village. She was taken to the cave and put straight onto the operating table. She remembered how they had to cut off her singed hair because of the burns and how, when they gave her something to make her sleep, she thought: 'How good'. But then she faced the horror of waking to remember that her children were dead. She spent several weeks being treated in the cave; she felt sure that one nurse who looked after her was English.

Teresina's narrative leads into my second theme: how the memories of these events of 1938 have been communicated to others. Teresina's story was, of course, known to her family and others in the village, but had not been told to a wider audience. For many years, under the dictatorship of Franco, the defeated had no voice. Franco's troops had arrived in La Bisbal de Falset on 31 December 1938. The villagers were told to come out of the caves, where they had taken shelter from bombardments, and to return to their homes. From their doorways, they watched as a large company of Moors marched through the narrow streets, singing in disconcertingly strange voices. The next day, the villagers were instructed to attend a mass in the church to celebrate their liberation. But for them, this so-called 'liberation' meant that they were no longer allowed to sing hymns in Catalan. Their language was banned, and their flag, and their traditional dances were forbidden. Years of fear and hunger followed, when the less that was said about the war, the better. The vanquished could not even mourn their dead in public.

Meanwhile, those who had returned from Spain to Britain continued to make vociferous objections to Franco's dictatorship. Patience Darton was one of those who on her return joined 'The British Medical Unit from Spain'. This group soon became part of the newly formed International Brigade Association (IBA). After the defeat of the Republic in the spring of 1939, the association campaigned for a return to democracy in Spain and for the release of political prisoners, sending speakers to meetings and producing pamphlets and articles. Nan Green was secretary of the IBA for many years. After the death of Franco in 1975 their main priority became the need to emphasise the continuing importance of the fight against fascism. Their experiences in Spain were often used to communicate this message to the next generation.

As a result, in Britain the cave hospital has become a small part of the historical legacy of the civil war, which, over the last six decades, has entered the wider public sphere in different ways. As early as May 1939, a photograph of the cave hospital was used to illustrate a series of articles for the *Nursing Mirror* by one of the nurses who had been there briefly, Lillian Urmston. In this series of seven articles, 'English Nurse in Spain', she wrote about nursing techniques for battlefield injuries and the advances in treatment that had been implemented during the civil war. The cave hospital, as we have seen, also featured in written memoirs. Those of Leah Manning were published in 1970, with her recollections of the visit to the cave. Unfortunately, many others remain unpublished.

A new and important development in this process began in 1976. A conference took place in Loughborough to commemorate the fiftieth anniversary of the war. The meeting was recorded by a group of oral historians, and they also carried out interviews with veterans who had been in Spain, and with some of those who had been involved in the Aid Spain campaigns in Britain. The recordings were then made available for others to use in a sound archive.[6] The Imperial War Museum began recording a series of interviews too, and Jim Fyrth added more to their collection in the 1980s when researching for his book *The Signal Was Spain*.[7] Together with the collection of photographs by Winifred Bates, we are lucky enough to have a substantial collection of sources on this subject.

Historians can use these sources in different ways. Paul Preston has drawn on Nan Green's memoirs as part of the biographical chapter on her that appears in his book, *Doves of War*.[8] Oral historians who are interested in the nature of memory may compare the narratives of a particular individual. For example, they sometimes examine two recordings made on separate occasions, especially when there has been long gap in between. It seems that even if small details are sometimes changed, the emotions that were felt at the time can remain as powerful as ever. Patience, for example, on different occasions recalled how, in the cave, she had been unable to help dying Finnish Brigaders. Nobody there spoke Finnish, and eventually they died from their terrible chest wounds, suffering for a long time despite the enormous quantities of morphine they were given. Many years separate the interview in the Imperial War Museum and the one I recorded with her in 1994. The two Finns have become three in the later account, but what has remained the same is her anguish at not being able to comfort them in their own language: 'Oh, I'll never forget them,' she told me. 'They were such beautiful creatures, great blonde things, you know, unable to say anything.' The distress she felt at the memory did not seem to have diminished over the years.

We are lucky enough to have this wealth of material for future generations, but in La Bisbal de Falset there was only one publicly accessible record of the events that took place in the cave. When I first went to the village and asked about the war, I was told that the town hall had a list with the names of the dead from the cave who had been buried in an unmarked communal grave in the local cemetery. Amongst all the Spanish names on the list were some names that were obviously those of foreign volunteers. But there was little other material available.

When I went back to carry out interviews, I took with me copies of the photographs from the archive at the Imperial War Museum, London, that they had never seen before. There was great delight on discovering that Teresina was in one of them. It seemed that perhaps, after so many years of trying to forget the war, a shift in attitudes was taking place. It was now time to break what had become known in Spain as the 'pact of oblivion', a response to the fear that examination of old wounds would lead to further bloodshed.

This reluctance to dwell on the war has continued until quite recent times. It seems that remnants of this feeling were still having an influence in the late 1980s. In 1987, a book of poems by Josep Perelló was published, illustrated by the well-known artist from the village, Francesc Masip. For the poem about the cave where the hospital had been, known locally as the cave of Santa Lucía, he first produced a rough draft which shows the demons of war pursuing the ranks of mortally wounded soldiers who had passed through the cave hospital. It was decided, however, that this image was much 'too strong', and it was replaced by a very different image. The demons have been replaced by smiling cherubim, and the trudging soldiers with a kneeling monk at prayer.

But by the time I went to the village in the year 2000, things were certainly changing regarding remembrance of the war in Spain, which brings me to my final theme: public remembrance.

The IBA publication *Memorials of the Spanish Civil War* tells the story of almost forty memorials to the Brigades in Britain, and since the book came out in 1996 many more have been added. There are now over eighty memorials relating to the civil war in the United Kingdom, some dating right back to the early years following the war. Most of them were brought into being by local groups that were drawn together for the purposes of remembrance. Research has been carried out on this process, particularly in relation to the First World

War, showing how groups based on 'fictive kinship' are formed. Although not linked by blood relationships or marriage, in such groups a shared aim produces a bond that links people together in a structure rather like that of an extended family.[9]

Nothing of this nature occurred in Spain until very recently, though monuments had been erected by the Francoist state, including the oppressive and pretentious 'Valley of the Fallen', a massive monument constructed by Franco after the war to honour the Nationalist dead and to be his own mausoleum. Much of the arduous and dangerous work of blasting the monument from out from the mountainside was carried out by Republican prisoners. But more recently there have been several cases in which the unmarked graves of the Republican dead have at last been acknowledged. For example, a memorial dating from the war was discovered and restored in the mountain range of the Pàndols in Catalonia, and was the subject of a documentary film made by David Leach. Members of the XV Brigade had built it before they were forced to retreat, inscribing the names of the dead in the cement.

In Corbera d'Ebre, a small town quite near La Bisbal de Falset, a very ambitious project is under way. The old town was left in ruins after the war and a new one built below. Now, the old town has been turned into a monument to the memory of the war. A new memorial to the International Brigades was inaugurated recently amongst the ruins and the first stone laid for the building of a museum. In contrast with the raw anguish of the epitaph engraved on the Pàndols memorial in 1938, 'We will triumph', the over-riding emphasis at Corbera reflects a different agenda. The entire site of the ruined town has become a sculpture park dedicated to peace.

Events like the homage to the Brigades in 1996 and projects such as the one in Corbera reflect how attitudes are now changing in Spain towards remembrance of the civil war. In La Bisbal de Falset, my interest in the history of the war was just the final trigger that led to a plan for a plaque in the cemetery on the unmarked grave. The mayor was helped by a group of enthusiastic supporters in the village. I worked to co-ordinate the efforts they were making with those of the IBA in Britain. The mayor soon came up with the idea of having two plaques, one in the cemetery and another in the cave itself. Unfortunately, our plans could not be as ambitious as the proposal put forward in the memoirs of David Zagier, a journalist working for a South African newspaper who had visited the cave in July 1938. He had been impressed by what he saw there, and particularly by the caring attitude of Dr Saxton towards his staff and patients, dubbing him 'Transfusion Saxton' for the work he was doing in saving lives.

He ended his passage about the cave hospital with his thoughts on how what he had witnessed there might be remembered. He wrote:

> *One day I thought as I gazed into the dark cave – a statue may be erected in front of this cave by the new and free Spaniards. A statue to honour a man called Dr Reginald Saxton.*[10]

Although we couldn't afford the statue of Reggie, we did have Reggie himself. For the inauguration of the plaques on 4 November 2001 he came back to the cave for the first time since the war, all the way from Canada. Other veterans made the journey up into the mountains too: Rosaleen Ross, who also travelled from Canada, Penny Feiwel, Sam Lesser and Steve Fullarton. Government recognition came through the participation of four regional officials and a speech from the representative of the Catalan Generalitat. I'm not sure how many hundreds of people attended, but I was pleased to see that there were considerable numbers of young people present.

The dynamics at play in remembrance groups have been examined by other historians looking from the outside. But, as a member of this particular group myself, I wanted to see how they worked from the inside. This, I hope, will add a further perspective to the research on remembrance that has already been done. In this instance, the common purpose of remembrance had drawn together a group of enthusiastic participants in Catalonia and a collection of interested people from Britain and Canada. Each of us had something to contribute and also something to gain from our involvement. This is not to imply that people became involved only in order to benefit in some way. However, the fortuitous conjunction of effort and reward does effectively increase the success of this type of project enormously. It is a mechanism which must underpin many groups formed for the purposes of remembrance. The effort exerted could be minimal, perhaps just a few hours as a spectator on the day of the ceremonies, or it could entail many hours of work and individual expenditure. The rewards could be of a personal or public nature, either transient or permanent. I will just give a few examples of this.

The Brigaders' contribution required the greatest commitment. It would be hard to find individuals with more determination and strength of mind, but the challenges that come with advanced age are indeed daunting. Impaired vision and hearing, failing legs and a host of other physical problems were all overcome in order to travel to a mountain village many miles from the nearest city. With characteristic courage, they journeyed into the unknown, trusting in the somewhat undefined arrangements I had made on their behalf, and in the goodwill of the people in La Bisbal de Falset. But, as veterans of the civil war, their reasons for attending the ceremonies were the most compelling of all. A mixture of several different personal and public motivating forces were evident. For Reggie Saxton, who had worked as a doctor in the cave, and Steve Fullarton, who had been a patient there, it was the chance to revisit a place that had been part of their experiences in the darkening days towards the end of the war, at a time when they had been tried and tested to the utmost as young men. Steve Fullarton also had a practical purpose for his return. He wanted to meet and thank Ramona, the village girl who throughout a long night had brought him water when he called out in thirst from his hospital bed. Sadly, she had died a few years earlier.[11] Personal loss was another reason for their wish to attend. They had known others who had fought and died at the Battle of the Ebro and could therefore find some small consolation in honouring their memory by being present at the inauguration.

However, honouring the dead is only a part of the function of public remembrance. In this instance, and on many similar occasions, the 'legend' of the Brigades was being used to transmit the message the Brigaders wished to convey to future generations. But, rather than conveying the simple message of 'never again' often associated with memorials from the Great War, the message of the International Brigade memorials is more positive, an affirmation of hope expressed in the belief that people can join together across national boundaries to resist oppression and fight for a better society. This can be seen in the words chosen for the plaque in the cemetery, which point out that those who were buried there were Spaniards and International Brigaders who had fought together to defend the Republic. By their presence at the inauguration, veterans of the Brigades created a much greater degree of public interest in the event. Several newspapers gave good coverage, Catalan television showed footage on the news and documentary film-makers took the opportunity to carry out interviews. This has all helped to disseminate their historical legacy a little more widely.

The families of Brigaders have often played a key role in the work of remembrance. The journey for the children of the Brigaders who attended this event was perhaps one that should be viewed more in emotional terms than in physical distance. Some were probing their fathers' past in Spain for the first time. Although these 'children' had reached middle age before the death of their parents, it was only then that they realised how little they understood about their parents' beliefs and experiences relating to the civil war. This realisation was likely to be accompanied by a sense of regret at not having found out more whilst their parents were alive. On this visit to Catalonia they found not only the battlefield sites relating to their family history, but also discovered that, indeed, bonds of 'fictive kinship' linked them to the other children of Brigaders. Their involvement with the group could help them to come to terms with loss, and perhaps to understand their parents a little better than before.

For the mayor and the village council in La Bisbal de Falset, all unpaid elected officials carrying out these duties in their spare time, the event entailed an unprecedented increase in workload. We had discussed the programme together in the initial stages, but the responsibility for ensuring that all went according to plan lay heavily on their shoulders. There is no doubt that this aim was achieved with distinction, and the acclaim that has greeted their efforts is fully justified. They too found rewards. The presence of the Brigaders, the four regional government officials and the assembled crowd from near and far, and the media coverage of the event, all increased the prestige of the village in the region. The success of the event amongst the local inhabitants can only have re-enforced the popularity of the council in the village.

For the other villagers of La Bisbal de Falset, attending the inaugurations was, if nothing else, an interesting diversion from the quiet daily life of the village. However, many of them had contributed much more than their mere presence on the day. Not only had most of the funding come from the town hall budget, but the villagers of all generations had also undertaken the practical tasks for the preparations for the ceremonies, and on the day itself. That the occasion had meant a great deal to them was evident from the number of times I was warmly thanked and told that the day had been unforgettable. Some were moved by the re-emergence of childhood recollections, by the memories of people they had loved and lost in the war, or by the discovery of a village history previously unknown to them. An extract from a letter I received from the former mayor of the village, Enric Masip i Gorgori, perhaps conveys most clearly the depth of feeling that emerged:

> *I feel I should let you know the great impact that the events we celebrated have had upon the village. November 4ᵗʰ 2001 has left an indelible imprint in La Bisbal de Falset – it was the recuperation of an important part of our history, we realised that we were recovering part of our own lives, above all in the beautiful, emotional and moving ceremony in the cemetery, during which many of us were unable to avoid feeling a knot in the throat and tears in the eyes. Personally speaking, from the moment in which I was asked by Lluis, the mayor, to collaborate in the work of preparation for the ceremonies, I can say that, without doubt, there have been very few things that I have done with more enthusiasm, or that have filled me with as much satisfaction as this, both in my private life and during the sixteen years that I was mayor of the village.*[12]

He closed the letter by stressing that meeting the Brigaders had captured the interest of the young people in the village and that, 'after so many years of unjustly imposed forgetfulness', this should be 'a cause of satisfaction for us all'.

Both in Britain and Spain, the number of new memorials to the International Brigades and to those who supported the Spanish Republic show that the civil war continues to hold a powerful and pertinent symbolic meaning for society today.

This lecture was delivered on 2 March 2002 at the Imperial War Museum, London, based on research for a book that was subsequently published in Catalan as Més enllà del camp de batalla *(Valls: Cossetània Edicions, 2004) and in English as* Beyond the Battlefield: Testimony, Memory and Remembrance of a Cave Hospital in the Spanish Civil War *(Abersychan: Warren & Pell, 2005).*

NOTES

1. Nan Green, manuscript of *A Chronicle of Small Beer*, pp.70-1 (Published by Nottingham Trent University in 2004).
2. Ibid, pp.69-71. Major Vidkun Quisling was a Norwegian collaborator during the Second World War.
3. Patience Edney, Imperial War Museum Sound Archive, 8398.

4. Ibid.

5. Winifred Bates, 'A Woman's Work in Wartime', unpublished short memoir, Marx Memorial Library, Box 29/D/7.

6. Tameside Local Studies Library, Astley Cheetham Public Library, Stalybridge, Cheshire.

7. Jim Fyrth, *The Signal was Spain: The Aid Spain Movement in Britain, 1936-39* (London: Lawrence & Wishart, 1986).

8. Paul Preston, *Doves of War: Four Women of Spain* (London: HarperCollins, 2002).

9. Jay Winter and Emmanuel Siven (eds.), *War and Remembrance* (Cambridge: Cambridge University Press, 1999).

10. David Zagier, unpublished memoir, 'Seven Days Amongst the Loyalists', pp.114-7.

11. Letter from Steve Fullarton to Angela Jackson, 25 November 2001.

12. Letter to Angela Jackson and the International Brigaders from Enric Masip i Gorgori, 18 November 2001.

September 1936: Stalin's Decision to Support the Spanish Republic

Ángel Viñas

The blow which the French and British governments inflicted on the Spanish Republic by denying it their support and tabling the non-intervention policy turned out to be devastating; and it was only partially and belatedly offset by the assistance tendered by the Soviet Union. How this help came about has been controversial. The long-standing lack of reliable documentary sources gave carte blanche to the most fanciful interpretations in the English-speaking world, where the reception of the reconstruction of the past undertaken by Spanish[1], German[2] and Russian[3] historians has yet to take place.[4]

BIASED HISTORY

The key elements of conventional history, particularly of a neo-Francoist bent, can be summarised as follows:

- Communists intervened in Spain almost as soon as the civil war broke out.
- Stalin never seriously considered the option of abiding by the non-intervention policy to which the Soviet Union subscribed at the end of August 1936.
- The Comintern was in the vanguard of Soviet intervention, having allegedly taken its decision in July 1936 to set up the International Brigades.
- Arms and advisers were sent by the Soviet Union to Spain before direct military assistance was provided.

The facts tell a different story. On 25 July 1936, Prime Minister José Giral wrote to the Soviet ambassador in Paris:

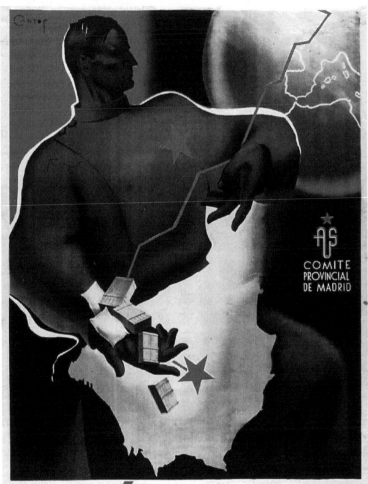

LA URSS SEÑALA A LAS DEMOCRACIAS
EL CAMINO DE LA PAZ

*Wartime poster produced by Cantos in Madrid for the AUS
(Friends of the Soviet Union) with the caption: 'The USSR shows
the democracies the way to peace'.*

The government of the Spanish Republic needs to equip its army with modern weapons in enough quantity to sustain the fight against the insurgents who are waging a civil war against our nation's legitimate authorities and constitutional government and are receiving abundant supplies of foreign arms and munitions. As our government is aware that the USSR has the capacity to supply military hardware, it has decided to approach Your Excellency to respectfully ask you to inform your government of my government's wish and need to obtain a considerable volume of military hardware of every type from the USSR.[5]

Two aspects of this telegram stand out. Firstly, the ambassador is not addressed by his name, suggesting a lack of preparation by the Spanish side. Secondly, the Republicans already knew that Franco had looked abroad to secure arms. This was the case, even though neither Hitler[6] nor Mussolini[7] had yet decided as much. It suggests that Republican agents were alert to developments in the international scene.

However, some writers still adhering to a Cold War framework of interpretation, who have inflated the importance of this telegram, have failed to notice the first real sign of active interest that the Soviet leadership took in events in Spain.[8] This was the decision of the Politburo of 22 July, three days before the Spanish telegram was sent, concerning fuel supplies to the Republic on discounted terms.[9] The historical, political and international importance of that decision hardly needs emphasising. It occurred just five days after the launch of the military coup. It was not a low-ranking decision, but one taken at the highest possible level. Lastly, just a day earlier the Republican government had sent a request for fuel to London, which the British turned down that same day, 22 July.[10]

In operational terms, all this means that the Kremlin must have found out about the Spanish request and reacted at lightning speed, a surprising occurrence in Soviet foreign policy at that time. We also know, thanks to Rybalkin, that the Republican representatives in Paris persisted in requesting arms from the USSR. Despairing at the lack of progress in negotiations with the French, Fernando de los Ríos, then joint leader – with the socialist vice-president of the Cortes, Luis Jiménez de Asúa – of the Spanish delegation sent to contact the French government, repeatedly informed the Soviet embassy that he was prepared to travel to Moscow at any time to sign any appropriate agreements in order to obtain whatever hardware the Soviet Union might deem fit to supply. It is unlikely that such approaches would have been made without the knowledge of at least Giral and the Minister of Foreign Affairs, Augusto Barcia. However, neither Barcia nor de los Ríos, subsequently ambassador to Washington, ever commented on this matter.

Although much of the correspondence between the Spanish embassy in Paris and the Madrid government has not yet been found, it is still possible to identify the period during which such contact must have taken place. Some references are available in Russian archives. The repeated requests for military hardware predate the arrival in Paris of the journalist and *Pravda* correspondent Mikhail Koltsov. Indeed, on about 6 August he was approached by Giral's son, who was then involved in the attempts to obtain arms. This implies there were channels of communication between the two embassies, enabling Giral junior to make an urgent approach to Koltsov, perhaps when the Russian went to apply for his visa or to visit the Spanish embassy.[11]

Nevertheless, the Soviet leadership, which was doubtless informed of these contacts, turned a deaf ear to the Spanish requests. It was one thing to send fuel, but quite another to supply arms.[12] However, it was common knowledge that the assistance that the fascist powers were giving to General Franco was by then on the increase.

THE VIEW OF WESTERN DIPLOMATS AND WHAT WAS REALLY HAPPENING

Research by historians has traditionally been based upon the reports that Western diplomats sent home concerning the initial Soviet response. Some of these had a major impact. The telegrams by the Italian chargé d'affaires, Vincenzo Berardis, reveal that Mussolini took his decision to help Franco in the knowledge that the Russians did not seem to be prepared to act. Like his colleagues, Berardis, an analytically-minded diplomat whose reports are still an interesting source, noted that until late July the highly regimented Soviet press confined itself to publishing fairly neutral reports about events in Spain and the international response they were generating. Then suddenly, at the beginning of August, 'spontaneous' demonstrations took place in support of the Spanish Republic.

None of the diplomats from countries with a particular interest in what was taking place in Spain had anticipated that the Kremlin would intervene swiftly and actively in the turmoil. Rather, they nearly all conveyed a mood of profound uncertainty and deep concern. The French chargé d'affaires, Jean Payart, who also later served in Republican Valencia, simply noted that the Soviet government was keen to give the impression that it was well disposed towards the proposed non-intervention in Spanish affairs. The French Foreign Minister, Yvon Delbos, had launched this initiative in early August. The only condition that Moscow imposed was that other countries already lending support to the rebels, particularly Portugal, must also sign up to the pact. In fact a fierce debate had broken out in Moscow as to what the Soviet Union should or should not do. It is a debate on which very little light has been shed, and it is surprising that historians should have lent so heavily on the accounts given by Walter Krivitsky, who by then had been undercover in The Hague for more than a year as an NKVD (Soviet political and security police) agent.[13]

At an operational level the debate began within the Comintern (which was taken completely by surprise by the military coup).[14] From here, it soon spread to the Sovnarkom (Council of Commissars) and the ultimate decision-makers: the Politburo and Stalin. There was a logic to all this. The Comintern was a useful tool, but ultimately a mere tool, of Soviet foreign and security policy, which until then had been defined in the Politburo (although Stalin often took crucial decisions on his own), and was largely implemented by the Sovnarkom by overt and covert means. The Comintern fulfilled the not insignificant task of providing a connection with national communist parties, which it tried to keep in line with Soviet requirements. It should be stressed that Stalin did not merely allow this debate to take place but also encouraged it. Otherwise it would have been stopped quite early. Rationally the hypothesis must be raised that the aim was likely to have been the achievement of greater clarity in order to deal with a complex situation where a false move might have damaged the interests of Soviet foreign and security policy.

On 23 July Georgi Dimitrov stated that it would be a great error to follow a line that might bring about the dictatorship of the proletariat. In accordance with thinking predating the coup, what was required instead was to reinforce the democratic Republic with the assistance of a People's Army based on loyal military elements. This is something that tends to be overlooked by all those writers (and there are many) who still follow in the steps of authors such as Krivitsky and Bolloten.

On 7 August, a report to Dimitrov from the assistant director of the information department, Pyotr A Chubin, highlighted the involvement of the fascist powers in Spain, including in the operational sphere (troop transport, air cover and logistical support).[15] He reached the conclusion that, if this had not been the case, the uprising could not have made such progress. This was a slight exaggeration but not a complete misreading of the situation. Sooner or later the foreign legionnaires and the native Moroccan forces which made up the Army of Africa would have crossed the Strait of Gibraltar, as the Republican fleet was barely operational. In truth, they had already started to do so. Naturally, the air bridge provided by German aircraft enabled them to move more rapidly to the peninsula, thereby facilitating the reinforcement of the columns that ruthlessly annihilated the feeble resistance put up by the disorganised Republican militia. These two operations enhanced Franco's status among the insurgents.

Chubin recommended that whatever assistance the democratic world was prepared to lend to the Republic should be provided as quickly as possible. He pointed out that the fascists were not sitting on their hands but were crushing their opponents with overwhelming savagery. No doubt his assessment drew on recent experiences. Chubin was not calling for Soviet intervention, as this was not his decision to take. However, there were other courses of action that could be activated through the Comintern. Dimitrov agreed with his subordinate's assessment.[16] Instructions were rapidly sent to the national communist parties calling on them to bring pressure to bear on their respective governments (the British intercepted the message sent to the Communist Party of Great Britain, which contained a fair amount of wishful thinking). For its part, the PCF (French Communist Party) had already been agitating for such action for some time.

The Comintern instructions were based on an analysis that was not inaccurate: the intervention of the fascist powers in favour of the rebels, on the one hand, and the failure of the democratic countries to assist the Republic, on the other, had created a situation that was allowing the insurgents to gain the upper hand. This analysis coincided with the assessments made by British military intelligence, which immediately began to scrutinise what was happening in the field of operations that had by then opened up in Spain.[17] It was also clear to MI3 (Military Intelligence Section 3) that foreign assistance to the rebels had been the factor that had contributed most to their progress.

For the Soviet leadership the major problem was that the reports from the Comintern agents in Madrid on the political and social situation were too sparse (and of dubious quality) to form a well-founded judgement as to the operational trends and outlook. The early reports painted an almost rosy picture that was soon disavowed by subsequent events. So the Sovnarkom urgently drew on the assets of the Red Army military intelligence service (GRU).[18] Whether the GRU or the NKVD foreign department had any agents operating in Spain by then is open to debate. It would hardly have been surprising. Pre-war developments had been closely monitored by Italian intelligence, but also by German and French intelligence (which were both taken by surprise).

In the Russian military archives are kept the reports that the GRU prepared throughout August and September 1936.[19] General Semyon Petrovich Uritsky, its director, submitted them to the People's Commissar for Defence, Marshal Vorochilov. They were written by his assistant, Nikonov, supported by other staff, most frequently one named Yolk. The first report is dated 7 August, the same day on which Chubin issued his own. This raises the question of whether it was a coincidence or whether both were produced in response to orders from superiors. Nikonov and Yolk presented a fairly positive picture of the Republican resistance, whose resources (in terms of men, equipment – and aircraft, above all) were, they said, greater than those of the rebels. Their assessment underestimated the forces on the ground and ignored qualitative factors, which were absolutely crucial. The same military value cannot be attributed to a chaotic army and a few completely disorganised and far from combat-ready militias as that of insurgent forces led by the Spanish Foreign Legion and colonial troops.

MOSCOW NEEDS INFORMATION TO ACT

At the beginning, Moscow did not have a very good understanding of what was happening in Spain. One of the first decisions was to establish an embassy in Madrid, to which GRU agents were sent under appropriate diplomatic cover.[20] They included the senior military adviser Jan Berzin (a pseudonym) and the military attaché, Vladimir Goriev, as well as one of his assistants. The commercial attaché, I Winzer (or Vintser) came from the NKVD foreign department. While the selection of personnel was undertaken hurriedly, the appointments were not formalised by the Politburo until 22 August. The initial team, headed by ambassador Marcel I Rosenberg, travelled to Madrid in great haste. This was a time during which the GRU reports were painting a picture of a gradually deteriorating Republican position, whereas Franco's star was in the ascendant.

A month later, an old Bolshevik, Vladimir Antonov-Ovseyenko, was appointed consul-general to Barcelona. In the first few days of October, just after his arrival, he was informed that he was to be given a military 'attaché' and an assistant, who would be designated vice-consul and second secretary respectively.[21] It is most likely that they were also GRU agents, although documentary evidence of this has not been identified. The NKVD and the Comintern also ended up with a presence in Barcelona, as well as Madrid and Valencia. In any case, the appearance of Soviet representatives in the nation's capital allowed the Giral government to intensify its requests for assistance, given the instantaneous communications through the new embassy. Unfortunately the messages themselves have not been found, although some of their contents are known.

Three actions that went unnoticed demonstrate which way the wind was blowing. The first was a consequence of the Politburo's decision of 17 August authorising a group of fifty Spaniards to visit the USSR in order to get acquainted with Soviet facilities and military units.[22] The second was the authorisation for two military experts to be sent to Spain to advise the PCE (Spanish Communist Party). This was not exactly shocking news, and the relevant message to Madrid was intercepted by the British. The third move proved to be more significant. It was the very first operational example of the way in which high-level Soviet interest in military assistance was being developed. It is to be found in a letter that Nikolai Krestinsky, Assistant Commissar for Foreign Affairs, sent to Stalin on 9 August (two days after Chubin and Nikonov/Yolk's reports). This was also forwarded to Vorochilov, Kaganovich, Orkjonikize (Commissar for Heavy Industry) and Chubar, who was then Acting Commissar for Foreign Trade.[23] According to this document, there had already been discussions in Moscow as to whether assistance should be given through agents who might acquire military hardware in the United Kingdom. This was a route that had not been available for very long, and vanished a few days later when the British government decided to implement a strict policy of non-intervention.

Krestinsky opposed direct shipments in view of the political and diplomatic risks involved. This suggests that by then the idea raised by

Giral had been dropped, and that the role played by his son, through Koltsov, had proved inconsequential. Krestinsky suggested an alternative: military hardware for the Republic could be obtained through third countries, probably in Latin America. He mentioned Mexico as a specific option. Perhaps he was unaware that the Mexicans were already acting independently in London, where their approaches were not well received, and in Paris, where they also achieved little.

In the meantime, Stalin's attention continued to focus on oil supplies. On 14 August, just before going on holiday to his Sochi dacha on the Black Sea, he phoned Krestinsky and ordered him to do the necessary in order to intensify the operation by mobilising Soviet representatives in Paris. Three days later the Politburo quickly fulfilled his wishes.[24] A Spanish vessel, the *Remedios*, which just happened to be in the Romanian port of Constanța, where it had travelled to load 6,000 tons of petroleum purchased through the Belgian company Petrofina, received urgent instructions from Madrid to sail for Batum, in Georgia, and to take on Soviet fuel. This operation did not succeed, but others did.[25]

It is clear that action on this scale, while important, was inadequate. On 26 August an extraordinary meeting of the Politburo was convened, although little is known of the agenda. It was then, for the first time, that the possibility was raised of assisting the Republic through the creation of an international volunteer corps.[26] This was the kernel for the International Brigades, but at that time it was an idea that required further consideration. The logical framework would be the Comintern and not the Sovnarkom. The actions of the latter, which were much more compromising for the Soviet Union, were kept discreetly in the background.

The 26 August meeting has long been known. However, fabricated accounts have continued to be written, based on the old story that the decision to create the International Brigades was taken at a meeting in Prague a month earlier, and was as a result of another meeting held in Moscow on 21 July, when it was supposedly suggested by the Red International of Labour Unions (Profintern).[27]

STALIN STEPS ON THE ACCELERATOR

Two events put pressure on the Kremlin. On the one hand, there was the continuous deterioration of the Republican military position, which is evident from the increasingly alarmed tone of the GRU

138 *Looking Back at the Spanish Civil War*

reports.[28] On the other, there was the support given to Franco by the Germans and the Italians. The fascist powers not only did not stop when the non-intervention policy started being applied; they increased their assistance, while spreading rumours about the alleged Soviet interference in Spanish affairs. For Stalin, German and Italian behaviour must have demonstrated that Berlin and Rome were resolved not to take their international commitments seriously. The Italian intervention may have not bothered him too much. The Third Reich's involvement was quite another matter.

The Soviet response consisted in allowing the PCE to join a new Spanish government under Largo Caballero on 4 September, dropping Stalin's initial willingness to continue supporting Giral. As on other occasions during the civil war, local requirements led the Spanish communists to propose a course of action which Moscow had not contemplated.

Much has been made of Rosenberg's first actions in Madrid. Perhaps understandably for an inexperienced ambassador in a hot posting, and someone who was utterly ignorant of Spain and the Spaniards, he immediately dabbled in Spanish politics. Naturally, he reported back to Moscow and soon received a very harsh response. On the same day as the new government was formed, Litvinov sent him a message reprimanding him for meddling in domestic politics. This scolding must have hurt Rosenberg, one of the commissar's favourites during his previous appointments in Paris and at the League of Nations secretariat.

Rosenberg's faux pas was compounded by Goriev, who felt a similar temptation to 'give instructions' to the Spanish military. Litvinov informed the ambassador that the Defence Commissariat had criticised the attaché for his suggested line of action. The order was that Spanish military or non-military politics were to remain strictly in Spanish hands.[29]

Although unfortunately we still have no reliable information about the Republican requests, which were increased after Rosenberg's arrival, a second response from Stalin two days later is documented. On 6 September he telegraphed Kaganovich, his right-hand man in the Politburo, with three instructions. The possibility of selling Mexico fifty high-speed bombers so that they could be sold on to Spain must be urgently examined. Some twenty pilots were to be chosen for training the Spaniards in handling such aircraft. Lastly, some 20,000 rifles, 1,000 machine-guns and about twenty million bullets should be sold.[30]

This telegram shows that Krestinsky's suggestions were still influencing Stalin's thinking. Nevertheless, his 'suggestion' was not particularly well thought-out. The idea that a country such as Mexico, which had no modern aviation whatsoever, might sell Spain fifty high-speed bombers was laughable. It is also worth pondering how long it would have taken to make this 'sale', to ship the aircraft to Mexico and then from Mexico to Spain. No wonder that most of Stalin's instructions were not carried out in the way he intended. However, there is tenuous evidence suggesting that an American company was approached. The reasons are not hard to understand. Shipping aircraft from the United States to Mexico would have been much quicker to do and easier to conceal than from the Soviet Union. Other instructions were easily accomplished. This was the case with dispatching a few pilots. It has long been known that in September at least three fighter pilots, nine bomber pilots and navigators and two engineers set off for Spain. A few army officers were also chosen.[31]

A further GRU report must have put pressure on the Soviet leadership. It underlined the negative side of Republican resistance. Although there was no lack of enthusiasm, indiscipline (particularly amongst the anarchists), lack of a unified command and poorly trained troops explained why Toledo's Alcazar had not yet been taken. From the report it could be gleaned that the time was ripe for intervention because otherwise the fate of the Republic would be sealed.

Stalin's original wishes made room for a more comprehensive approach. This was examined with due alacrity and put into practice in five ways.[32] The first action was the establishment of the International Brigades. The second was the shipping of equipment to support combat, such as large numbers of trucks. The third was the supply of old war materiel available in Soviet arsenals. The fourth took the form of modern war materiel, in particular aircraft and tanks. And the fifth was purchases of second-hand weaponry in certain European countries. All these actions, which are listed separately for analytical purposes only, were considered over more or less the second half of September 1936.

According to Krivitsky's account, on 14 September a meeting took place in the Lubianka (headquarters of the feared NKVD) in order to discuss aid for Spain. This meeting has been a standard feature of history-writing in the West. Krivitsky claimed that Uritsky and Abram Slutsky, his NKVD foreign department counterpart, participated. If it ever took place, this meeting was the follow-up to another infinitely more important meeting, which was held not in the Lubianka but in the Kremlin itself. The Kremlin meeting was chaired by Molotov and attended by his number two at the Sovnarkom, Andrei Andreevich Andreev, and Kaganovich, as well as Mikhail Abramovich Moskvin, from the Comintern executive committee. This participation shows the involvement of the two essential branches of Soviet power, namely the Politburo and the government, as well as the Comintern. Genrikh Yagoda, Commissar for Internal Affairs and NKVD supremo, was also present, with Slutsky. It is obvious that Krivitsky's account was wrong. And Krivitsky also ignored another meeting at the Comintern where, according to Dimitrov's diary (page 32), the issue was raised of how more assistance could be given to the Spaniards through smuggling. It is more than likely that this referred to the acquisition of equipment via third countries. Krivitsky's claims that he took the initiative in arranging such an operation through a network of shell companies is as bogus as his allegations of sending on his own undercover agents to deal with Spanish affairs.

As Howson has demonstrated, many of Krivitsky's assertions are untrue.[33] Soviet documents show what lay behind these acquisitions. Vorochilov informed Stalin on 13 December that arms were bought from Czechoslovakia, France and Switzerland. The Soviets used their own resources to pay a sum of almost $2 million. The arms were rifles, sub-machine-guns, heavy machine-guns and cartridges. They were all second-hand and were repaired and shipped out in good condition, and at a substantial discount.

What about the International Brigades? The decision to create them was taken during the Comintern presidium and executive committee meetings held between 16 and 19 September. This was a logical development. Since the first days after the coup Republican ranks had been augmented by volunteers from all kinds of origins. At the outset this happened in a pretty haphazard way, but little by little the process became more orderly. Establishing the precise date when the International Brigades came into being is important for demolishing one of the key items central to the Francoist mythology. Backdating it to July allows it to be argued that:

(a) Like Hitler and Mussolini, the USSR was implicated from the outset – thereby reducing the political, military and ultimately historical significance of the involvement of the fascist powers.

(b) There was substance to the myth that the Republic was going to fall headlong into the communist abyss, in line with the mass propaganda put out by the conservative media over the previous months.

(c) The fascist powers were justified in assisting Franco since it was in response to an aggressive move on the part of the Soviet Union, the 'bogeyman' of the time.

What the Comintern decision meant was that the organisational capacity of the various communist parties the world over would be put to work recruiting communist and non-communist volunteers and sending them to Spain. Among the volunteers there were those who already had combat experience from the First World War, while others had served in their own national armed forces. However, most lacked any military experience, although the cadres did not. In September 1936 there was nothing to suggest that the Brigades would take on the significance that they later did, still less that they might be used as shock troops for the Republican army. They could never compete with the iron fist, in the form of the Condor Legion, which Hitler placed at Franco's disposal the month after the Brigades were created; or with the Moroccan soldiers recruited by Franco even in the French protectorate.[34]

Action then shifted again to the Sovnarkom. GRU reports were piling up in Soviet leaders' in-trays painting a bleak picture of the situation. One, dated 15 September, stressed that the Republicans were still being held back by the lack of a unified operational command, their fissiparous tendencies, the autonomy with which their forces were acting and the poor levels of interaction between them. The Government showed signs of frailty. The defence of Madrid, which Franco's columns were approaching, had barely begun. Meanwhile, supplies for the insurgents were continuing to flow in from Germany and Italy, sometimes through Portugal. These reports were largely accurate.

Another report of 19 September was highly critical of Largo Caballero's government. Reinforcements were arriving in a disorganised and sporadic way. Victories were boosting the morale of the rebels, yet if they suffered defeats they might show signs of disintegration. On 22 September the Comintern representative in Spain, Victorio Codovilla, came forward with an important analysis. He had attended the meetings in Moscow the previous week and was doubtless familiar with the atmosphere prevailing there. Given the intervention of the fascist powers, he stressed, the struggle could last a long time. But if such aid did not continue as before (a somewhat hypothetical assumption), if the programme of the Republican government was put into practice, if the command and operations were unified, and if forces were diverted from one front to another, 'fascism' would be destroyed.[35] Goriev also relayed his impressions. With the customary qualifications, his message concluded in a rather optimistic tone: everything was not lost.

Meanwhile, Largo Caballero's government continued to push for support. Its correspondence with the Soviet embassy in Madrid has not yet been found, but it must have been more complex than generally believed. This is reflected, for example, in the way that the growing Soviet involvement finally took shape. It also encompassed the supply of trucks. An initial operation was put in place on 5 October.[36] This suggests some advance preparation, probably dating back to September, because on the 28th of that month the Spanish oil monopoly company Campsa signed a bill to pay for supplies to be made to the Madrid city council. The truck transaction involved a far from negligible order: 1,000 vehicles, at a price of $1,250 each, plus $60 per set of spare parts, to be shipped to a Spanish port and payable in three instalments at seventy, eighty-five and 100 days.

It was at this time, when things were looking rather bleak for the harassed Republic, that Stalin took the decision to get militarily involved. Thanks once more to Rybalkin, we know what he did. At 3.45pm on 26 September he phoned Vorochilov from Sochi and 'suggested' to him that urgent consideration be given to the possibility of selling the Republicans the following hardware: between eighty and 100 T-26 tanks without any markings that might reveal that they had been manufactured in Soviet plants; and fifty to sixty SB bombers equipped with foreign-made machine guns.[37] All of them were to go with the personnel required to operate them. The sale was to be made 'through Mexico'. This no longer meant a country. 'Mexico' had by then become the code word for Spain.

The next day, the GRU prepared another report on the progress of military operations. It highlighted the advances made by the insurgents, low Republican morale, and a minor improvement in the political situation in Madrid; it argued that the fall of Toledo to Franco would have major repercussions, as was indeed the case. That same 27 September, the Defence Commissariat confirmed to Stalin that 100 tanks, 387 specialists, thirty planes without machine-guns, and complete crews for fifteen additional aircraft were ready to go, together with the corresponding munitions (half of the tanks were available immediately).

This shipment was larger than the initial ones that Hitler and Mussolini had sent to Franco. It might indicate that Stalin was seeking to enable the Republicans to offset the superior modern weaponry that the rebels had already received. At the Politburo meeting of 9 October Vorochilov was given the task of making preparations for further shipments, a clear sign that Moscow was soon aware that the initial shipment would fall short of what was needed.

THE BACKGROUND TO STALIN'S DECISION

The time sequence as described above leads to the conclusion that Stalin's decision was to a great extent a response to the intervention of the fascist powers in Spain. Unlike Hitler, the Soviet dictator did not act with lightning speed. His behaviour was also much more cautious than Mussolini's. Although little by little Stalin started to lay the ground for a potential intervention, and did so by both overt and covert means, it still took two months before, from his holiday retreat, he ordered a fairly modest move – while as yet unidentified contingency plans had been drawn up in Moscow.

When Stalin gave the go-ahead, Franco was on the point of taking command of the insurgents. He had achieved so many military successes and occupied such a large area of Spanish territory that, for all intents and purposes, it was by then hardly possible to dislodge him. It is impossible not to assume that Stalin gave his green light in full awareness that, without Soviet aid, the Republic was facing imminent defeat, due to the assistance given to Franco by the fascist powers, the ineffectiveness of Republican resistance and the existing discord amongst the forces supporting the government. Stalin's intervention in the Spanish hornets' nest took place in full knowledge of the hopelessness of the Republican position. While the reasons which moved the fascist dictators can be identified more or less accurately, the Soviet motives are more difficult to disentangle.

This, in fact, is one of the issues which has been a bone of contention for many years. And the way in which it has been 'solved' has determined for many writers how they would interpret Soviet involvement in the civil war. For communist historians and fellow travellers, conceptual difficulties never arose. Following a tradition dating back to the war itself, assistance to the Republic always appeared to them to be an inevitable demonstration of solidarity in the fight against fascism that was led by the Soviet Union. On the opposing side were writers influenced by a wider range of ideological beliefs. They have offered a completely opposed interpretation. For the anarchists, Trotskyists and POUM (Partido Obrero de Unificación Marxista) supporters, all highly active in publicising their theories, particularly over the internet, Stalin wanted to drown the potential for the genuine emancipation of the Spanish proletariat, quelling the intoxicating revolution that was then breaking out spontaneously. For conservatives and the right, the Soviet dictator aspired to create in Spain a forerunner of what were to become the people's democracies of central and eastern Europe.

Two crucial considerations must not be underestimated. Firstly, there was the realisation on the part of the Soviets that the fascist powers had extended their policy of aggression into Spain. While opinions in Moscow might diverge as to the causes of this, they probably did not range widely; ultimately, almost all the decision-makers were in agreement that at least the German version of fascism represented a threat to the security of the Soviet Union. The problem was how to fight its aggression in operational terms, and, more specifically, what to do about the case of Spain. Secondly, the Spanish Civil War provoked a great upsurge in left-wing opinion worldwide. Clearly some of this was in response to campaigns waged by the national communist parties; but some of it was not. Yet the combination of both these phenomena had a crucial impact upon two basic dimensions of Soviet policies: on the one hand its efforts to build a more robust collective security system (essentially meaning the containment of the Third Reich) on the best possible terms for the USSR, and on the other hand its self-image as leader of the international left. On both counts there were opposing points of view.

Litvinov advocated non-intervention in Spain. After the Franco-Soviet pact of 1935, which yielded a political rapprochement but never contained a military protocol, he aspired to promote the kind of dynamics that might lead France – and ultimately the United Kingdom – to establish a barrier against the expansionist designs that he correctly attributed to Hitler. Two ideas danced before Litvinov's eyes. As the USSR's pacts with France (and Czechoslovakia) were essentially inadequate, due to their lack of a defence component, the first idea was for a more comprehensive agreement with the French

Popular Front government. The second idea was to work for a 'grand coalition' comprising France, Czechoslovakia, Romania, Yugoslavia and Turkey that might encourage Hitler to back off. He believed that this might earn some respect from the UK and Italy, even if they did not sign up. It was probable that Poland could be relied on. Only Hungary would align itself with Germany. Such a coalition was all the more urgent as the steps that Hitler was taking were liable, in turn, to isolate the Soviet Union.[38] This was certainly what was happening with Italy. These ideas were rejected by the Politburo. It was in this context that Stalin took his decision to help the Spanish Republic.

Litvinov was aware that there was a contradiction between supporting a Republic from which the UK was keeping its distance, on the grounds that it saw it as an example of Soviet penetration, while simultaneously soft-talking the British into joining a common front against the Third Reich. Neither were the Soviet leaders who really mattered unaware of this – and nor did they conceal it from the Republicans. In a famous letter dated 21 December 1936, Stalin, Molotov and Vorochilov drew Largo Caballero's attention to the advisability of 'preventing Spain's enemies from seeing her as a communist republic and thereby forestalling their open intervention, which constitutes the gravest possible danger to Republican Spain'. If an increasingly Soviet-inclined regime were to be established in Spain, the UK, France and the USA would adopt a stance not of neutrality but of opposition. Hence the insistence on bolstering a bourgeois democratic parliamentary regime that might give Spain a better chance of victory. This crucial realisation had already been made at a very early date by Pablo de Azcárate, later on ambassador to the Court of St James. At the Foreign Office, however, this interpretation hit a brick wall.

STRATEGIC, POLITICAL AND IDEOLOGICAL CONSIDERATIONS

As Stalin's thinking developed at his summer retreat, he was heavily influenced by geostrategic and geopolitical considerations, to which some writers, such as Denis Smyth, have drawn particular attention.[39] If Spain were to be strangled by fascism, this would represent a danger to France, which constituted the first link in the Soviet-proposed chain to restrain the expansionist appetite of the Third Reich.[40] It is barely worth adding that in that case Hitler would be encouraged to adopt a more aggressive policy. Sooner or later this would be directed against the USSR. According to the analysis of Soviet policy carried out by the British embassy in Moscow, the USSR's relationship with France was something that also appeared essential to UK diplomats when they tried to ascertain the Kremlin's viewpoint. If the French felt themselves to be in danger, the Soviet security strategy, to which France was pivotal in 1936, would be threatened. This was a scenario that needed to be contained: those reports that reached Stalin's in-tray in Sochi repeated many of the same messages. Two of these were crucial: given aid, the Republic was not necessarily a lost cause; but a potential victory would only be possible if the substantial material support that the insurgents were receiving from the fascist powers were to be matched.

As Geoffrey Roberts has pointed out, this does not mean over-looking the fact that Stalin was aware of the limitations of the focus on collective security.[41] Assisting the Republic caused friction, and the Soviet diplomats and intelligence services would have had to have been stupid not to have realised that the more support they gave the Republicans, the greater would be the suspicion with which the democracies would view their intervention in Spanish affairs.

Ultimately, the protection of Soviet security was dependent upon proclaiming a single message loud and clear: the only way of dealing with the fascist powers was to not submit to intimidation. Maisky records a 'spontaneous' exchange of opinion that he had in June 1937 with the chairman of the Non-Intervention Committee, Lord Plymouth.[42] The ambassador responded to the latter's allegation that, however imperfect it might have been, the committee's work had greatly reduced the danger of a European war by saying that, quite to the contrary, it had increased it. Hitler and Mussolini had convinced themselves that they had no reason to fear any serious opposition, and this had reinforced their sense of impunity. In reality events were evolving not as the British diplomat believed, but rather more as his interlocutor was arguing. Roberts points out that the Soviet defence budget was increased by 340 per cent between 1932 and 1937 and that it doubled again between 1937 and 1940.[42] This involved a considerable effort that must at least have helped to sustain the atti-tude that the Soviets should not allow themselves to be overcome by the threat that the fascist powers represented.

Nevertheless, while the political and strategic element is likely to have been the main component in Stalin's decision, this does not mean that there were no other factors involved. Stalin had some fundamental concerns in August and September 1936. He had launched a merciless assault on Trotskyist deviationism, and his direct, immediate and continuous personal involvement in the dynamics leading to the execution of Kamenev, Zinoviev and their co-accused is documented in minute detail. This was something that Comintern officials were not unaware of.

A large proportion of Chubin's report was devoted to the Trotskyist movement and its relationship with events in Spain. Chubin highlighted the fact that Trotskyists in France had been keen to point out that they had already anticipated the path that events would take in Spain. In particular, they claimed that the ground for the rebellion had been laid by the errors and equivocations of the Popular Front, and that it would not be the bourgeois Republic that would save Spain but the revolution of the proletariat. From this viewpoint, the impression taken was that Spain constituted a fertile field for the successful realisation of Trotskyist theories and predictions. This was not something that could be contemplated with equanimity at the Kremlin.

Later, Lieutenant-Colonel Simon, chief of the Deuxième Bureau in Moscow, suggested that the reasons for the persecution of the Trotskyists must have gone deeper than those alluded to publicly.[44] In his view, the stabilisation of the Soviet regime was at stake, and Stalin was prepared to adopt any measures necessary to ensure the continuity of his project. Simon believed that it was probably also a precautionary measure. Discontent had spread within the USSR, and perhaps Stalin had wanted to come down hard in order to avoid it surfacing and being expressed openly. At that time, supporting a regime hounded by fascism could be presented as a clear demonstration of the righteousness underpinning the two volte-faces that had been made previously – in joining the League of Nations and giving support to a collective security policy; and, after the Seventh World Congress of the Comintern, in opening the doors to the participation of communist parties in Popular Fronts.[45] Looking at Spain, it is possible to claim that in Stalin's view there might have been a perfect confluence of strategy and ideology.

Therefore we should not dismiss Stalin's ideological perspective as knee-jerk analysis laced with paranoia. In Sochi, when on 6 September he initiated the about-turn in policy towards Spain, he informed Kaganovich of his own thoughts as to how *Pravda* should have covered and explained the trial of the 'Zinovievist/Trotskyist' faction – and how it had failed to do this. He claimed that those executed were nurturing the most sinister intentions and were guilty of the worst possible sin against the Soviet code:

> ... *the defeat of socialism in the USSR and the restoration of capitalism ... The struggle against Stalin, Vorochilov, Molotov ... and others is a struggle against the soviets, against collectivization, against industrialization ... Because Stalin and the other leaders are not isolated individuals but the personification of all the victories of socialism in the USSR, the personification of collectivization, of industrialization and of the flourishing of culture, that is to say the personification of the efforts of workers, peasants and of the working class intelligentsia to secure the defeat of capitalism and the triumph of socialism.*[46]

When it comes to the supreme boss, such claims should not be underestimated, and writers who have studied Stalin during that era have taken great care not to do so. These are statements that allow us to weigh the practical significance of ideology in Stalinist policies. It is clear that he wanted his first great political purge to be seen from the perspective that he had clearly explained to Kaganovich. *Pravda* had omitted to do this and he regretted it. He claimed that a great opportunity had been lost.

Neither was this mere theoretical discourse. On 11 September Stalin approved the proposed expulsion of the Assistant Commissar for Heavy Industry, despite the fact that just a few weeks earlier, with other 'suspicious elements', he had taken part in a press campaign denouncing Zinovievists and Trotskyists and calling for the execution of the accused. At the meeting of the Comintern presidium on 16 September one of the most important issues had been to identify the lessons that should be learned from the trial as regards the communist parties and the international workers' movement. And it was no less significant that soon after, on 25 September, Stalin ordered the removal of Yagoda from his post as Commissar for Internal Affairs and his replacement by an even more dreadful figure, Nikolai I Yezhov, who quickly became his right-hand man in launching a massive campaign of purges and terror. Following quickly on the heels of that, on 29 September, the same day on which the Politburo formally approved the shipment of military supplies to Spain, Stalin signed the decree concerning 'Trotskyist and Zinovievist counter-revolutionary elements', aimed purely and simply at their complete annihilation.[47]

The ideological discussion proceeded along the same lines. During the Comintern presidium debates a few days earlier, Togliatti (who was to become Stalin's key man in Spain) had based his thinking on Dimitrov's diagnosis that the struggle against Trotskyism was an essential element in the fight against fascism. To his eternal shame, Togliatti went even further: as Pons has recorded, Trotskyism could not be seen as a current within the workers' movement. It had become no more and no less than the vanguard of the counter-revolution. It had to be combated not by focusing on isolated groups, but by conducting dramatic purges on the agents of class enemies embedded within the proletarian movement.

So this was the atmosphere hanging over the Politburo, the Sovnarkom and the Comintern in September 1936. In a word, it is far from absurd to assume that Stalin might not have wanted to be reproached 'from the left' for having the slightest leniency towards the fascist aggressors. Put plainly, no significant aspect of communist or Soviet policies during that period can be understood without reference to the action against Trotskyism. If to this we add the idea that had arisen during the early days of the Spanish Civil War, that the Soviet Union could not lose its leadership over the anti-fascist and left-wing masses, it is not hard to see that Stalin might have found it impossible to remain inactive indefinitely. So, what if the Republic were to fall before the assault of the fascist powers? Ultimately, what was at stake was the prestige of the USSR and of the international communist movement.

Objectively, as Soviet jargon had it, the intervention in Spain in September 1936 fulfilled various purposes of some significance. To note these is not a matter of cataloguing them, still less of ranking them by importance. It is possible to do this with a certain degree of confidence in the case of Hitler and Mussolini, but is not so easy with Stalin, as we lack primary sources recording his thoughts in Sochi. Those purposes were:

1. To serve notice on aggressors, particularly the Third Reich, to act with caution when it came to attempts at intimidation.
2. To serve as a demonstration of the 'correctness' of the ideas that Stalin had gradually been developing about the nature of a potential future conflict in which German fascism would constitute the principal threat.
3. To give France the impression that the Soviet Union was a reli-

able partner, eager to protect collective security at a time when it was vulnerable.
4. To help reinforce the role of France in Soviet planning.[48]
5. To show the left worldwide, and its own population, that the Soviet Union was not leaving the Spanish proletariat in the lurch.
6. To help reduce the likelihood of a 'fascist' victory in the domestic 'war' that had broken out, whereby its 'Trotskyist variant' might succeed in getting through the Stalinist system.

To this end, the fact should be mentioned that during the weeks immediately following Stalin's decision there was a glut of detentions, as if, as the French military attaché pointed out, the authorities wanted to persuade public opinion that the detainees were conniving with foreign organisations hostile to the Soviet state. These included senior military personnel, although they were not as well-known as those who fell victim to purges over the following years, as well as many foreign communists, especially Germans.

For many writers, Stalin's vacillations are explained by the need to satisfy two contradictory pressures: on the one hand to help the Republic without thereby alienating the community of democratic powers, and on the other to avoid antagonising the Third Reich too much. Yet ultimately, in tandem with the outbreak of the great wave of terror, there was no other measure that was capable of simultaneously fulfilling a whole series of aims, in which strategic considerations, foreign policy and ideology were inextricably entwined; it formed the only permissible 'line' that the Stalinist system was inclined to follow. To these aims would soon be added others, linked in part to the merciless fight that Stalin was launching against all forms of deviationism – to his 'left' and to his 'right' – and to the war experience that would be gained in fighting the feared Nazi aggressor on the distant battlefields of Spain. This is a somewhat more complex scenario than one involving the notion that Stalin wanted from the outset to establish a base from which to support the creation of a bogus 'people's republic', before the concept even existed.

In the above analysis no mention has been made of the gold issue. This refers to the well-known but usually misinterpreted fact that the Spanish government took the decision to send to the USSR almost three-quarters of the gold reserves of the Bank of Spain. The council of ministers approved the motion tabled by Largo Caballero and Juan Negrín, then Minister of Finance, on 6 October 1936. Previous contacts had been initiated by Negrín with ambassador Rosenberg, with the approval of the Prime Minister. This unusual operation has given rise to great discussions in the literature, mostly without any kind of documentary support. In my view, the fact that Spanish gold was going to be sent to Moscow may have made Stalin's decision a little easier: the USSR would not take any financial risk. It is, however, unlikely that this was the main factor. Unfortunately, however, I was not allowed access to the relevant documentary evidence in Moscow. More research needs to be done in Russian archives before coming to more definitive conclusions on this aspect. For the time being, many of the myths created by the acrimonious discussion amongst Republicans about the reasons they had lost the war, and by historians bent upon superimposing on the Spanish Civil War the ideological framework of the Cold War, have been documentarily disproved.[49]

This chapter was written following the author's unscripted lecture at the Imperial War Museum, London, on 8 March 2008.

NOTES

1. See the trilogy by Ángel Viñas: *La soledad de la República: el abandono de las democracias y el viraje hacia la Unión Soviética* (2006); *El escudo de la República: el oro de España, la apuesta soviética y los hechos de mayo de 1937* (2007) and *El honor de la República: entre el acoso fascista, la hostilidad británica y la política de Stalin* (2008). All published by Editorial Crítica, Barcelona. Previously, Antonio Elorza and Marta Bizcarrondo, *Queridos camaradas: la Internacional Comunista y España, 1919-1939* (Barcelona: Editorial Planeta, 1999).
2. Frank Schauff, *Der verspielte Sieg: Sowjetunion, Kommunistische Internationale und Spanischer Bürgerkrieg* (Frankfurt: Campus Verlag, 2004) (also available in Spanish).
3. Yurii Rybalkin, *Operasia 'X': Sovetskaya Voennaya Pomoshtsh Respublikanskoi Ispanii* (Moscow: Airo XX, 2000); available in Spanish as *Stalin y España: la ayuda militar soviética a la República* (Madrid: Marcial Pons Historia, 2007).
4. Regrettably, the only reliable, although limited in scope, work in English available is *The Soviet Union and the Spanish Civil War* (interactive e-book, Columbia University Press, 2004); translated into Spanish as *La Unión Soviética y la guerra civil española: una revisión crítica* (Barcelona: Editorial Crítica, 2003).
5. Archives of the Spanish Ministry of Foreign Affairs, R-2296/7.
6. For the German case see A Viñas, *Franco, Hitler y el estallido de la guerra*

civil: antecedentes y consecuencias (Madrid: Alianza, 2001 (previous versions go back to 1974 under the title *La Alemania nazi y el 18 de julio: antecedentes de la intervención alemana en la guerra civil*; same publisher).

7. Mussolini had interfered in Spanish domestic politics as far back as 1932. He was inimical to the Republic from the outset. For a recent overview see Morten Heiberg, *Emperadores del Mediterraneo: Franco, Mussolini y la guerra civil española* (Barcelona: Editorial Crítica, 2003). For Mussolini's decision itself, see Paul Preston 'Mussolini's Spanish Adventure: From Limited Risk to War', in Paul Preston and Ann L Mackenzie (eds.), *The Republic Besieged: Civil War in Spain* (Edinburgh: Edinburgh University Press, 1996).

8. For instance Ronald Radosh, Mary R Habeck and Grigory Sevostianov (eds.), *Spain Betrayed: The Soviet Union in the Spanish Civil War* (New Haven: Yale University Press, 2001) have failed to mention that the telegram, presented as a great discovery, had already been exhumed by a Russian historian ten years earlier.

9. This is one of Rybalkin's great discoveries. He found the relevant document in the Russian presidential archives, to which no Western civil war researcher has enjoyed access to my knowledge. It is also one of the Rybalkin discoveries appropriated by Antony Beevor, who cites exactly the same source but fails to assess its significance. It is also surprising that Beevor has extensively drawn on Rybalkin without mentioning him as a source. The seven references that Beevor makes to the central archives of the Russian Defence Ministry feature among Rybalkin's sources. This is a coincidence difficult to believe in, as Russian departmental archives are usually inaccessible, with the partial exception of the Foreign Ministry files. Beevor's references to the GARF (Government Archives of the Russian Federation) are also cited by Rybalkin. In academia this behaviour usually goes by the name of plagiarism. It is a sad fact that an otherwise distinguished English military historian feels compelled to use such elementary tricks. Beevor's work has been consulted in the Spanish version, *La guerra civil española* (Barcelona: Editorial Crítica, 2005).

10. For an analysis of the circumstances see my *Mitografía y guerra civil: seis ensayos desmitificadores* (to be published in 2011).

11. None of this appeared in the published version of Koltsov's diary.

12. It is worth recalling that, almost from the outset, Franco argued that the uprising had been launched 'to save Spain from communism'. The rebels' National Defence Junta even enshrined this extraordinary notion in some of its decrees laying the foundations for a legal system of its own.

13. In his utterly unreliable book *In Stalin's Secret Service* (New York: Harper & Brothers, 1939). His specious arguments have been taken up by, among others, Gary Kern, *A Death in Washington: Walter G Krivitsky and the Stalin Terror* (New York: Enigma Books, 2003). A previous exploitation of Krivitsky's tales by Stephen Koch, *Double Lives: Spies and Writers in the*

Secret Soviet War of Ideas Against the West (New York: The Free Press, 1994) is even more fanciful.

14. Stanley G Payne, *Union Sovietica, comunismo y revolución en España, 1931-1939* (Barcelona: Plaza y Janés, 2003), p.169, has claimed that there was less surprise in Moscow than in Berlin or Rome. This is a leap in the dark. Rome and London knew about the insurgents' plans. No evidence has yet been produced to show that the Soviets were aware of them, although I would not exclude this possibility.

15. Chubin's report was published as doc.33 in the collection of the General History Institute of the Russian Academy of Sciences and of the Russian Federal Archive Service, *Komintern i grazhdanskaja vojna v Ispanii: Dokumenti*, (Moscow: Nauka, 2001).

16. The fact that Radosh et al should have made no mention of these reports demonstrates two things: firstly, they did not look too hard; secondly, if they did see them then maybe they opted not to incorporate them into their collection because they clashed with their ideas, which can ultimately be traced back to Krivitsky.

17. Historians have usually overlooked these reports. They were produced by a group of analysts grouped under the innocuous name of Air Intelligence Service (AIS). The National Archives, Kew: HW 22 /1.

18. I fail to understand how Payne (p.169) claimed that 'access to high-level Soviet government documents remains prohibited', despite citing Rybalkin's book in his bibliography.

19. RGVA (State Military History Archives): 33987/3/845.

20. This challenges the accuracy of Krivitsky, who claimed that he selected the first Soviet intelligence agents from The Hague and sent them to Hendaye and Lisbon. As recently as 2003, Kern (p.62) followed this line verbatim despite its utter implausibility. Moscow followed a standard procedure. The representative of the French Second Bureau was the military attaché while his assistants were responsible for operational tasks.

21. AVP RF (Foreign Policy Archives of the Russian Federation): 097/ 1/102/ doc.14, p.19.

22. RGASPI (State Political and Social History Archives): 17/16/ 21, doc.240.

23. The letter is in AVP RF: 010/11/53, doc.71, pp.29ff.

24. RGASPI: 17/162/20, doc.244.

25. This is a still clouded subject. New data has recently come to light which I have used in my *Mitografia y guerra civil.*

26. Georgi Dimitroff, *Tagebücher 1933-1943,* (ed. Bernhard H Bayerlein) (Berlin: Aufbau-Verlag, 2000), p.126. There is another less detailed edition, by Ivo Banac, *The Diary of Georgi Dimitrov* (New Haven: Yale University Press, 2003).

27. This canard goes back to civil war propaganda in Britain by the Francoist side. It has been taken up by Fernando Ballesteros Castillo, *Las Brigadas*

Internacionales: de Thorez a Togliatti, pasando por Tito (Madrid: Editorial San Martín, 2006), p.31.

28. Our hypothesis is that Stalin and the Soviet leadership would rely more on the GRU reports than on news items appearing in the Soviet and foreign media.

29. Litvinov's reprimand is in AVP RF: 010/11/53 doc.71, pp.56ff. Elorza/Bizcarrondo (p.460) have cited only part of this telegram but in such a way that neither the reprimand itself nor Rosenberg and Gorev's temptations are apparent.

30. Telegram reproduced in RW Davies; Oleg V Khlevniuk; EA Rees; Liudmila P Kosheleva and Larisa A Rogovaya (eds.), *The Stalin-Kaganovich Correspondence, 1931-1936* (New Haven: Yale University Press, 2003), p.351.

31. By then Italian and German troops were operating alongside Franco. Although the numbers involved were yet not great, their contributions were extremely important.

32. Unfortunately the original documentary evidence remains unknown.

33. In Gerald Howson, *Arms for Spain: The Untold Story of the Spanish Civil War* (Spanish edition) (Barcelona: Península, 1998), pp.159 and 292-7.

34. The issue of the foreign assistance to both sides in terms of personnel and equipment is a highly contentious one. For a detailed analysis see my 'Armas y hombres para España. La cuestión de los apoyos exteriores en la guerra civil: un balance crítico', in Enrique Fuentes Quintana (dir.) and Francisco Comin (coord.), *Economia y economistas españoles durante la guerra civil* (Barcelona: Galaxia/Gutenberg, 2008).

35. This report is reproduced in *Komintern*, doc.35, pp.119-45.

36. All the documentation about aid of this type is kept in the Juan Negrín archive in Paris (AJNP).

37. Many writers, of whom Beevor is the latest, state that the opposite was the case and that Vorochilov called Stalin. They are wrong. They have misinterpreted Rybalkin, who consulted the record of the call.

38. Silvio Pons, *Stalin and the Inevitable War, 1936-1941* (London: Frank Cass, 2002), p.46.

39. See "We Are with You': Solidarity and Self-interest in Soviet Policy towards Republican Spain, 1936-1939', in Preston and Mackenzie (eds.), *The Republic Besieged.*

40. It should be added that the PCF press had been stressing that, in fighting for Spain, the Republicans were also fighting for French security: see Pierre Broué, *Staline et la Révolution* (Paris: Fayard, 1993), pp.74ff. On 12 August French Communist leader Jacques Duclos emphasised that it should not be allowed that France be surrounded.

41. See 'Soviet Foreign Policy and the Spanish Civil War', in Christian Leitz and David D Dunthorn (eds.), *Spain in an International Context, 1936-1959* (New York: Berghahn Books, 1999), pp.88ff.

42. In *Cuadernos españoles* (Moscow: Progreso, without date), pp.132ff.
43. See 'The Fascist War Threat and Soviet Policies in the 1930s' in the compilation edited by Andrea Romano and S Pons, p.152.
44. The details are in a secret report produced by Lieutenant-Colonel Simon referring to the events of October and November and dated 5 December 1936. SHD (Service Historique de la Défense, Vincennes), 7N 3122.
45. It should be noted that the Popular Front in Spain was not imposed by the communists or the Soviet Union. It grew out of specific Spanish circumstances.
46. RW Davies et al, pp.349-50.
47. Oleg V Khlevniuk, 'The Objectives of the Great Terror, 1937-1938', in Julian Cooper; Maureen Perrie and EA Rees (eds.), *Soviet History, 1917-1953* (Basingstoke: Macmillan, 1995), p.159.
48. It should not be forgotten that in September/October 1936 the Russians tried to make military progress with France, so as to build up a common stance against Germany and to reduce the extent to which Paris was dependent upon London (Sabine Dullin, *Des hommes d'influences: Les ambassadeurs de Stalin en Europe* (Paris: Payot, 2001), pp.156ff).
49. A new book by A Viñas and Fernando Hernández Sánchez, *El desplome de la República* (Barcelona: Editorial Crítica, 2009) deals with the end of the civil war, the role of the communists and their relations with Juan Negrín. These are topics which rank among the most hotly debated in civil war historiography. The interpretations still abundant in the English-speaking world are confronted in the book with the relevant documentary evidence.

Laurie Lee in the International Brigades: Writer or Fighter?

Richard Baxell

During the Spanish Civil War of 1936-1939, more than 2,500 British and Irish volunteered to help the democratically elected Republican government in its struggle against the rebel forces of General Franco and his German and Italian allies. This was by no means 'a poets' war' – the overwhelming majority of the volunteers came from working-class backgrounds – yet the two most widely known British volunteers are both writers. The first is George Orwell, whose graphic memoir *Homage to Catalonia* portrayed Orwell's involvement in the war and the internecine struggles between Republican factions that came to a head in Barcelona in May 1937. The second is the hugely popular English poet and author, Laurie Lee, whose story of his time in Spain has also generated considerable attention. Unfortunately, however, this is not solely due to Lee's stature as a writer, but also to the controversy that has developed over the accuracy and veracity of his account. As a recent biography of Laurie Lee has shown, he could be, in the words of his brother, a rather 'secretive' and 'devious' person.[1]

When Laurie Lee died in May 1997, he received fulsome obituaries in the British press, worthy of his status. *The Independent* described him as 'One of the great writers of the century whose work conjured up a world of earthly warmth and beauty'.[2] Lee wrote widely: in addition to novels and poetry, he wrote travel books, essays, a radio play and several short stories. He received a number of literary awards and was honoured with an MBE for his work as caption-writer-in-chief for the Festival of Britain in 1951. For most people, however, Lee is probably best known for his autobiographical trilogy.[3]

The first volume, *Cider with Rosie*, was published in 1959, and chronicles Lee's upbringing in rural Gloucestershire. It presents a picture of

The young Laurie Lee.
Courtesy Kathy Lee

rural Britain that was fast disappearing, 'an elegy to a passing era'. The theme of change is central to the book; both for Laurie Lee – who moves towards adulthood with the discoveries of the pleasures to be had with his cousin Rosie Burdock underneath a hay cart – but also for the small village of Slad, and other such 'rural idylls':

> *Time squared itself, and the village shrank, and distances crept nearer. The sun and moon, which once rose from our hill, rose from London now in the east ... In the faces of the villagers one could see one's change, and in the habits their own change also. The horses had died; few people kept pigs any more but spent their spare time buried in engines. The flutes and cornets, the gramophones with horns, the wind harps were thrown away – now wireless aerials searched the electric sky for the music of the Savoy Orpheans. Old men in the pubs sang, 'As I Walked Out', then walked out and never came back.*[4]

Lee's memoir continues in the second part of the trilogy, which describes how Lee himself 'walked out and never came back'. *As I Walked Out One Midsummer Morning*, published in 1969, is an account of Lee's experiences tramping and busking through Spain, which began in July 1935 and ended with the outbreak of civil war in July 1936, and his repatriation back to the UK on a British navy destroyer. Like *Cider With Rosie, As I Walked Out...* ends on a note of change, though this time for Spain:

> *An officer came up on deck and offered me a drink. 'Shame to break up your holiday like this,' he said. Later, a German airship passed above us, nosing inquisitively along the coast, the swastika black on its gleaming hull. To Spain, so backward and so long ignored, the nations of Europe were quietly gathering.*[5]

Both books have received great critical acclaim. *Cider With Rosie* has been described as a 'work of art' and *As I Walked Out...* as 'a beautiful piece of writing'. And, in addition to this critical acclaim, both books have long been extremely popular. *Cider with Rosie* has sold over six million copies worldwide and has twice been televised in Britain. It is also, of course, a novel that many children read whilst at school.

The third and final part of the trilogy is *A Moment of War*, Lee's account of his experiences in Spain during the civil war. Lee waited until 1991, more than fifty years after the end of the war, to publish

A Moment of War and, like the earlier parts of the trilogy, it met initially with enthusiastic reviews. John Sweeney, writing in the *Literary Review*, described it as: 'A great, heart-stopping narrative of one young Englishman's part in the war in Spain … it is crafted by a poet, stamping an indelible image of the boredom, random cruelty and stupidity of war.'[6] And, in a review in the *Sunday Telegraph* entitled 'Girls are more exciting than guns', Byron Rogers claimed that 'This [book] will tell you more about the civil war than Hemingway or any history book.'[7]

Lee begins his account some time in December 1937, with a description of his two-day trek over the Pyrenees into Spain, accompanied by his numerous belongings. After crossing the border, Lee is promptly arrested as a suspected spy. His interrogator informs him: 'No señor! Not over the Pyrenees. Not with all that circus equipment you are carrying. Books, cameras – and a violin, dear Jesus … It was the violin that did it. And the German accent. You would never fool anyone you know.'[8]

Lee is imprisoned under threat of execution and spends a week confined with a deserter from the Spanish Republican army. His future looks bleak when his companion is removed from the cell and executed. Somehow, however, Lee's story is eventually confirmed and he is released and escorted to Figueras (the mustering point for volunteers who have arrived in Spain from the north), where Lee describes being admitted into the International Brigades and having his passport confiscated. At Figueras he meets a number of other volunteers for the International Brigades, whom he describes thus:

> *The French crooks crouched in corners, shrugging and scowling; the Poles sat in princely silence sunning their beautiful cheekbones. The Czechs scribbled pamphlets and passed them to each other for correction; while the Russians seemed to come and go mysteriously as by tricks of the light. The British played cards and swore.*[9]

Lee then goes on to describe his experiences at Figueras, which include a romantic interlude with a young Spanish girl from Andalusia, called Eulalia:

> *The girl wore the tight black dress of the villages, and had long Spanish-Indian eyes… Her eyes were like slivers of painted glass, glinting in the setting sun. I heard the boys upstairs stamping and singing to the breathy*

music of an old accordion. But I couldn't join them. I was trapped down here, in this place, this cellar, to the smell of coñac and this sleek animal girl ... She held my hands still for a moment. 'Frenchman,' she said thickly. 'English,' I replied, woodenly. She shrugged, and whispered a light bubbling profanity – not Catalan but pure Andaluz. Her finger and thumb closed on my wrist like a manacle. Her body met mine with the quick twist of a snake.[10]

Lee then goes on to describe his rudimentary military and political training, about which he is rather less flattering than about Eulalia:

We finished the days training with an elaborate anti-tank exercise. A man covered a pram with an oil-cloth and pushed it round and round the square, while we stood in doorways and threw bottles and bricks at it. The man pushing the pram was Danny, from London. He was (rather) cross when a bottle hit him.[11]

Lee is then transferred to Albacete, the International Brigade base, accompanied by other British volunteers, whom Lee portrays rather unfavourably as 'the ex-convicts, the alcoholics, the wizened miners, dockers, noisy politicos and dreamy undergraduates busy scribbling manifestos and notes to their boyfriends'.[12] Lee believes them to be motivated by: 'Failure, poverty, debt, the law, betrayal by wives or lovers – most of the usual things that sent one to foreign wars'.[13] However, he does at least temper this rather slanderous accusation by pointing out that the volunteers were all united by a deep hatred of fascism.

At the International Brigade base Lee is arrested again, this time over the stamps in his passport from his previous trip to Spain, which showed him to have been in Morocco during the spring of 1936, just preceding the uprising. Lee is interrogated by an American called Sam (whom some have assumed to be a reference to Tony de Maio, an American who was later accused of having executed American prisoners in his charge[14]). Sam asks him: 'Just what were you doing there at that time – for Gawd's sake?'

Despite the incriminating stamps, Lee is eventually freed following the intervention of the guide who had accompanied him over the Pyrenees, and a 'favourable word from a mysterious high voice of authority in Madrid' (probably a reference to Bill Rust, the *Daily Worker* reporter and senior representative in Spain of the Communist

Party of Great Britain). Once again Lee rejoins his comrades, who are transferred to Tarazona de la Mancha, which had become the base for all the English-speaking volunteers in July 1937. Lee then relates his experiences as part of a machine-gun team, learning how to dismantle and practice firing the Russian Maxim gun. He also describes a visit from the General Secretary of the CPGB, Harry Pollitt. Despite a rousing speech, Pollitt is pestered by dispirited volunteers, desperate to return home.

After another encounter with the Andalusian girl Eulalia – who by a remarkable coincidence reappears in Tarazona – Lee is temporarily transferred from his company to another unit, charged with what he calls 'special duties'. These include arresting a farmer believed to be a fascist sympathiser and responsible for local sabotage, and the arrest of a young man (presumably an anarchist or POUMista) who is summarily shot by Lee's French commander, 'Kassell'.

When the Republicans launch their offensive at Teruel, Lee returns to his company and describes how Bill Rust visits the British volunteers bearing a cap he had collected from Teruel, which had just fallen to the Republicans. Early in January 1938 Lee leaves the battalion once again when he is transferred away from his unit to Madrid, to make radio broadcasts for the United States, accompanied by the American 'Sam'.

He returns from Madrid to Tarazona to find that the British Battalion has been moved up to the front lines at Teruel, and the base's Spanish commanders order Lee to rejoin his unit. Whilst on route to Teruel, Lee describes how he and his companion, a Portuguese volunteer, are deserted by their driver and take shelter in a barn. Here they narrowly escape being shot by three British volunteers, to whom Lee and his companion attach themselves. However, caught in a Nationalist artillery barrage, the British volunteers are forced to retreat and they leave Lee with a Spanish Republican unit. Lee remains with the Spaniards for several days before they are overrun by Francoist forces, and he describes his involvement in desperate hand-to-hand combat, which results in him killing a rebel soldier: 'There was the sudden bungled confrontation, the breathless hand-to-hand, the awkward pushing, jabbing, grunting, swearing, death a moment's weakness or slip of the foot away.'[15]

He is repatriated back to Britain shortly afterwards on the orders of the political commissar at Tarazona, who advises him: 'You'll be much more use to us there. After all, you're not much use to us here.'[16]

Released from service in the International Brigades, he makes his way to Barcelona where, yet again, he is arrested as a spy and spends three weeks in prison. Once again Bill Rust manages to get him released and lets him stay in the safety of his flat in Barcelona, where he helps Rust organise a record card index of all the British volunteers. Lee then returns home to the welcoming arms of his girlfriend, and what he calls 'love without honour'.

In contrast to the earlier parts of the trilogy, *A Moment of War* has been dogged by controversy over its accuracy and truthfulness. This has been exacerbated by its rather belated publication, which some have seen as highly significant. John Dunlop, who fought with the British Battalion and the Anti-Tank Battery in Spain, has remarked pointedly that it took Lee twenty-two years (after the publication of *As I Walked Out …*) to publish 'what purports to be his part in the fight of the Spanish people', and he 'wonders why'. Bill Alexander, author of *British Volunteers for Liberty* and a commander of the British Battalion in Spain, also asked why he had waited so long, until a time 'when the possibility of verification and refutation has become more difficult'.

In fact, a number of the British members of the International Brigades have bitterly disputed Lee's version of events, with some going as far as to suggest that Lee wasn't even a member of the International Brigades in Spain at all. In a review of *A Moment of War* in 1991, Bill Alexander described the book as 'pure fantasy'. Alexander argued: '[Lee] never joined the British Battalion and the International Brigades. He wasn't at Teruel; he never got beyond Barcelona.'[17] For this reason Lee has become a figure of loathing for some veterans, who feel that he cashed in on the sacrifice of their friends and comrades. Of course, portraying the British volunteers as drinkers and gamblers duped into escaping the misery and failure of their lives in Britain was hardly likely to endear the book to former members of the International Brigades. However, it is not just veterans who have criticised the book.

Soon after Lee's death in late December 1997, a scathing article appeared in *The Spectator*, which echoed the long-held suspicions of the veterans. The article repeated Bill Alexander's criticisms of the book and stated categorically: 'The problem with Laurie Lee's story is that he never joined the International Brigade.'[18] Following the publication of this article a vigorous argument over Lee's role in Spain raged in the British press, particularly in the letter columns of *The*

Guardian.[19] Laurie Lee's widow, Kathy, understandably hurt that Courtauld's article should appear once Lee was not around to defend himself, wrote to *The Guardian* attacking Courtauld and angrily refuting his claims. Others supported her, with one letter writer criticising what he referred to as 'an old tankie' (meaning Bill Alexander) 'smearing an author's name after he's safely dead'.[20] However, Vernon Scannell, a poet and novelist who knew Lee, stated that both *Cider With Rosie* and *As I Walked Out One* … contained 'fanciful exaggerations and inventions common to the genre', and that *A Moment of War* should be understood with this in mind.[21]

Shortly afterwards, on 3 January 1998, Dr Barry McLoughlin, an Irish academic based in Vienna, who had extensive knowledge of the Comintern archives in Moscow, entered the debate. McLoughlin argued that the Moscow archives held documents that contradicted Courtauld and Alexander's view that Lee had never been in the Brigades.[22]

In May 1998, believing perhaps that attack is the best form of defence, one of Lee's supporters turned the spotlight on Bill Alexander. In a short article entitled 'Fighter or Faker?', Michael Eaude argued that Alexander's testimony was itself unreliable, and that Alexander's attacks on Lee were fostered by a desire to protect his own interpretation of the Spanish Civil War and the reputation of the British Battalion.[23] He argued that Alexander's work on the British volunteers was itself not the whole truth, as it avoided awkward details, such as the execution of deserters from the British Battalion.[24] Eaude claimed that:

> *[Alexander's] understandable loyalty to his comrades meant that the Brigades had to be whiter than white. That there were executions for desertion, drunkenness or 'Trotskyism' within the Brigades, or that lives were lost through ill organization, has been vehemently denied by Alexander.*[25]

The following year, in 1999, Valerie Grove published a biography of Laurie Lee which drew heavily on McLoughlin's research as evidence for Lee's involvement in the International Brigades. Though sympathetic to Lee, Grove nevertheless concluded that his account, whilst 'touching and vivid', was probably 'imaginative as to hard fact'.[26] How much of Lee's account is 'imaginative' and how much is 'hard fact' is still a matter of some contention.

As Bill Alexander and Simon Courtauld both recognised, the most glaring problem with Laurie Lee's account is with the chronology. As is often the case with reminiscences, Lee's memoir is rather vague when it comes to dates. He begins his story some time 'in December 1937', with a description of his two-day trek across the Pyrenees (which ironically, of course, he describes as not being believed by the Spaniards he met on his arrival in Spain).[27] The next reference to a date is to Christmas Day 1937, which Lee claims to have spent with the British Battalion at their headquarters in Tarazona de la Mancha. He refers to the battle currently raging in Teruel, in which Spanish Republican forces, operating without the International Brigades, have advanced into the town of Teruel. This certainly fits with the established chronology, for Teruel was indeed captured by Spanish Republican forces in December 1937, with the International Brigades kept initially in reserve.[28]

The problem lies in Lee's description of his experiences during the interim period. Within a period of, at the most, twenty-five days, Lee describes how he spends up to fourteen days in prison as a suspected spy, ten days at Figueras, two on a train from Figueras to the International Brigade base at Albacete, another two days in gaol in Albacete over the incriminating passport stamps, followed by 'a few days' transferring to Tarazona de la Mancha, an indeterminate amount of time on 'special duties' with the military intelligence unit, and finally 'several' more days with his regular unit. Even if Lee had crossed the Pyrenees at the very beginning of December 1937, the fortnight spent in gaol, the time travelling through Spain, the ten days at Figueras, let alone the period spent on 'special duties', simply could not all have taken place within the short timescale claimed. So either Lee is getting confused with his dates and chronology, or he is employing a certain amount of poetic licence. It is, of course, true that personal memoirs are notoriously unreliable when it comes to chronological order and the precise dates of events (particularly, of course, when they are written so long after the event), so perhaps it might be possible to give Lee the benefit of the doubt on this point. Unfortunately, however, there are numerous other significant errors and inaccuracies.

For example, Lee's description of military training at Figueras being voted on by volunteers seems highly unlikely to be correct. He states:

The next morning there was an outbreak of discipline in the barracks.
Soon, after daylight, scattered committees in groups, began to gather in

*the courtyard ... By majority votes it was agreed we should have more
exercise and drill.*[29]

It seems inconceivable that any such vote would have been allowed,
yet alone acted upon, in what, by this time, had become the highly
disciplined ranks of the International Brigades. As Bill Alexander has
stated, this might have been possible in the anarchic days of 1936
when some foreign volunteers were still fighting in militia columns,
but by December 1937 foreign volunteers had long been
incorporated into the International Brigades as part of the Spanish
Republican army. In fact, Lee's description of his time at Figueras
bears no relation to that of any other volunteer. The description of
being handed a 100 peseta note on arrival at Figueras, when
volunteers were only paid seven or eight pesetas per day, also seems
open to doubt.

Similarly, Lee describes meeting two commanders of the British
Battalion in Spain – Jock Cunningham and Tom Wintringham –
though both had returned to England before Lee's arrival
(Cunningham in August and Wintringham in November 1937).
Furthermore, he describes his company commander at Teruel as
'Terry, a forty-year-old non-commissioned officer from Swansea', yet
the commanders of the three British infantry companies in the
battalion at Teruel were Frank West, George Fletcher and Sam Wild,
all well-known figures in the British Battalion.[30] Whilst it is possible
that a volunteer might have used the nom-de-guerre of 'Terry' – a
number of British volunteers used pseudonyms whilst in Spain – there
is certainly no record of West, Fletcher or Wild ever doing so.

Lee's description of the visit to the battalion by Harry Pollitt, the
CPGB General Secretary, was cited by Bill Alexander as further
evidence of Lee's calumny. The account of the visit has caused
particular offence to British International Brigaders for, although Lee
refers to Pollitt's extraordinary gift as an orator, the impression gained
is that Pollitt is somehow able almost to bewitch the volunteers with
his rhetoric – at least until the end of his speech. At this point 'the
spell and magic' breaks, and the volunteers are suddenly:

*Plucking at his sleeves and pouring out their grievances, asking to be sent
back home. 'It ain't good enough, you know. I bin out 'ere over nine
months. Applied for leave and didn't get no answer. When they going to
do something comrade? ... eh?'*[31]

Lee must have been fully aware of criticisms of the Brigaders that labelled them as 'dupes' of the Communist Party, an image that this passage hardly helps to dispel. However, there is some substance to this account: despite Bill Alexander's remarks, it is true that there were a number of volunteers who wanted to return home and, with the incorporation of the International Brigades into the Spanish Republican army in September 1937, were unable to do so. John Angus, the British political commissar in charge of the 're-education centre' for deserters at Camp Lucas, is very candid about this;[32] and Bill Alexander himself accepts that the decree did cause some bitterness.[33] But Lee seems to be suggesting that there was a large number of volunteers begging Pollitt to be sent home, which seems unlikely. The period in the war which he is describing was, as many volunteers have remarked, a time when morale was high, not low. The Republicans had just launched an offensive at Teruel, which had astonished those in Spain and beyond who had believed the Republic was finished. As Lee himself later recounts: 'People talked of tides turning, and paths to victory reopening at last.'[34]

The Eulalia episodes (once at Figueras, then again during his time spent chasing spies at Tarazona) certainly seem, as Valerie Grove concluded, 'far-fetched', and it is difficult not to agree with Bill Alexander who always felt that Lee only included Eulalia in order to spice up his story and 'add a little sex'. As John Dunlop noted, the episodes bear a striking resemblance to an account in a book on the American volunteers by Arthur Landis, published nearly twenty-five years before *A Moment of War*.[35] Landis describes how a young poorly dressed Andalusian girl appeared at the headquarters of the No.3 Company of the Lincoln Battalion in March 1938. According to Landis, the young girl turned up again later in the year, when the Americans were preparing for the Ebro offensive. She was recognised by one of the Americans whom she had encountered at Jarama the previous year, discovered to be a spy, and executed.

Landis's description of the girl, and her frequent appearances and involvement in covert activities, certainly do bear a passing resemblance to the Eulalia episodes, but to say, as John Dunlop does, that Lee's 'story about "Eulalia" could have been lifted straight from a book by Arthur Landis' is probably to go too far. There is certainly a resemblance, but there are also clear differences between the stories. Of course, critics might argue that if Lee had 'lifted' the story he would have been a fool not to change some of the details.

The Eulalia story is one of a number of episodes in the book which, though not impossible in themselves, seem rather unlikely to have been Lee's personal experiences. By far the most damning of these is his description of his experiences working on 'special duties', hunting down spies and deserters in Tarazona. As Lee himself would have been the first to admit, his political views were fairly unsophisticated, and indeed he declared that he volunteered for Spain based on 'a general liking for all things Spanish'. Thus he would have been considered far too politically naïve and inexperienced to be sufficiently reliable for work with the SIM (the Republican secret police charged with rooting out spies), no matter how sympathetic he might have been to the Republican cause. Lee may have spoken Spanish, but he was not the only British volunteer to be able to do so, and British volunteers given political responsibilities in Spain were drawn from those who had a proven track record of political reliability before volunteering. Not all the British political *responsables* in Spain had the track record of a man such as Brigade political commissar Peter Kerrigan – who had studied at the Lenin School in Moscow between 1929 and 1930, been a delegate to the Seventh World Congress of the Comintern in 1935 and worked as an election agent for Willie Gallagher, the successful Communist Party parliamentary candidate for Fife – but Lee had no pedigree whatsoever, so the likelihood of his being considered sufficiently politically experienced and trustworthy to be entrusted with such responsibilities seems highly implausible at the very least.

Other inconsistencies and errors abound. In the original hard-back version of *A Moment of War*, Lee mentions meeting a veteran from the Battle of the Ebro, yet the battle did not begin until more than five months after Lee's departure. In the paperback version, which was published in 1992, the passage is wisely revised to read 'Aragon' instead of 'Ebro'. Elsewhere Lee describes Largo Caballero as the Spanish Prime Minister at the time he was in Spain, though Largo was dismissed in May 1937.

It seems clear that the litany of errors and inconsistencies establish that not all of the events described in *a Moment of War* could have taken place exactly as Lee said they did. Thus the book cannot be regarded as a reliable memoir of Lee's experiences in Spain. So, then, if the memoir was unquestionably 'imaginative as to hard fact', what do we actually know for certain about Lee's time in Spain?

That Lee went to Spain sometime around the end of 1937 by climbing over the Pyrenees is not disputed;[36] even Lee's sternest critics fully accept this.[37] The story of Lee's arrest and imprisonment on his entry into Spain are also generally agreed upon.[38] And documents held in Moscow cited by Barry McLoughlin do indeed show that Laurie Lee entered Spain in December 1937, actually on the 5th.[39] In fact, this information had been available for anyone who was looking for it, long before the Moscow archives were opened. A file held in the International Brigade Association archive in London provides conclusive evidence that Lee arrived in Spain in order to join the International Brigades.[40] The file is an alphabetical list of British volunteers compiled in September 1938, probably by Peter Kerrigan. In the list Laurie Lee's name and place of origin (Stroud) are clearly apparent, stating that he arrived in Spain in December 1937 and was later repatriated.

Once in Spain, Lee travelled to Figueras with several other English-speaking volunteers. The leader of the group to which Lee was allocated was an Irish volunteer, Bob Doyle, who reported that Lee's conduct was 'excellent' and that he showed 'a willingness to comply with regulations'.[41] Once there Lee was admitted into the International Brigades. Like all the other volunteers, he was allocated a number: Laurence Edward Alan Lee, an artist from Stroud, was British volunteer number 1502.[42]

From Figueras, Lee was transferred via Albacete to the British base at Tarazona de la Mancha, which he had reached by 15 December, at which time a report by an American officer in the International Brigades described him as 'a positive example to others'. The report also states that during his interrogation Lee admitted that his epilepsy meant that he would not be much use at the front and adds: 'He agrees that the added excitement would be too much for him'. The report recommended that Lee be given a post that was 'not strenuous'.[43]

Several sources place Lee at Tarazona from mid-December 1937. A report written at Tarazona on 23 December 1937 referred to the two epileptic fits that Lee suffered earlier at Figueras and stated: 'At present he is assisting in the cultural work at Tarazona'.[44] And in an interview held in the Imperial War Museum Sound Archive, British volunteer Tony McLean remembers meeting Lee in Tarazona.[45] According to McLean, who was working as a research clerk and military censor in the Brigades, Lee appeared to be doing very little at the base apart from amusing the locals with his fiddle playing. Like Bill Rust, McLean found Lee to be somewhat naïve about the issues surrounding the war. He apparently admitted to McLean: 'I'm not at all political. I just like Spaniards'. McLean – obviously fully aware of the controversy surrounding Lee – stated carefully: 'There's practically nothing to say that he was in the International Brigades. But he was.'

Unfortunately, Lee's activities in Spain during the remainder of January and the beginning of February 1938 are unknown. What is known is that he was granted an exit visa on 14 February and left Spain on 19 February 1938, with his passport stamped 'Sale sin dinero' ('Leaves with no money').[46] His tale of arrest in Barcelona appears to be essentially truthful, though the period of time he spent in gaol was more likely to have been the three days he described to a reporter in 1977 than the three weeks he describes in *A Moment of War*. During his time in Bill Rust's Barcelona flat he must indeed have worked on Rust's filing cards, for the cards have been discovered in an archive in Salamanca, just as Lee described them.[47] However, his claim (in the hardback edition) that the cards included details of British volunteers killed 'at Brunete, Guadalajara and the Ebro'[48] was, of course, mistaken, for the Ebro battle was months after Lee had left Spain. The later paperback edition was changed to read 'Brunete, Jarama and Guadalajara', but unfortunately the amendment is no great improvement, for the British Battalion did not participate in the Battle of Guadalajara.

The period immediately preceding Lee's departure on 19 February 1938 is frustratingly unclear. There appears to be no account of Lee's days in Spain in this period apart from his own and, though he had been declared medically unfit for front-line duties, there is no reason why he would not have been given another role. After all, a number of other volunteers were assigned to duties behind the line, because of age, wounds or illness.

But the central question is: did Lee actually participate in the fighting? His description of his participation in hand-to-hand combat on the edge of the Battle of Teruel and the killing of a Nationalist soldier is one of the most controversial passages. Certainly, as Lee's critics have pointed out, the evidence is that Lee never served with the British Battalion as a front-line soldier. However, as his wife Kathy quite rightly pointed out, Lee's account does not state that he fought at Teruel as part of the British Battalion, only that he was caught up in a mêlée whilst on route from Tarazona to rejoin his company some time 'early in January'. Ironically, Lee's tale of his exploits at Teruel is not impossible, at least in terms of timing. The British Battalion fought at Teruel from 14 January to 3 February 1938, when they were pulled out for rest and recuperation. Nevertheless, it seems probable that this part of the tale is an invention, for it seems wholly unbelievable that the relatively untrained epileptic poet would have been any match for, in his words, a 'frantically spitting Moor', one of Franco's battle-hardened, elite soldiers. But, so far, this has been impossible to verify. Probably the only person who knew the truth was Laurie Lee himself.

Tony McLean, the British volunteer who met Lee at Tarazona, always remained convinced that Lee took no part in the actual fighting, and many other volunteers felt the same. In fact it was the inclusion of this passage which indirectly led to Courtauld's critical article. The citing by historian Tom Buchanan of Lee 'taking part in the desperate fighting at Teruel' in his book, *Britain and the Spanish Civil War*,[49] particularly irked Bill Alexander and encouraged him to talk to Courtauld.

The long delay in publication has been cited by Lee's supporters as a possible cause of many of the errors. However, as we have seen, it also raised suspicions amongst some of his critics. But the delay itself may not be as suspicious as some have believed. As Michael Eaude has pointed out, Lee's notebooks from his time in Spain were stolen from a BBC car in Seville in 1969, forcing him to rely on the vagaries of memory, and thus, he believes, partly explaining the delay in publication.[50] This might also explain Lee's nervousness following his submission of the manuscript. Lee insisted on the book being read by two literary advisors before publication, and changed the name of the book from the original *Winter of War* because, he said, he felt it to be 'too grand'.[51]

However, despite the long delay in publication, it is inconceivable that all the errors were simply an accident of a failing memory. Whilst Laurie Lee was undoubtedly in the International Brigades, there is no doubt that much of his account of his experiences in Spain is little more than wishful thinking. The combined weight of the errors and contradictions suggests that much of Lee's work is indeed, as Bill Alexander claimed, 'fantasy'. I would argue, therefore, that *A Moment of War* should be seen as Lee's version of what might or could have happened, rather than what did actually happen, a conclusion not unfamiliar to historians. As EH Carr argued in 1961 in his seminal work, *What is History?*: 'Documents do not tell us what happened, but only what [the author] thought had happened, or perhaps what he wanted himself to think had happened.'[52]

I was reminded of this when reading a book that was given to me by Sadie Thomas, whose brother and husband both served in the International Brigades in Spain – in fact her brother, Max Nash, was killed on the Ebro in July 1938. The book – *War and Peace* – is of course concerned with a very different war, but it is striking how easily Tolstoy's description of a young soldier recounting his war tales could be applied to Lee's account of his time in Spain:

> *He told them of his … affair just as those who have taken part in a battle generally do describe it, that is, as they would have liked it to have been, as they have heard it described by others and as sounds well, but not as it really was … He began his story meaning to tell everything just as it happened, but imperceptibly, involuntarily and inevitably he lapsed into falsehood … He could not tell them simply that every one went at a trot, and that he fell off his horse and sprained his arm and then ran as hard as he could from a Frenchman into the wood … His hearers expected a story of how, beside himself and all aflame with excitement, he had flown like a storm at the square, cut his way in, slashed right and left, how his sabre tasted flesh, and he had fallen exhausted, and so on. And so he told them all that.*[53]

The description by Valerie Grove of *A Moment of War* as 'an old man's book written with a young man's verve and a poet's imagination'[54] is, I think, a fair one. And it is difficult to disagree with Vernon Scannell when he argues: 'Whilst it's okay to make up love stories … This type of fantasising by Lee in a work which claims to be non-fiction is difficult to accept'.[55] Lee might have been wiser to have copied Milton Wolff, the commander of the American Abraham Lincoln Battalion, whose marvellous – though partly fictionalised – account of an American's experiences in Spain was entitled: *Another Hill: An autobiographical novel*.

Nevertheless, we should, perhaps, not be too hard on Laurie Lee. Whilst *A Moment of War* may not be a truthful account of his experiences in the Spanish Civil War, it was, at least, dedicated 'to the defeated' Republicans, something for which Bill Alexander, one of Lee's sternest critics, stated that he was always grateful. And, after all, it was not really Laurie Lee's fault that he did not fight with the British Battalion in Spain. He simply wasn't equipped for war, and was rejected for front-line service due to his epilepsy and consequently made many of his experiences up.[56] But it should not be forgotten that the young poet undoubtedly *did* cross the Pyrenees into Spain and he *did* join the International Brigades at a time when, in WH Auden's words, 'poets were going off like bombs'. That much alone must, surely, be worth something.

This lecture was delivered on 6 March 2004 at the Imperial War Museum, London.

NOTES

1. See Valerie Grove, *Laurie Lee: The Well Loved Stranger* (London: Viking, 1999).
2. Matthew Brace, 'Laurie Lee walks out for the last time', *The Independent*, 15 May 1997, p.1.
3. The three volumes, *Cider with Rosie* (London: Hogarth Press, 1959), *As I Walked Out One Midsummer Morning* (London: Deutsch, 1969) and *A Moment of War* (London: Viking, 1991) are also published collectively as *Red Sky at Sunrise* (London: Viking, 1992).
4. Lee, *Cider with Rosie*, p.230.
5. Lee, *As I Walked Out*, p.176.
6. Review of *A Moment of War* by John Sweeney, 'Cider Freak Let Loose on the Poor Spaniards', *Literary Review*, October 1991, p.37.
7. Review of *A Moment of War* by Byron Rogers, 'Girls are more exciting than guns', *Sunday Telegraph*, 20 October 1991, p.x.
8. Lee, *A Moment Of War*, pp.9-10.
9. Ibid, p.28.
10. Ibid, pp.33-4 and p.36.
11. Ibid, p.41.
12. Ibid, p.45.
13. Ibid, p.46.
14. Grove, p.515.
15. Lee, *A Moment Of War*, p.161.
16. Ibid, p.162.
17. See Bill Alexander's review of *A Moment of War* in Box D-3, file C/34, International Brigade Memorial Archive (IBMA), Marx Memorial Library (MML).
18. Simon Courtauld, 'A Not Very Franco Account', *The Spectator*, 3 January 1998, p.17.
19. The controversy surrounding Courtauld's article on Lee was given front-page coverage in *The Guardian* of 31 December 1997 and generated a number of letters to the paper over the next few days (see below). It was also picked up in other national quality newspapers, such as *The Independent* and *The Times*.

20. Paul Burroughs, letter to *The Guardian*, 2 January 1998, p.14.
21. Vernon Scannell, 'A moment of truth', *The Guardian*, 1 January 1998, p.13.
22. Barry McLoughlin, 'Laurie Lee was in Brigades', *The Guardian*, 3 January 1998, p.18.
23. Michael Eaude, 'Fighter or Faker?', *The Guardian* (review section), 13 May 1998, p.8.
24. It is true to say that Bill Alexander was always keen to present the International Brigades in a positive light. As a recent study of the British volunteers has pointed out, Bill Alexander, along with Frank Ryan and Bill Rust (who also published works on the British volunteers), are 'keepers of the story by which they wanted the battalion to be remembered'. James K Hopkins, *Into the Heart of the Fire: The British in the Spanish Civil War* (Stanford: Stanford University Press, 1998), p.xi. However, Eaude is muddying the water. After all, it is not Alexander's account that is under examination here.
25. Eaude, p.8.
26. Grove, p.516.
27. Lee, *A Moment of War*, p.1.
28. For an overview of the Teruel battle see, for example, Hugh Thomas, *The Spanish Civil War*, 3rd ed. (London: Penguin, 1990), pp.788-94. For the involvement of British volunteers in the battle, see Bill Alexander, *British Volunteers for Liberty* (London: Lawrence & Wishart, 1982), pp.160-8 and Richard Baxell, *British Volunteers in the Spanish Civil War* (London: Routledge/Cañada Blanch, 2004), pp.92-4.
29. Lee, *A Moment of War*, p.38.
30. George Fletcher and Sam Wild both later commanded the British Battalion; Frank West was a political commissar. The only British volunteers called 'Terry' who are listed as fighting at Teruel were Terry Grant from Nottingham (whose real name was James Poole-Burley), who died in Aragón in March 1938, and Terry McCartney, a thirty-two-year-old from London.
31. Lee, *A Moment of War*, p.94.
32. John Angus, *With The International Brigade in Spain* (Loughborough: Loughborough University, 1983), p.7.
33. Alexander, pp.79-80.
34. Lee, *A Moment of War*, p.120.
35. Arthur Landis, *History of the Abraham Lincoln Brigade* (New York: Citadel Press, 1967), p.408.
36. As Courtauld states: 'There is no dispute about Lee's return to Spain, or that he was held prisoner for two weeks.' Courtauld, op cit. Likewise, John Dunlop states that 'it is definitely true that somehow or other he got himself put into jail in Barcelona having been arrested without papers'. John Dunlop, review of *A Moment of War*, in Frank Graham, *Battles of Brunete and the Aragon* (Newcastle: Frank Graham, 1999), p.59.

37. See Alexander's review, p.1.
38. Whilst it is true that no records of Lee's arrest have been found in any Spanish archives – prompting Valerie Grove into suggesting that 'the death cell episodes must be imagined' (Grove, p.516), Bill Rust, the *Daily Worker* correspondent who, like Bill Alexander, wrote a book on the role of the British in Spain, *Britons in Spain* (London: Lawrence & Wishart, 1939), later confirmed to Alexander that he had indeed heard of Lee's predicament in Spain and arranged his release. (See Alexander's review, p.1).
39. Moscow Archives (MA) (International Brigade Memorial Trust), 545/6/91 p.142.
40. MML, IBMA Box D-7, file A/1.
41. Grove, p.96.
42. MA 545/6/91 p.142 (IBMT).
43. MA 545/6/162 p.33 (IBMT).
44. Ibid.
45. Interview with Tony McLean, Imperial War Museum Sound Archive, 838, reel 3.
46. Grove, pp.104-5.
47. I am grateful to Professor Robert Stradling for this information.
48. Lee, *A Moment of War*, p.174
49. Tom Buchanan, *Britain and the Spanish Civil War* (Cambridge: Cambridge University Press, 1997), p.164.
50. A Spanish veteran recently voiced his suspicion to me that Lee never actually wanted to write *A Moment of War*, but was pressured into writing it by his publisher who had paid Lee an advance. Having spoken to a representative from Viking, who published the book, I feel this can probably be discounted. Lee was notorious for changing publishers at whim – see Diana Athill, *Stet: An Editor's Life* (London: Granta, 2001) – and apparently teased a number of publishers with tales of the manuscript, which he claimed to be carrying around in his briefcase. Eventually Lee offered the manuscript to Viking for an undisclosed sum. Telephone conversation with Toby Lacey of Viking, 14 March 2002.
51. Ibid.
52. EH Carr, *What is History* (London: Macmillan, 1961), p.19.
53. Leo Tolstoy, *War and Peace* (London: Macmillan, 1959). Book III, chapter VI, p.258.
54. Grove, p.108.
55. Scannell, p.13.
56. MA 545/6/162 p.33 (IBMT).

The Crimes of Franco

Paul Preston

The remains of General Franco lie in the gigantic mausoleum of the Valle de los Caídos (Valley of the Fallen), built with the sweat and blood of 20,000 slave labourers. For Franco's monument to his own greatness, and to the fallen of his own side in the Spanish Civil War, it took nearly twenty years to carve the 850-foot long basilica out of the hillside of the Valle de Cuelgamuros in the Guadarrama mountains north-east of Madrid, and to erect the immense cross which towered 500 feet above it.[1] The fate of his enemies could not have been more different.

Apart from those killed on the battlefields, tens of thousands were officially executed, judicially murdered, between the autumn of 1936 and 1945, when the Axis defeat imposed some caution on the Caudillo. An indication of the scale of the repression is given by the fact that the thirty-seven of Spain's fifty provinces that have been fully or partially researched to date have come up with the names of more than 100,000 persons. This suggests that, in terms of the identifiable dead, the final figure may be in the region of 130,000. However, there were others, perhaps another 50,000, who were killed without even the simulacrum of a trial. Some were thrown alive from cliffs into the sea, or from high bridges into deep rivers. Others were shot against the walls of a cemetery or by a roadside, and were buried in shallow graves where they fell, or thrown into disused mineshafts. For decades their families lived in terror, unable to grieve properly, unsure of the fate of their mothers or fathers, their husbands or sons.

Those whose names have been identified are those who were executed after a pseudo-trial, and/or buried in a cemetery where records were kept. To those must be added those murdered whose names cannot be known. It may never be possible to calculate the exact numbers killed along the road travelled by the African columns that raped, looted and murdered their way from Seville to Madrid.

Sculpture by Alejandro Rubio Dalmati at the memorial at Lardero, La Rioja, to the more than 2,000 civilians from the province who were murdered by the fascists following the military coup in July 1936.

What of those killed in the open fields by the patrols of mounted Falangists and Carlists who 'cleaned up' the countryside when the columns had moved on? What of those who, having fled from their own towns and villages, were murdered elsewhere with no one to recognise their corpses?

The problem is illustrated by one appalling example concerning the fate of unknown refugees. By September 1936, in southern Spain, there were more and more refugees in flight. As towns and villages along the road from Seville to Mérida had been taken by the African columns, many workers and their families had already fled westwards. At the same time, some had fled northwards from the repression in Cádiz and Huelva. Others had gone southwards from Badajoz and Mérida after the capture of both cities. The result was a large number of desperate refugees in the western part of Badajoz, cut off to their east by the Seville-Mérida road and to the north by the Mérida-Badajoz road, to the south by the advancing columns, and to their west by the Portuguese frontier. By mid-September, about 8,000 men, women, children and old people had collected, in open country near the town of Valencia del Ventoso, where the local population did its best to feed them at rapidly organised soup kitchens.

On 18 September, faced with the prospect of being driven into Nationalist hands, the trade union and political leaders among them organised the refugees into columns to undertake a desperate forced march towards Republican lines. It was decided to divide this desperate human mass into two groups. The first contingent consisted of approximately 2,000 people, the second of 6,000. The first had a dozen men armed with rifles and about 100 with shotguns, the second about twice as many. These exiguous forces had to protect two lengthy columns of horses, mules and other domestic animals and carts containing whatever possessions the refugees had managed to grab from their homes before taking flight. Alongside walked young children, women with babes in arms, others pregnant, and many old people.

Moving at different speeds, the groups spread out. Most successfully crossed the road from Seville to Mérida, and some made it to Castuera in the Republican zone. However, the bulk of the refugees, the slowest, threw up dust clouds which made it easy for rebel reconnaissance aircraft to pinpoint their position. The headquarters in Seville of General Gonzalo Queipo de Llano, the rebel commander in the south, were fully informed of their movements, the civilian composition of the columns and their sparse armament. Nevertheless, preparations were made to attack them as if they were well-equipped military units. They walked into an elaborate ambush. Machine guns were placed on the hills overlooking their route and, when the refugees were within range they opened fire. Large numbers were killed during the fighting. More than 2,000 were taken prisoner and transported to Llerena. Many hundreds scattered into the surrounding countryside. Families were separated, some never to meet again. Some wandered in unfamiliar territory for weeks, only to be killed or captured by search parties of Civil Guard and mounted Falangists. A few made it through to the Republican zone. In Llerena, where the prisoners were held, a massacre took place, with prisoners machine-gunned in the bullring.[2]

Most of those killed in the so-called 'Column of 8,000' are not among the named dead. Despite the difficulty of reaching definitive figures, an indication of the scale of the killings is given by the outstanding historian of the repression in the south, Francisco Espinosa Maestre, who has located the names of 6,610 murdered in the repression just in the west half of the province of Badajoz. Espinosa Maestre estimates that the total numbers in that western half of the province could easily exceed 12,000.[3]

The violence of the military rebels was part of a deliberate policy. The first of the secret instructions, issued in April 1936, by General Emilio Mola, the director of the coup, declared:

> *It has to be born in mind that the action has to be violent in the extreme to reduce as soon as possible the enemy which is strong and well-organised. Of course, all leaders of political parties, societies and trade unions which are not linked to the movement will be imprisoned and exemplary punishment carried out on them in order to strangle any rebellion or strikes.[4]*

In his proclamation of martial law in Pamplona on 19 July 1936, Mola said:

> *Re-establishing the principle of authority unavoidably demands that punishments be exemplary both in terms of the severity with which they will be imposed and the speed with which they will be carried out.[5]*

Shortly afterwards he called a meeting of all of the *alcaldes* (mayors) of the province of Pamplona (Navarra) and told them:

It is necessary to spread terror. We have to create the impression of mastery, eliminating without scruples or hesitation all those who do not think as we do. There can be no cowardice. If we vacillate one moment and fail to proceed with the greatest determination, we will not win. Anyone who helps or hides a communist or a supporter of the Popular Front will be shot.[6]

The killings did not just take place in areas where there was resistance. It is noteworthy that, in places where the military coup was immediately successful, the killings were in the thousands. In the three overseas bases of the Canary Islands, Ceuta and Melilla 2,768 people were killed; in Galicia 3,000, in Zamora 3,000, in Valladolid 3,430 and in Navarra 2,789.

In late 2002, building works in one of the patios of the municipal cemetery of Toledo unearthed a huge mass grave containing hundreds of bodies of persons who had disappeared at the end of September 1936, after the capture of the city by Franco's forces. In addition to the casualties among the Republican militiamen and troops during the attack on Toledo, afterwards there was a sweeping purge of prisoners, the wounded and civilian personnel suspected of left-wing leanings. Without mass DNA testing it is impossible to know the exact numbers of Republicans killed in the days following the siege. Nevertheless, according to the cemetery's register, between 27 September and 13 October, 727 bodies were buried. There were twenty-one batches of corpses with no details other than the numbers contained in each batch, and labelled 'desconocidos' ('unknown'). There were eight corpses on 27 September and then sixteen batches between 1 and 3 October, making up a total of 564 victims, which presumably includes those killed during the fighting on 27 September and the prisoners and civilians killed over the next six days. The last five batches, one each on 4, 5, 6, 7 and 13 October, saw another 163 bodies.[7]

All over Spain, archaeological activity is producing evidence of the horrors of the civil war. Equally typical was what happened between July 1936 and December 1937 near the village of Concud in the province of Teruel. Into Los Pozos de Caudé, a pit six feet wide and 250 feet deep, were hurled the bodies of 1,005 men and women, including adolescent boys and girls. Few of them were political militants. Their crime was simply to be considered critical of the military coup, related to someone who had fled, to have a radio or to have read liberal newspapers before the war. It has taken sixty-eight years for their families to find out the truth. Fear prevented anyone from even going near the pit, although occasionally at night bunches of flowers would be left nearby. Once the socialists were in power, people began openly to leave floral tributes. Then, in 1983, a local farmer came forward and said that he had kept a notebook with the numbers of shootings that he heard each night throughout the Spanish Civil War. They came to more than 1,000.[8]

Media interest in Caudé and other common graves began in 2002, when a young Navarrese sociologist, Emilio Silva-Barrera, began to investigate the fate of his grandfather who had disappeared in León in the first months of the war. Overcoming the wall of silence and fear built by the Franco regime, which survived the transition to democracy, Silva discovered the truth. At dawn on 16 October 1936, his grandfather, with twelve other Republicans, was murdered by Falangist gunmen near Priaranza del Bierzo. Their bodies were buried in a field next to the roadside where they fell. A shopkeeper, Emilio Silva-Faba was the father of six children aged between three months and nine years, his offence his membership of the centre-left Republican party. His grandson then located the burial place, and persuaded a group of archaeologists and forensic medical experts to take part in exploratory digs. DNA tests of the exhumed bones have now identified Emilio Silva-Faba.[9]

As a result of that 'success', Emilio Silva, together with Santiago Macías Pérez, a local historian from León, founded an organisation, the Association for the Recovery of Historical Memory (Asociación para la Recuperación de la Memoria Histórica – ARMH), to continue the work. By 2005, twenty-six digs were ongoing and 109 bodies had been recovered. The association had 2,500 requests for help in locating the remains of relatives. It is impossible to calculate with certainty the number of bodies lying in shallow graves across Spain, but the association estimates that the requests reflected about 10 per cent of the total. There exist gigantic common graves: in Extremadura, where mass killings took place at the concentration camp of Castuera, in Asturias in both Oviedo with 1,600 and Gijón with 2,000, and in various parts of Andalusia. In Catalonia, the regional government has located fifty-four such graves, with 4,000 corpses in Barcelona alone. There are graves in every part of Spain. As they are excavated, relatives stand nervously, like those awaiting the rescue parties in mining disasters or earthquakes. For those who never knew what had happened to their loved ones, even though they know that they were murdered, they still await the definitive confirmation with horror and trepidation. When it comes, as sometimes it does, it permits the shuddering release of pent-up and unacknowledged grief.

It was a Spanish investigating judge, Baltasar Garzón, who pursued General Pinochet on behalf of the 'disappeared' in Chile. Yet in Spain, where there are more than ten times as many cases, despite the private initiative of Emilio Silva who has taken the case to the United Nations, the government of the Partido Popular refused to put resources into the search. Under the PSOE socialist party that is changing. Nevertheless, there is still no census of the dead, no team of historians working on the problem, no funds for DNA testing. The government does, however, contribute to the upkeep of the graves of Falangist volunteers who fought with the Germans on the Eastern Front. Moreover, right-wing historians have been responding to the work of the ARMH with a resurrection of the Francoist propaganda that implies that the 'reds' simply got what they deserved. With the most virulent of their number regularly riding high in the best-seller lists, the Spanish Civil War is being fought all over again on paper.[10]

The admirers of General Franco, Spanish and foreign, focused on a series of 'triumphs' which, not surprisingly, were also loudly trumpeted by his regime's propaganda apparatus. The most regularly cited of these accomplishments are a victory in the Spanish Civil War allegedly won by superior generalship, the bringing of law and order to an anarchic nation, the maintenance of Spanish neutrality in the Second World War and the masterminding of the Spanish economic miracle of the 1960s. In fact, to his dying day, Franco vengefully kept Spain divided between the victors and the vanquished of 1939. This benevolent father of his nation regarded the civil war as 'the struggle of the *patria* (fatherland) against the *anti-patria*', and the defeated as the 'scum (*canalla*) of the Jewish-masonic-communist conspiracy'.

The view of Franco as a magnanimous patriot is difficult to reconcile with the psycho-pathological language used by Francoists to depict their left-wing compatriots as subhuman – dirty, filthy, stinking depraved scum, slime, whores and criminals. This language justified the need for 'purification', a euphemism for the most sweeping physical, economic and psychological repression. The cost in blood of saving a nation's soul mattered little to the victors.

The horrors already mentioned reflect the fact that, just as happened with the Nazi *Volksgemeinschaft* and in the Soviet gulags, the

Franco dictatorship embarked on a process of national 'reconstruction' through the execution, forced exile, imprisonment, torture and economic and social humiliation of hundreds of thousands of people. The persecution of the compatriots deemed to belong to the 'anti-Spain' (leftists or liberals and their extended families, all of whom became non-persons without civil rights) affected millions. From the very first days of the war, terror had been a crucial instrument of the military rebels, but to this Franco added a determination to annihilate as many Republicans as possible. Despite the German and Italian hopes for a rapid Nationalist victory, Franco's objective was the gradual and thorough occupation of Republican territory, boasting to a senior Italian officer: 'In a civil war, a systematic occupation of territory accompanied by the necessary purge (*limpieza*) is preferable to a rapid rout of the enemy armies which leaves the country still infested with enemies.'[11] On 4 April 1937, at the beginning of the campaign against the Basque Country, he declared ominously to Mussolini's ambassador, Roberto Cantalupo:

> ... *we must carry out the necessarily slow task of redemption and pacification, without which the military occupation will be largely useless. The moral redemption of the occupied zones will be long and difficult because in Spain the roots of anarchism are old and deep.*[12]

The kind of moral redemption which he had in mind, already seen in the massacres which had followed the captures of Badajoz in August 1936 and Málaga in February 1937, more than explained the need for slowness. It would guarantee that there would never be any turning back, not only through the physical elimination of thousands of liberals and leftists but also in the long-term terrorising of others into political support or apathy. Franco was fully conscious of the extent to which the repression not only terrified the enemy but also inextricably tied those involved in its implementation to his own survival. Their complicity ensured that they would cling to him as the only bulwark against the possible revenge of their victims.

In the south, the horrors were perhaps greatest, as a colonial army applied against the civilian population the techniques of terror used in the African wars. The ferocity of the terror was unrelated to the strength of working-class resistance. In the case of Badajoz, where the resistance was fierce, nearly 4,000 people were killed in one week. Two thousand of them were shot in the local bullring in a twenty-four hour period. Piles of corpses were soaked in petrol and burned in the local cemetery, thereby rendering it impossible for there to be an accurate account of those killed. The repression was also bloody in the working-class district of Triana in Seville, where the workers opposed the coup; but in Huelva, where the right took over relatively easily, the repression took more than 6,000 lives. What happened in Huelva was representative of what took place in all parts of rebel-held territory, not just in those places that had to be conquered by military force. It took place where the military rebels succeeded immediately, and where there was virtually no resistance. This was not the work of uncontrolled elements, as happened in the Republican zone, where the military rebellion triggered the total collapse of the entire apparatus of law and order. The Falangists and others carrying out the systematic killings could at any time have been restrained by the military authorities. Yet, the military actively encouraged thousands of civilian vigilantes to carry out a dirty war.

The purpose of terror as a weapon to generate fear far and wide was made clear by the broadcasts of both General Mola in the north and, more systematically, by General Queipo de Llano in the south. His obscene descriptions of the bloody atrocities were heard nightly from Seville, and may have contributed to provoking some atrocities by his listeners. The savagery visited upon the towns conquered by Spanish colonial forces was simply a repetition of what they did when they attacked a Moroccan village. In a broadcast on 23 July, Queipo de Llano declared:

> *We are determined to apply the law without flinching. Morón, Utrera, Puente Genil, Castro del Río, start digging graves. I authorise you to kill like a dog anyone who dares oppose you and I say that, if you act in this way, you will be free of all blame.*[13]

As news of the murders reached towns that were threatened by right-wing forces, reprisals were taken against the right-wing elements that were assumed to be planning to do the same. But the uncontrolled militias were not the same as the disciplined troops of the rebels, who were encouraged by their officers to carry out atrocities. The Republican authorities made every effort to control the 'uncontrolled' elements. The official Republican response was typified by a broadcast made by Indalecio Prieto, the moderate socialist leader, on 8 August 1936. He declared:

Even if the terrible and tragic reports about what has happened and is happening in areas dominated by our enemies are true, even if day after day we receive lists of the names of comrades, of beloved friends, whose attachment to an ideal was enough to ensure them a treacherous death, do not, I beg you, I entreat you, do not imitate their behaviour. Meet their cruelty with your pity, meet their savagery with your mercy, meet the excesses of the enemy with your generous benevolence. Do not imitate them! Do not imitate them! Be better than them in your moral conduct! Be better than them in your generosity. I am not asking you, let it be clear, to lose strength in the struggle, ardour in the battle. I call for toughness in combat, breasts of steel, as some of our brave militias call themselves, breasts of steel, but responsive hearts, capable of shuddering in the face of human suffering, capable of pity and tender feeling, without which is lost the very essence of human greatness.[14]

Deaths in the Republican zone were carefully registered. Those in the Nationalist zone were not. Accordingly, there are thousands of those who just disappeared. Most deaths were not registered and many were simply buried in collective common graves. Nevertheless, the latest figures suggest that the assassinations in the Nationalist zone were between three and four times those committed in Republican territory.

The horrors of the military repression in Seville and the rest of western Andalusia in 1936 were gradually extended to the rest of Spain as Franco captured ever more territory. Considerable cruelty was carried out against women in the name of the Francoist concept of redemption – rape, confiscation of goods, execution because of the politics of a son or husband. An image of Nationalist women as virgins or good mothers, unblemished, passive, submissive pious guardians of the moral order, was propagated through the Church and the Falange's women's organisation, the Sección Femenina. There was a contrasting imagery directed against 'red' women who were depicted both as whores and 'not women'. These accusations, a reflection of the fear provoked in right-wing men by the liberation of women by the Republic, were specifically directed against politically active women like Dolores Ibárruri and Margarita Nelken, and more generally against women on the left. In La Coruña, the civil governor, Francisco Pérez Carballos, was shot on 24 July 1936. His wife, Juana Capdevielle San Martín, was in an advanced state of pregnancy. She was arrested and imprisoned. When she heard the news of her husband's fate, she miscarried. She was released, but some days later she was picked up by a Falangist paramilitary squad, raped and murdered.[15] It was common for the widows and the wives of prisoners to be raped. Many were forced to live in total poverty, and frequently, out of desperation, to sell themselves on the streets. The increase in prostitution benefited Francoist men, who thereby slaked their lust and at the same time reassured themselves that 'red' women were a fount of dirt and corruption.

As each area of Spain was conquered, there began a process of political and social purge. This was often justified in terms of left-wing atrocities, despite the fact that in many places the military coup had succeeded within days, if not hours, and there had been no such atrocities. Hundreds of thousands who escaped the random killing were kept in conditions of extreme degradation in prisons and concentration camps. Torture accounted for large numbers of suicides in prison, and the authorities, feeling cheated by these 'escapes' from their justice, often reacted by executing a relative of the prisoner. Central to the repression was the systematic economic exploitation of both the rural and industrial working classes. Many thousands were forced to work – and die – in inhuman conditions in penal detachments and work battalions. The threat of imprisonment forced millions of workers to accept starvation wages.

The social humiliation and exploitation of the defeated was justified in religious terms as the necessary expiation of their sins, and also in social-Darwinist terms. The defeated were denounced as degenerate, and their children were taken away, and military psychiatrists carried out experiments on women prisoners in search of the 'red gene'. In prisons, massive efforts were made to break not only the bodies of prisoners but also their minds. The man who supervised the process was Major Antonio Vallejo-Nájera, the head of the psychiatric services of the Nationalist army. He set up the Laboratory of Psychological Investigations to engage in psychological studies of prisoners in concentration camps to establish 'the bio-psychic roots of Marxism'. The results of his investigations provided the delighted military high command with 'scientific' arguments to justify their views on the subhuman nature of their adversaries, for which he was promoted to colonel.[16]

A good example of what redemption by Franco really meant could be found in the experience of Catalonia after the region's capture in

January 1939. Occupied Catalonia experienced an all-pervading terror in a period when merely to stay alive was a major achievement for many. Research into daily life for the defeated in rural Catalonia in the 1940s is deeply shocking, revealing an appalling catalogue of hunger and illness, arbitrary repression and fear – fear of arrest, fear of denunciation by a neighbour or by a priest. The entire process was underpinned by the complicity of thousands of people who for many reasons – fear, politics, greed, jealousy – became informers and denounced their neighbours. The sheer misery of life for the defeated in Franco's Spain accounts for the notable rise in the suicide rate, which was often the consequence of economic and sexual extortion by the powerful. Considerable cruelty was visited upon women under the rhetorical Francoist umbrella of 'redemption' – rape, imprisonment as retribution for the behaviour of a son or husband and confiscation of goods. Soldiers billeted on poor families often took advantage of the unprotected women of the household. There was no shortage of priests ready to defend the honour of male parishioners and to denounce their female victims as 'reds'.[17]

Violence against the defeated was not limited to prison, torture and execution, but extended to the psychological humiliation and economic exploitation of the survivors. Franco's policy of economic self-sufficiency, or autarky, contributed to the repression and humiliation of the defeated and to capital accumulation, although its rigidity also delayed eventual growth. Considering himself to be an economist of genius, Franco embraced autarky oblivious to the fact that Spain lacked the technological and industrial base which had made such a policy feasible for the Third Reich. Autarky in Spain brought economic and social disaster. The shortages consequent upon closing Spain to the world provoked the emergence of a black market, the *estraperlo,* which exacerbated the differences between rich and poor. Inevitably, it was those close to the regime who benefited, and the defeated who suffered. State interventionism in every aspect of the planting, harvesting, processing, sale and distribution of wheat was so corrupt that it made fortunes for officials while creating shortages that saw food prices rocket. Access to work and ration cards meant getting identity cards and safe conducts, which involved certificates of 'good behaviour' from local Falangist officials and parish priests. Inevitably, the defeated suffered materially and were further humiliated while the sense of well-being of the victors was enhanced.

The social consequences of autarky and the workings of the black market fitted well with the Caudillo's rhetorical insistence that the defeated could find redemption only through sacrifice. There was a clear link between the repression and the capital accumulation that made possible the economic boom of the 1960s. The destruction of trade unions and the repression of the working class ensured starvation wages that permitted banks, industry and the landholding classes to record spectacular increases in profits. Moreover, the organisation which enabled prisoners to redeem their sentences by work, the Patronato para la Redención de Penas, effectively forced thousands of Republican prisoners into slave labour. The penal detachments provided forced labour for mines, railway building and the reconstruction of the so-called 'devastated regions'. Military penal colonies were set up for long-term public work projects such as the Guadalquivir Canal, dug out over 180 kilometres and twenty years.[18]

The greatest symbol of the exploitation of Republican prisoners was Franco's personal caprice, the gigantic basilica and towering cross of the mausoleum of the Valle de los Caídos. Twenty thousand were employed, and several were killed or badly injured, in its construction, a gigantic mausoleum for Franco and a monument to those who fell in his cause. And the Valle de los Caídos was merely one of several enterprises in which Republican prisoners were forced to work to perpetuate the memory of the Francoist victory in permanent form. The ruined Alcázar of Toledo was rebuilt as a symbol of the Nationalist heroism displayed during its three-month siege. In Madrid, the entrance to the University City, the site of the savage battle for the capital, was marked by a gigantic Arch of Victory. The Valle de los Caídos, however, dwarfed them all. The human cost of forced labour, and the deaths and suffering of the workers and their families, were matched by the fortunes made by the private companies and public enterprises that exploited them.

After years in which the atrocities of Francoism were silenced in the interests of the consolidation of democracy, it is now possible to put together the overall picture of the Spanish holocaust. Mass graves are one of the most horrendous legacies of the way in which Franco established his power. The true extent of the appalling conditions of the Francoist prison regime is only now beginning to emerge. The daily conditions of starvation and torture, and the terror of waiting for the firing squad, are things that have long been familiar through the memoirs of survivors. Yet it is only recently that the stories are being heard about what happened to the women and children forced into

Franco's prisons at the end of the civil war. Many of the thousands of women imprisoned by the regime at the end of the war were young, some with very young children, some pregnant, some raped and made pregnant by their guards. The consequence was a substantial prison population of children who were punished for the perceived crimes of their mothers. Many died in the goods trains into which they were packed to be moved from one prison to another. Many died of hunger, of cold or of disease. In the provincial prison of Zaragoza, forty-two newborn babies died in one week. Many children were mistreated, locked up in dark rooms and forced to eat their own vomit. Thousands were forcibly taken from their mothers and given for adoption or to be brought up in religious establishments. Usually, albeit not always, the removal of a child signified that the mother was about to be shot. Pregnancy did not save a young woman from execution – one judge commenting: 'We cannot wait seven months to execute a woman'.[19]

An important part of the story concerns the Spaniards who were victims of Nazism as a result of actions taken by the Franco regime. For many Republicans, forced into exile by the regime, there was no escape from the Nazi war and terror machine. Thousands of exiled Spaniards found themselves among the millions of non-German forced labourers obliged to work for the German war effort. Nearly 15,000 Spaniards were forced to work in the construction of the Atlantic Wall in 1940/41, while approximately 4,000 were deported to the German-occupied Channel Islands. From October 1941, these 'Spanish communists', as Hitler described them, were forced to build strong-points on the various islands. Only fifty-nine survived.

In addition to those forced to work for the Nazis, there were many Spaniards who ended up in German concentration camps. The most detailed examination of the fate of the Spaniards who ended up in Mauthausen in Austria concluded that of the over 30,000 Spanish refugees who were deported from France to Germany, nearly 15,000 were imprisoned in Nazi camps. Of these by far the largest contingent, around 50 per cent, ended up in Mauthausen (making up the second largest contingent of prisoners there), with other groups transported to Auschwitz, Buchenwald, Dachau and other parts of the Nazi camp system. Around half of the Spaniards that were deported were killed. Although the number of Spanish victims of the Nazi terror machine pales into relative insignificance compared to the total number of victims, it is significant that the Franco regime not only did nothing to prevent Spaniards suffering the fate of other Europeans, but actively encouraged the Germans to detain and deport exiled Republicans.[20]

It was not just exiled leftists who, thanks to the Franco regime, fell into the clutches of the Nazis. A major propaganda operation was mounted to deceive large numbers of Spanish workers, driven by hunger, to work in the Third Reich. Franco owed Hitler a considerable debt, and the needs of the German war industry for labour provided a method of payment. A visit to Germany by Gerardo Salvador Merino of the Falangist union organisation resulted in propaganda about the high standards of living in Germany, high wages and possibilities for saving. No mention was made of the fact that the money earned by Spanish workers would go towards payment of the civil war debt. Within weeks of the German invasion of the Soviet Union, the Blue Division of Falangist volunteers was on its way to fight in Russia. In addition to the combatants, an agreement was made on 21 August 1941 between the Deutsche Arbeitsfront (German Labour Front) and the Falange for 100,000 Spanish workers to be sent to Germany. In fact, after the first batch of 7,000 went, their reports of the conditions made it more difficult for the Falange to find volunteers.

The reconstruction of this repression has been rendered difficult by the one-sided destruction of archival material. This begs the question: if Francoism had so much to be proud of, why were the police, judicial and military archives of the 1940s so ruthlessly purged? In the 1960s and 1970s, the archives of provincial police headquarters, of prisons and of the main Francoist local authority, the civil governors, disappeared. Conveys of trucks removed the 'judicial' records of the repression. As well as the deliberate destruction of archives, there were also 'inadvertent' losses when some town councils sold their archives by the ton as waste paper for recycling.[21] Despite the losses, enough has survived to permit the reconstruction of the 'legal' repression. The efforts of the Association for the Recovery of Historical Memory, both through their archaeological digs and through their encouragement of people to come forward and recount their memories, are contributing to the nationwide reconstruction of the 'unofficial' repression. Finally, it is possible to have a reasonably approximate overview of the human cost of the military coup of 1936. This has been a cumulative process. Since the death of Franco, huge efforts have been made by local historians to recover surviving documentation, more thoroughly in some areas than in others. It is on this basis that serious estimates of the figures involved can now be made.

The responsibility for the crimes committed by the military rebels has to be sought in a huge pyramid of collaborators, built on the eager participation of right-wing army officers, landowners, village Falangists and priests, through to the military commanders of entire provinces, on up to Mola, Queipo de Llano and Franco. At the top of the pyramid was Franco. The 'legal' or 'constitutional' system that his advisors began to create from 1 October 1936 attributed absolute power to him. Accordingly, his personal responsibility was the greatest, but it was not an issue that caused him qualms of conscience. In his death-bed testament, he wrote:

> ...*with all my heart, I pardon all those who declared themselves my enemies, even if I did not regard them as such. I believe, and I wish it to be the case, that I never had any other than those who were the enemies of Spain.*[22]

Clearly, in this regard, he was happy to believe his own propaganda. Following the example of Josef Goebbels, Franco's propagandists presented the repression, the executions, the overflowing prisons, the concentration camps, and the slave labour battalions as the scrupulous yet compassionate justice administered by a wise and benevolent Caudillo. One after another they lined up to sing the praises of the Caudillo's lofty and noble impartiality. Typical of them was the repentant leftist Joaquín Pérez Madrigal, who intoned:

> *Franco, Franco, Franco, is the liberator of the Fatherland, the restorer of Law, the distributor of Justice, he who weighs out wealth, love and all things good. Franco, Franco, Franco, has reconquered Spain, he is the saviour of all Spaniards. Of all Spaniards! Franco is the Victor, the Founder, the bringer of Justice and the Magnanimous one.*[23]

Altogether more specific was the greatest sycophant of them all, Franco's one-time commander and, by the time of the civil war, propaganda chief, General Millán Astray. Under the title 'To bring justice is the most august mission of the Head of State (Franco, the Bringer of Justice)' ('Ejercer la justicia es la más augusta misión del Jefe del Estado (Franco, el Justiciero)'), Millán Astray reverently described how Franco dispensed justice:

Twice when our eyes met, they were damp with tears, not because the sentence had been death, but because the magnanimity of Franco's heart had imposed itself and, in the interests of a justice free of hatred, he had blocked out anything that might stand in the way of serene justice and had commuted the sentence. In all the many cases that the courts had suggested commutation of the death sentence, he agreed. In those cases where he approved the death sentences, the evidence of horrendous crimes against the Fatherland and against fellow man had been so overwhelming that his duty of defending the very existence of the Fatherland and the safety of peaceful citizens meant that there was no possibility of clemency. In all other cases, generosity was the order of the day. No one, other than those who had committed murder and their crime had been fully proven, had been condemned to death.[24]

For his biographer, the newspaper editor Luis de Galinsoga, Franco, 'as well as being the Generalísimo of the forces, Head of State and, for every grief-stricken Spaniard, the distributor of help, the guardian and the shoulder to cry on', was also 'the supreme administrator of justice'.[25] The administration of justice to which the awe-struck Millán Astray and Galinsoga referred was based on Franco's examination of the files on those Republican prisoners who had not been summarily executed as they were captured, or murdered behind the lines by Falangist terror squads, but subjected to cursory courts martial. Usually, large numbers of defendants would have been tried in batches, accused of generalised crimes – most often 'military rebellion', that is to say, having failed to support the uprising of July 1936 – and given little or no opportunity to defend themselves. The death sentences passed merely needed the signature under the word 'enterado' ('acknowledged') of the general commanding the province. As a result of Italian protests, from March 1937 death sentences had to be sent to the Generalísimo's headquarters for confirmation or pardon. The last word on death sentences lay with Franco, not as head of state, but as commander-in-chief of the armed forces. The fact that pleas for clemency were usually examined by Franco after the condemned had already been executed led to the joke by Franco's chaplain that the Generalísimo wrote 'enterrado' ('buried').

In this area, his close confidant was Major, later Lieutenant Colonel, Lorenzo Martínez Fuset of the military juridical corps, who was auditor del Cuartel General del Generalísimo (legal adviser to headquarters). The tiny, balding Martínez Fuset was an amiable individual with a child-like smile, much liked by his fellow-officers. He was utterly devoted to Franco, to the point of adulation.[26] Contrary to the syco-phantic myth of a tireless and merciful Caudillo agonising late into the night over death sentences, the reality was more prosaically brutal. In Salamanca or in Burgos, after lunch or over coffee, or even in a car speeding to the battle front, the Caudillo would flick through and then sign sheaves of them, often without reading the details but nonetheless specifying the most savage form of execution, strangulation by garrote.

Occasionally he would make a point of decreeing 'garrote y prensa' ('garrote reported in the press').[27] Franco did insist on seeing the death sentences personally, but he reached his decisions in the most cursory manner. On the various occasions when Ramón Serrano Suñer was present when Martínez Fuset arrived with folders of death sentences, he would offer to leave. Franco usually told him to stay, saying: 'It's just routine stuff, Ramón'. While the Caudillo and his brother-in-law continued to work, Martínez Fuset would read out the name, age and profession of the condemned. Occasionally, without raising his head from the papers that he was examining with Serrano Suñer, Franco would ask: 'political party?', and then state the manner in which the death sentence was to be implemented, garrote or firing squad. That killing should be so casual would have seemed utterly natural to a man brutalised by the colonial wars in Africa, who had had himself proclaimed responsible only to God and to History.[28]

In mid-July 1939, Count Galeazzo Ciano, Mussolini's son-in-law and the Foreign Minister of Fascist Italy, arrived in Barcelona. He was returning the official visit made to Italy one month earlier by Ramón Serrano Suñer, Franco's brother-in-law. Having been an enthusiastic advocate of Franco's cause during the civil war, he was assured of a warm welcome. However, he was not impressed. Among the enter-tainments provided for such an illustrious guest was a tour of battle grounds. Near one of them, he was shown a group of Republican pris-oners working. Their condition provoked the bitter commentary: 'They are not prisoners of war, they are slaves of war.' Later he was received by Franco in the Palace of Ayete in San Sebastián. On his return to Rome, he described Franco to one of his cronies:

> *That queer fish of a Caudillo, there in his Ayete palace, in the midst of his Moorish Guard, surrounded by mountains of files of prisoners condemned to death. With his work timetable, he will see about three a day, because that fellow enjoys his siestas.*[29]

It certainly seems to be the case that Franco's sleep was never interrupted by any concern for his prisoners nor by any sense of guilt as he
signed death sentences.

*This lecture was delivered on 12 March 2005 at the Imperial War
Museum, London.*

NOTES

1. On the creation of the Valle de los Caídos, see Paul Preston, *Franco: A
   Biography* (London: HarperCollins, 1993), pp.351-2, 679-80; Daniel
   Sueiro, *El Valle de los Caídos: los secretos de la cripta franquista*, 2ª edición
   (Barcelona: Argos Vergara, 1983), passim.
2. The fate of the *Columna de los 8000* is known thanks to the pioneering
   researches of Francisco Espinosa and José María Lama. They published
   their initial findings in 'La columna de los ocho mil' in *Revista Municipal
   de Reina* (Badajoz), agosto, 2001. See also Francisco Espinosa Maestre, *La
   columna de la muerte: el avance del ejército franquista de Sevilla a Badajoz*
   (Barcelona: Editorial Crítica, 2003), pp.195-9; José María Lama, *La
   amargura de la memoria: República y guerra en Zafra (1931-1936)*
   (Badajoz: Diputación de Badajoz, 2004), pp.431-40. Numerous eye-
   witness accounts were gathered in the remarkable documentary film *La
   columna de los ocho mil* made in 2004 by the Asociación Cultural
   Mórrimer of Llerena.
3. Espinosa Maestre, *La columna*, pp.238, 321, 328-430.
4. Felipe Bertrán Güell, *Preparación y desarrollo del alzamiento nacional*
   (Valladolid: Librería Santarén, 1939), p.123.
5. Emilio Mola Vidal, *Obras completas* (Valladolid: Librería Santarén, 1940),
   p.1173.
6. Juan de Iturralde, *La guerra de Franco, los vascos y la Iglesia*, 2 vols. (San
   Sebastián: Publicaciones del Clero Vasco, 1978), I, p.433. See also Hugh
   Thomas, *The Spanish Civil War*, 3rd edition (London: Hamish Hamilton,
   1977), p.260.
7. 'Toledo. «Patio 42»: una fosa común olvidada', *Diario de León*, 27
   September 2004. For more information, see the website of the Asociación
   para la Recuperación de la Memoria Histórica: www.memoriahistorica.org.
8. Emilio Silva and Santiago Macías, *Las fosas de Franco: los republicanos que
   el dictador dejó en las cunetas* (Madrid: Ediciones Temas de Hoy, 2003),
   pp.151-65.
9. Silva and Macías, *Las fosas*, pp.21 et seq.
10. This is a reference to the voluminous writings of Pío Moa Rodríguez and
    César Vidal. For an acute analysis of their political function, see Francisco
    Espinosa Maestre, 'Sobre la matanza de Badajoz y la lucha en torno a la

196   *Looking Back at the Spanish Civil War*

interpretación del pasado' in *El fenómeno revisionista o los fantasmas de la derecha española* (Badajoz: Los Libros del Oeste, 2005), pp.77-100.

11. 'Franco to Faldella, 14 February 1937', reproduced in Ismael Saz Campos and Javier Tusell Gómez (eds.), *Fascistas en España: la intervención italiana en al guerra civil a través de los telegramas de la 'Missione Militare Italiana in Spagna' (15 diciembre 1936-31 marzo 1937)* (Madrid/Rome: Consejo Superior de Investigaciones Científicas, 1981), pp.211-3.

12. Roberto Cantalupo, *Fu la Spagna: ambasciata presso Franco, Febbraio-Aprile 1937* (Milan: Mondadori, 1948), p.231.

13. *La Unión*, 23 July 1936.

14. *El Socialista*, 9 August 1936.

15. Carlos Fernández Santander, *Alzamiento y guerra civil en Galicia (1936-1939)*, 2 vols. (Sada, A Coruña: Ediciós do Castro, 2000), p.86, 94, 156; V Luis Lamela García, *A Coruña, 1936: memoria convulsa de una represión* (Sada, A Coruña: Ediciós do Castro, 2002), pp.35, 50, 106.

16. Ricard Vinyes, Montse Armengou and Ricard Belis, *Los niños perdidos del franquismo* (Barcelona: Plaza y Janés, 2002), pp.31-5; Alberto Reig Tapia, *Ideología e historia: sobre la represión franquista y la guerra civil* (Madrid: Akal, 1984), p.28.

17. Conxita Mir, *Vivir es sobrevivir: justicia, orden y marginación en la Cataluña rural de posguerra* (Lleida: Editorial Milenio, 2000), passim.

18. On the use of slave labour in general, see Isaías Lafuente, *Esclavos por la patria: la explotación de los presos bajo el franquismo* (Madrid: Ediciones Temas de Hoy, 2002). On the use of prisoners in the construction of the Guadalquivir canal, see Gonzalo Acosta Bono, José Luis Gutiérrez Molina, Lola Martínez Macías and Ángel del Río Sánchez, *El canal de los presos (1940-1962): trabajos forzados: de la represión política a la explotación económica* (Barcelona: Editorial Crítica, 2004).

19. On the treatment of women in prison, see Ricard Vinyes, *Irredentas: las presas políticas y sus hijos en las cárceles franquistas* (Madrid: Ediciones Temas de Hoy, 2002); Fernando Hernández Holgado, *Mujeres encarceladas: la prisión de Ventas, de la República al franquismo, 1931-1941* (Madrid: Marcial Pons, 2003) and Tomasa Cuevas Gutiérrez, *Prison of Women: Testimonies of War and Resistance in Spain, 1939-1975* (Albany: State University of New York Press, 1998).

20. On the fate of the Spanish exiles in general, see Antonio Vilanova, *Los olvidados: los exilados españoles en la segunda guerra mundial* (Paris: Ruedo Ibérico, 1969), pp.1-231. The most complete study of the workers sent to Germany by the regime is by José Luis Rodríguez Jiménez, *Los esclavos españoles de Hitler* (Barcelona: Editorial Planeta, 2002). On Spaniards in the German concentration camps, see the standard work by David Wingeate Pike, *Spaniards in the Holocaust: Mauthausen, the Horror on the Danube* (London: Routledge/Cañada Blanch, 2000).

21. On the loss of documentation, see Francisco Espinosa Maestre, *La justicia*

de Queipo: *violencia selectiva y terror fascista en la II División en 1936: Sevilla, Huelva, Cádiz, Córdoba, Málaga y Badajoz* (Sevilla: Centro Andaluz del Libro, 2000), pp.13-22; Silva and Macías, *Las fosas*, pp.119-21.

22. Francisco Franco Bahamonde, *Pensamiento político de Franco*, (ed. Agustín del Río Cisneros), 2 vols. (Madrid: Ediciones del Movimiento, 1975), I, p.xix.

23. Joaquín Pérez Madrigal, *Tipos y sombras de la tragedia: mártires y héroes, bestias y farsantes* (Ávila: Imprenta Católica Sigirano Díaz, 1937), pp.11-2.

24. General José Millán Astray, *Franco, el Caudillo* (Salamanca: M Quero y Simón Editor, 1939), pp.61-2, 214.

25. Luis de Galinsoga and General Franco Salgado, *Centinela de Occidente (Semblanza biográfica de Francisco Franco)* (Barcelona: Editorial AHR, 1956), p.302.

26. Eugenio Vegas Latapié, *Los caminos del desengaño: memorias políticas (II) 1936-1938* (Madrid: Tebas, 1987), pp.88-9.

27. Herbert Rutledge Southworth, *Antifalange: estudio crítico de 'Falange en la guerra de España' de Maximiano García Venero* (Paris: Ruedo Ibérico, 1967), p.202; Ramón Garriga, *La España de Franco: las relaciones con Hitler*, 2ª edición (Puebla: Editorial Cajica, 1970), pp.7-8; Ramón Garriga, *Los validos de Franco* (Barcelona: Editorial Planeta, 1981), pp.42-3, 72-3.

28. Article 47 of the statutes of FET y de las JONS (the reconstituted Falange party created by Franco to merge the various political groups supporting the 1936 rebellion), which was published in August 1937, states: 'El Jefe Nacional de Falange Española Tradicionalista y de las JONS, Supremo Caudillo del Movimiento, personifica todos los Valores y todos los Honores del mismo. Como Autor de la Era Histórica donde España adquiere las posibilidades de realizar su destino y con él los anhelos del Movimiento, el Jefe asume, en su entera plenitud, la mas absoluta autoridad. El Jefe responde ante Dios y ante la Historia.'

29. Duilio Susmel, *Vita sbagliata di Galeazzo Ciano* (Milano: Aldo Palazzi Editore, 1962), p.158.

The Spanish Civil War: History and Memory

Julián Casanova

'The elections held last Sunday clearly show me that I do not have the love of my people today,' wrote King Alfonso XIII in a farewell note to the Spanish people, before leaving the royal palace on the night of Tuesday 14 April 1931. So began the Second Spanish Republic, with street celebrations and a festive atmosphere, in which revolutionary hopes were combined with hunger for reform.

The Republic had vast problems in consolidating itself and had to confront strong challenges from above and below. It had two years of relative stability, followed by a further two years of political uncertainty, and a final few months of disturbance and insurrection. The first challenges, which were the most visible as they usually ended up as confrontations with the police, came from below, initially as social protests and later as insurrections from anarchists and socialists. However, the coup de grâce, the challenge that finally overthrew the Republic through force of arms, came from above and from within, that is to say, from the military command and the powerful ruling classes that had never tolerated it.

HISTORY

In July 1936 a large section of the Spanish army took up arms against the Republican regime. What was planned was an uprising, with all the violence necessary, and a quick victory. However, things did not turn out that way and the result of this uprising was a long civil war, lasting nearly three years.

Divisions in the army and police forces thwarted the victory of the military rebellion, as well as the achievement of its main objective: the rapid seizure of power. But by undermining the Republican government's

'The Nationalists', poster by Juan Antonio Morales for the Republic's Ministry of Propaganda in 1936.

power to keep order, this coup d'état transformed itself into open violence, such as had never been seen before, by the groups that supported it and those that opposed it. Thus began the civil war.

The Spanish Civil War is notorious for the dehumanisation of the adversary, for the terrible violence it generated. Lawless, arbitrary shootings and massacres eliminated enemies, real or presumed, on both sides. The Francoist policy of extermination of the left was fervently approved by a large number of conservative people. Meanwhile, where the army coup failed, many on the left saw this as the hour of revolution and of final judgement against the rich, and class hatred and vengeance spread like wildfire. The Church suffered a cruel and violent persecution: almost 7,000 members of the clergy were murdered.

The military created, from the first moment of the coup, a climate of terror in whcih almost 100,000 people were murdered during the civil war. More than 60,000 people were murdered on the other side. And 50,000 people were killed in the uncivil peace that followed the civil war. At the end of the war, in 1939, half a million people languished in prisons and concentration camps.

There were various conflicts involved in the Spanish Civil War. It was a war of classes, between different conceptions of the social order, between Catholicism and anti-clericalism, and between different conceptions about nation, and the ideas and creeds that then dominated the international scene. In the civil war there crystallised the worldwide battles between landowners and workers, Church and state, obscurantism and modernisation, that were also being fought out elsewhere between communism and fascism, while the debilitated democracies looked on.

However, a civil war accompanied by a social revolution as intense as the Spanish one did not take place anywhere else during the interwar years. The anarchists were to live their golden age, although short-lived. They spread a complex network of revolutionary committees all over Republican Spain. They collectivised land and factories. They created militias. They took part in the government of Catalonia and the Republic. And they dreamed of a world without class, or political parties, or states.

Those who survived the harsh repression after the defeat in 1939 went to their graves remembering a revolution that was of the people, that saw collectivisation, and that had no masters or authority, a revolution that was unique in the history of humanity. Dozens of accounts, documentaries, books, novels and films have kept the flame burning in spite of the efforts of the detractors on the Republican and Francoist sides, who from the beginning accused the CNT-FAI of every crime imaginable. This is the double face of anarchism: the dark face, the violence; and the happy face, the egalitarian dream.

From the outset, the Church and most Catholics placed all their resources – and there were a good many of them – at the disposal of the insurgent military. The military did not have to ask the Church for its support: it offered it gladly. Nor did the Church have to take its time in deciding. Both parties were aware of the benefit of the role played by the religious element, the military because they wanted order, the Church because it was defending the faith.

The international situation was not conducive to peace and this affected the war, in its origin an internal conflict. International support on both sides was vital in keeping the war going in the first few months.

When the war began, the democratic powers were attempting to 'appease' the fascists, especially the German Nazis. So the Spanish Republic had to wage war against an army favoured by the international situation. Dictatorships under the rule of a single man and a single party had been substituted for democracy in many countries; and, except in Russia, all these parties were of the right. Six of the continent's democracies were invaded by the Nazis the year after the civil war ended. Spain, then, was no exception in a continent ruled by the authoritarian right. But this cannot excuse a wide sector of Spanish society, the political and union leaders, soldiers and churchmen, who did nothing to develop a civil culture of respect for the law, for electoral results, for freedom of expression and association and for civil rights.

At the end of August 1936, all the twenty-seven European states except Switzerland, whose constitution decreed its neutrality, had officially subscribed to the Non-Intervention Agreement. The monitoring of this agreement was conducted by a Non-Intervention Committee, set up in London on 9 September 1936 under the chairmanship of the Conservative Lord Plymouth, the Parliamentary Under-Secretary to the Foreign Office, and a Non-Intervention Subcommittee made up of representatives from the states bordering Spain and the major arms producers, including Germany, France, Great Britain and the Soviet Union.

In practice, non-intervention was a complete farce, as it was termed by people at the time, who saw that it put the Republic at a disadvantage with the military rebels. This policy put a legal government and a group of military rebels on the same footing. The war was not a Spanish domestic matter. It became internationalised, thereby increasing the brutality and destruction. This was because Spanish territory became a testing ground for new weaponry that was being developed during the rearmament years prior to the great war that was on the horizon. Indeed, the Spanish Civil War ended on 1 April 1939 and the Second World War broke out five months later.

Tens of thousands of foreigners fought in the Spanish Civil War. It was, in fact, a European civil war, with the tacit sanction of the British and French governments. A little over 100,000 fought on Franco's side: 78,000 Italians, 19,000 Germans, 10,000 Portuguese, plus more than 1,000 volunteers from other countries, not counting the 70,000 Moroccans who made up the 'native regulars'. On the Republican side, figures given by Rémi Skoutelsky show that there were nearly 35,000 volunteers in the International Brigades, and 2,000 Soviets, of whom 600 were non-combatant advisors. Contrary to the myth of the communist and revolutionary threat, what in fact hit Spain through open military intervention was fascism.

In the closing years of Franco's dictatorship, certain pro-Franco military historians, such as Ramón and Jesús Salas Larrazábal and Ricardo de la Cierva, attempted to show that the Republicans and the military rebels had received the same amount of material, that foreign participation was not enough to tip the balance in favour of Franco, and that the idea that non-intervention had harmed the Republicans was made up by the communists and the international left who sympathised with the Republic. This is also an argument raised now by neo-revisionism and neo-Francoism in Spain.

However, the foremost experts of the financing of the war and its international dimension, from Ángel Viñas to Martín Aceña, and including Gerald Howson and Enrique Moradiellos, have pointed out the imbalance in favour of the Nationalist cause not only in terms of war materials but also in terms of logistic, diplomatic and financial aid. The Republic had money from the sale of gold reserves at its disposal, an amount very similar to that provided to Franco in foreign aid, but the problem lay in the difficulties it had in legally purchasing arms from democratic countries. As Howson has pointed out, gold and foreign currency were not enough, because the embargo and restrictions imposed by the Non-Intervention Agreement forced successive governments under José Giral, Francisco Largo Caballero and Juan Negrín to fall into the clutches of arms dealers who demanded exorbitant prices and commissions, and blackmailed politicians and civil servants. As a result, the Republic often had to buy overpriced and obsolete equipment, disarmed planes, or bombers that had no bomb bays. Russia, Poland and other countries were continually swindling the Republic.

The international intervention of Nazi Germany and Fascist Italy, and the retraction, for the most part, of the Western democracies, determined in a major, if not decisive, way the evolution and duration of the conflict and its end result.

Many Spaniards saw the war as a horror right from the start; others felt they were in the wrong zone and tried to escape. Some Republican figures did not take sides in the war, forming a 'third Spain'. But millions of people were forced to take sides, though some got their hands dirtier than others. There is no simple answer to the question of why such barbarity broke out. Spain began the 1930s with a Republic and ended the decade under a right-wing, authoritarian dictatorship. Whatever we may say of the violence that preceded the civil war, it is clear that in Spanish history there is a before and after to the coup d'état of July 1936. And then, for at least two decades after 1939, there was no attempt at positive reconstruction, as occurred in the countries of western Europe after 1945.

The two sides in the war had such different ideas of how to organise the state and society, and were so committed to their aims, that settlement was difficult. Nor did the international scene afford much room for negotiation. The new dictatorships had to face movements of mass opposition, and to control them required new instruments of terror. It was no longer enough to prohibit political parties, censor the press or deny individual rights. Murder, torture and concentration camps were the brutal result.

Why did the military rebels win the war? They had the best-trained troops in the Spanish army, economic power and the Catholic Church on their side and, with them, international sympathy blew their way. This was Spain as portrayed in the poster by Juan Antonio Morales, 'Los Nacionales', published by the Republican government's Under-Secretary for Propaganda: a general, a bishop and a capitalist with a swastika, a vulture and colonial troops in the background. They could not lose.

Thus there is no simple answer as to why the climate of euphoria and hope in 1931 was transformed into the cruel, all-destructive war of 1936. The Republic lasted for eight years, five in peace and three at war, and interpreting them still arouses passionate opinions rather than historical debate.

MEMORY

The history of the civil war and the dictatorship is no longer the exclusive preserve of historians, and there are now hundreds of people who wish to address this past in political terms and, in the case of the heirs of the victims of Francoism, ethical terms. Ditches have begun to be opened in search of the remains of murder victims who were never registered, and there have been some magnificent documentaries that unearth aspects of this past that have been concealed until now. At least 20,000 people murdered by the military and the fascists in the first months of the war were never registered, and their families – grandchildren rather than children – want to know what happened, and to recover their bones.

However, this examination of the sedition committed by the military and by Francoism has also brought about a reaction from well-known journalists, apologists for Francoism, and amateur historians who have resurrected the essential arguments of Francoist spin: it was the left, with its violence and hate, that started the civil war, and what the right and the principled did, with the military coup in 1936, was in response to 'Popular Front terror'. Thus, all the complex, painstaking explanations of historians were now boiled down to two issues: who started the civil war and who carried out the most cold-blooded killings? Once again, propaganda replaced historical analysis.

There is now a new social dimension for history, with testimony playing the main role. But the most significant events of the civil war and the dictatorship had already been investigated previously, and the most important questions have now been answered. This is the result of painstaking work by dozens of historians who, over the past forty years, have been conducting constant research in archives, press repositories and libraries. Without these documents and books, thousands and thousands of them, we would know very little about this period.

This is why it is so important to compile and preserve all the documents and testimonies of this past. The struggle for information and truth, and the refusal to forget, must be, as has been the case in recent years, the distinguishing marks of our democracy. But, as well as publicising the horror that the war and the dictatorship generated, and making reparation to the victims that have been forgotten for so long, we must make archives, museums and educational programmes in schools and universities the three basic hubs of public memory policy. Beyond the testimonial and dramatic recall of those who suffered political violence, future generations will learn history through the documents and photographic and audiovisual material that we manage to preserve and hand down to them. This is the responsibility of the politicians of the PSOE socialist party who govern Spain now, and of those in the opposition, the right, who refuse to administer this past of death and terror. Because with no archives, there is no history.

Franco's victory was also a victory for Hitler and Mussolini, and the Republic's defeat a defeat for the democracies. Now, seventy years later, we have to teach the young that violence and intransigence are the worst legacy of that period. Only dialogue, political debate, democracy and freedom can heal the wounds of the past and help to create a better present.

This lecture was delivered on 3 March 2007 at the Imperial War Museum, London.

About the contributors

Richard Baxell is the author of *British Volunteers in the Spanish Civil War: The British Battalion in the International Brigades, 1936-1939* (2004, updated in 2007). He studied history as an undergraduate at Middlesex University, before taking an MA at the Institute of Historical Research and a PhD at the London School of Economics and Political Science. A trustee of the International Brigade Memorial Trust, he is currently writing a book on British anti-fascist fighters from 1932 to 1945.

Julián Casanova is Professor of Contemporary History at the University of Zaragoza. Among his books are *Anarchism, the Republic and Civil War in Spain: 1931-1939* (2005); *La Iglesia de Franco* (2001); and *República y guerra civil* (2007). He has been Hans Speier Visiting Professor at the New School University, New York and Visiting Professor at Facultad Latinoamericana de Ciencias Sociales, Quito, Ecuador, and at the Universidad Industrial de Santander, Bucaramanga, Colombia.

Helen Graham is Professor of Modern European History at Royal Holloway, University of London. She has published extensively on topics related to Spain in the 1930s and 1940s, including the civil war, the Popular Front, women in the Republic and Franco's post-war penal policy. Her books include *Socialism and War: The Spanish Socialist Party in Power and Crisis 1936-1939* (1991); *Spanish Cultural Studies: An Introduction* (with Jo Labanyi) (1995); *The Spanish Republic at War 1936-1939* (2002); and *The Spanish Civil War: A Very Short Introduction* (2005).

Angela Jackson is the author of *British Women and the Spanish Civil War*, a doctoral thesis first published in 2002 and updated in 2009 for a paperback edition. She lives in Catalonia, where much of her research has focused on the interactions between International Brigaders and local people. Her books include *Beyond the Battlefield:*

'Democratic Spain needs you. Join the anti-fascist people's militias!'

Testimony, Memory and Remembrance of a Cave Hospital in the Spanish Civil War (2005); a novel, *Warm Earth* (2007); and *At the Margins of Mayhem: Prologue and Epilogue to the Last Great Battle of the Spanish Civil War* (2008). As president of the association No Jubilem La Memòria, she works to promote research and education on the subject of the civil war in the Priorat region of Catalonia.

Enrique Moradiellos's many books include a definitive work on the contribution of Great Britain to the defeat of the Spanish Republic, *La perfidia de Albión: el gobierno británico y la guerra civil española*, which was published in 1996. Among the other books are *El reñidero de Europa: las dimensiones internacionales de la guerra civil española* (2001); *1936: los mitos de la guerra civil* (2004); *Franco frente a Churchill* (2005); and *Negrín* (2006). He has lectured at Madrid's Complutense University and at Queen Mary and Westfield College, London University, and is currently Professor of History at the University of Extremadura in Caceres.

Paul Preston is Príncipe de Asturias Professor of Spanish History at the London School of Economics and Political Science, where he is also the Director of the Cañada Blanch Centre. He is the author of many books on Spain and the Spanish Civil War, including the biographies *Franco: A Biography* (1993); and *Juan Carlos: A People's King* (2004); as well as *¡Comrades! Portraits from the Spanish Civil War* (1999); *Doves of War: Four Women of Spain* (2002); *The Spanish Civil War: Reaction, Revolution and Revenge* (2006); and *We Saw Spain Die: Foreign Correspondents in the Spanish Civil War* (2008). He is a Fellow of the British Academy and in 2000 was appointed CBE. In 2007 he was awarded Spain's highest civilian honour, the Gran Cruz de la Orden de Isabel la Católica.

Francisco J Romero Salvadó is a senior lecturer at Bristol University, where he teaches modern Spanish history and politics. He has written widely about the social and political origins of the Spanish Civil War and its aftermath in books such as *Twentieth Century Spain: Politics and Society, 1898-1998* (1999), *Spain, 1914-1918: Between War and Revolution* (1999); *The Spanish Civil War: Origins, Course and Outcomes* (2005); and *Revolution, Social Conflict and Reaction in Spain, 1916-1923* (2008). He is currently working on a historical dictionary of the Spanish Civil War.

Ángel Viñas is Professor of Political Economy at Madrid's Complutense University. Among the books he has written is a three-volume history of the Spanish Republic at war: *La soledad de la República: el abandono de las democracias y el viraje hacia la Unión Soviética* (2006); *El escudo de la República: el oro de España, la apuesta soviética y los hechos de mayo de 1937* (2007); and *El honor de la República: entre el acoso fascista, la hostilidad británica y la política de Stalin* (2008). In addition, he has had a career as a diplomat, having served as the European Community's ambassador to the United Nations from 1992 to 1996, as well as holding diplomatic posts for the Spanish government in Washington, Bonn and Brussels. He was also a director at the European Commission for almost fifteen years.

Jim Jump is a freelance journalist based in London. He is the son of a British International Brigader and a Spanish Republican refugee and is a trustee of the International Brigade Memorial Trust and editor of its newsletter. He edited *Poems from Spain: British and Irish International Brigaders on the Spanish Civil War* (2006) and co-edited a Spanish anthology of poems by International Brigaders from the British Isles, *Hablando de leyendas: Poemas para España* (2009). He also edited a bilingual collection of poems by his father, James R Jump, *Poems of War and Peace/Poemas de guerra y de paz* (2007).

This memorial in Sartaguda lists the names of more than 2,700 Republican supporters who were executed in Navarra following the military uprising in 1936.

Select index of names and places

Abrahams, Basil 90n
Aceña, Martín 203
Aitken, George 73, 77, 78, 85, 89n, 91n
Alba, Duke of 93, 106
Albacete 9, 67, 72, 161, 165, 169
Alexander, Bill 163-7, 171, 172, 174n, 175n
Alfonso XIII, King 199
Almodóvar, Pedro 28n
Álvarez, Manuel 118
Andalusia 160, 182, 186
Andreev, Andrei Andreevich 140
Angus, John 167
Antonov-Ovseyenko, Vladimir 136
Aragón 27n, 36, 40, 174n
Aranjuez 34
Asturias 26n, 182
Auden, WH 173
Auschwitz 190
Azaña, Manuel 47, 51-2, 53, 57
Azcárate, Pablo de 145

Babia 28n
Badajoz 26n, 27n, 179-80, 184-5

Baldwin, Stanley 57, 99
Barayón, Amparo 9, 13-15, 16-18, 20, 21, 26, 27n
Barcelona 9, 37, 52, 67, 98, 105, 136, 157, 163, 170, 174n, 182, 194
Barcia, Augusto 132
Basque Country 54, 184
Bates, Winifred 117, 118, 120
Batum 137
Bauer, Otto 48-9
Baxell, Richard 9
Beevor, Anthony 152n, 154n
Belsize Park 40
Berardis, Vincenzo 132
Berlin 16, 103, 138, 153n
Berzin, Jan 135
Bethune, Norman 35
Bilbao 118
Blackburn 7, 33
Bloomfield, Tommy 68
Blum, Léon 55, 56, 57, 63n, 100
Blumel, André 57
Bolloten, Burnett 133
Bonnet, Georges 59
Brennan, Gerald 47
Briskey, Bill 69

Brome, Vincent 71
Brunete (inc. battle) 35-6, 73, 86, 170
Buchanan, Tom 171
Buchenwald 190
Burdock, Rosie 159
Burgos 27n, 194
Burleigh, George 35

Cabanellas, Miguel 53
Cádiz 179
Calvo Sotelo, José 47
Camberwell 40
Canary Islands 181
Cantalupo, Roberto 184
Capdevielle San Martín, Juana 186-7
Carr, EH 171
Casa de Campo 35
Casanova, Julián 9
Caserta 42
Castro del Río 185
Castuera 179, 182
Catalonia 40, 54, 113, 114, 122, 123, 125, 182, 187-8, 201
Cercas, Javier 29n
Ceuta 181
Chamberlain, Neville 59, 100, 103-5
Channel Islands 190
Charlesworth, Albert 77, 89n
Chinchón 34, 75, 78
Chubar, Vlas 136
Chubin, Pyotr A 134, 135, 136, 147
Ciano, Count Galeazzo 58, 194

Cierva, Ricardo de la 203
Clancy, George 88n
Clarke, Tom 71
Cochrane, Paddy 8c
Cockburn, Claud 82
Codovilla, Victorio 141
Colman, Julius 'Jud' 69, 80, 82
Concud 181
Constança 137
Conway, Chris 'Kit' 72
Cooney, Bob 92n
Copeman, Fred 71, 82-3, 84-5, 86, 89n, 91n
Corbera d'Ebre 122
Córdoba (Cordova) 73
Courtauld, Simon 164, 171, 173n, 174n
Crome, Len (Lazar Krom) 7, 11, 31-43, 44n, 111
Crome, Peter 7, 42
Crook, David 67, 74, 75
Cuenca 27n
Cunningham, Jock 69, 78-9, 91n, 166

Dachau 190
Daladier, Edouard 59
Darton, Patience (see Edney, Patience)
de Maio, Tony 161
Delbos, Yvon 133
Delgado, José 50
Díaz Fernández, Carlos G 38, 40
Dickenson, Ted 78
Dimitrov, Georgi 133-4, 140, 149

Dobson, Harry 118
Dollfuss, Engelbert 50
Domanski, Mieczyslaw (see Dubois)
Dover 34
Doyle, Bob 8c, 9, 169
Dubois (Mieczyslaw Domanski) 35, 36
Dumont, René 39
Dundee 71
Dunlop, John 163, 167, 174n
Durruti, Buenaventura 9
Dvinsk (Daugavpils) 31

Eaude, Michael 164, 171, 174n
Ebro (inc. battle) 9, 37, 38, 40, 111, 112c, 115-17, 124, 167, 168, 170, 172
Eden, Sir Anthony 57, 99, 100, 103-5
Edinburgh 31
Edney, Patience 111, 114
Edwards, Jack 8c, 9
El Bierzo 28n
El Escorial 35
Espinosa Maestre, Francisco 180

Feiwel, Penny 8c, 9, 123
Fernández, Aurora 117
Fidalgo, Pilar 17-18, 25
Figueras 67, 160, 165-6, 167, 169
Fleming, Alexander 42
Fletcher, George 166, 174n
Franco, Francisco 7, 10, 11, 13, 19, 21-2, 25, 33, 34, 35, 41, 45, 47, 50, 52, 53-4, 55, 56, 57, 58, 59, 74, 76, 79, 93, 95, 96, 98, 99, 100, 101, 102, 103-5, 106-7, 111, 113, 114, 119, 122, 131, 132, 134, 136, 138, 141, 142, 143, 152n, 157, 171, 177, 181, 182, 183-4, 186, 187-90, 191-5, 197n, 203, 206
Fry, Harold 73, 77-8
Fullarton, Steve 123, 124
Fyrth, Jim 120

Gal (Gallicz), Colonel 78, 80, 83
Galicia 27n, 181
Galinsoga, Luis de 193
Gallagher, Willie 168
Gandesa 38
Garzón, Baltasar 183
George VI, King 41
Gibraltar (inc. Strait of) 55, 56, 96, 99, 134
Gijón 182
Gil Robles, José María 47, 49-50
Gilbert, Tony 68, 71, 76, 92n
Giral, José 129, 132, 136, 137, 138, 204
Gloucestershire 157
Goebbels, Josef 192
Goicoechea, Antonio 49
Gorbachev, Mikhail 42
Goriev, Vladimir 135, 138, 142
Graham, Frank 83
Graham, Helen 9, 65

Gramsci, Antonio 53
Grant, Terry 174n
Green, Nan 37, 38, 115, 118, 119, 120
Gregory, Walter 68, 81
Grove, Valerie 164, 167, 172, 175n
Guadalajara (inc. battle) 27n, 35, 170
Guadarrama 177
Gurney, Jason 68, 71, 73, 76, 89n

Hailsham, Lord 106
Haldane, JBS 84
Halifax, Lord 105, 106
Hankey, Sir Maurice 98-9
Hemingway, Ernest 35, 84, 160
Hidalgo, Diego 54
Hitler, Adolf 10, 33, 47, 49, 50, 56, 98, 99, 102, 103, 131, 140, 141, 143, 144-5, 146, 149, 190-1, 206
Hodson, Ada 112c, 118
Hopkins, James 72
Howson, Gerald 140, 203
Huelva 179, 185
Huerta, J 46c
Hüttner, Helen 41, 43
Hüttner, Jonny 43
Hyndman, Tony 73

Ibárruri, Dolores (La Pasionaria) 115, 186
Islington 40

Jackson, Angela 9
Jacobsen, Fernanda 34-5
Jarama (river, valley and battle) 9, 34, 35, 65, 71, 74-87, 90n, 91n, 167, 170
Jiménez de Asúa, Luis 63n, 131
Jolly, Douglas 38
Jones, Jack 8c, 9
Jones, John 'Bosco' 79

Kaganovich, Lazar 136, 138, 140, 147, 148
Kalmanovitch, Jacob Maurice 'Hans' 37, 43n
Kamenev, Lev 147
Kenton, Lou 8c
Kerensky, Alexander 97
Kerrigan, Peter 66c, 72-3, 80, 168, 169
Koltsov, Mikhail 132, 137
Kosor 44n
Krestinsky, Nikolai 136-7, 139
Krivitsky, Walter 133, 139-40, 153n
Krom, Helena 42
Krom, Jacob (Jascha) 33, 42
Krom, Sima 42

La Bisbal de Falset 38, 111-14, 118, 119. 121, 122, 124, 125-6
La Coruña 186
La Mancha 68
La Pasionaria (see Ibárruri, Dolores)
La Rioja 178c

Lance, Christopher 34-5
Landis, Arthur 167
Lardero 178c
Largo Caballero, Francisco 47, 138, 141, 142, 145, 150, 168, 204
Lee, Kathy 164, 170
Lee, Laurie 7, 9, 157-73, 175n
Leeson, George 70, 89n
León 28n, 182
Lesser, Sam 8c, 9, 123
Levy, Bert 89n
Libava 31
Limerick 88n
Linden, Maurice 35
Litvinov, Maxim 138, 144-5
Llerena 180
London 7, 8c, 10, 33, 40, 42, 57, 67, 68, 69, 70, 74, 79, 93, 95, 99, 100, 101, 106, 109n, 114, 121, 131, 137, 153n, 155n, 159, 161, 169, 174n
Lopera 69
Lorca, Frederico García 17
Los Pozos de Caudé 181-2
Loughborough 120

Macartney, Wilf 66c, 69, 72-3, 88n
Macaulay Stevenson, Sir Daniel 33
McCartney, Terry 174n
McCrae, Jock 75
McDade, Alec 86
MacFarquhar, Roderick 34-5

McLean, Tony 169-70, 171
McLoughlin, Barry 164, 169
Macías Pérez, Santiago 182
Madrid 16, 27n, 34-5, 37, 50, 53, 56, 67, 69, 74-5, 78, 79, 80, 85, 87, 90n, 98, 101, 102, 109n, 130c, 132, 135-6, 137, 138, 141, 142, 161, 162, 177, 189
Madrigueras 66c, 67-8, 72, 73-4, 76, 82
Maes, Magdalena 13, 21
Maisky, Ivan 41, 146
Málaga 184
Manning, Leah 111, 118, 120
Manzanares 75
Margesson, David 101
Marsé, Juan 24, 25
Martínez Fuset, Lorenzo 193-4
Marty, André 37-8, 39, 40
Masip, Francesc 121
Masip, Teresina 114, 118, 121
Masip i Gorgori, Enric 126
Mauthausen 190
Melilla 181
Mérida 179
Meyer, Alfred 42
Miaja, General 75
Millán Astray, José 192-3
Mir, Conxita 23
Moa Rodríguez, Pío 60n, 195n
Mola, Emilio 47, 50, 51, 53, 180, 185, 192
Molotov, Vyacheslav 140, 145, 148
Monks, Joe 88n

Monte Cassino 41
Moradiellos, Enrique 57, 203
Morales, Juan Antonio 200c, 204
Morata de Tajuña 83
Morgan, Charles 80
Morón 185
Moscow 40, 69, 131, 133, 136,
    137, 138, 141, 143, 146,
    147, 151, 164, 168, 169
Moskvin, Mikhail Abramovich
    140
Munich (agreement) 106, 107
Mussolini, Benito 10, 47, 49,
    50, 56, 58, 98, 99, 102,
    103-4, 105, 106, 111, 131,
    132, 140, 143, 146, 149,
    152n, 184, 194, 206

Naples 42
Nash, Max 172
Nathan, George 72, 88n
Navarra 180, 181, 212c
Negrín, Juan 57, 59, 150-1,
    155n, 204
Nelken, Margarita 186
Newcastle upon Tyne 83
Newcomb, Professor 42
Nicholas II, Tsar 31
Nikonov 135, 136
Nottingham 68, 174n
Nyon 58

O'Callaghan, George 88n
Old Castile 13
Oldham 77
Ondaatje, Michael 15, 26

Orkjonikize, Grigoriy 136
Orwell, George 157
Overton, Bert 69, 77-8
Oviedo 182

Pamplona 180
Pàndols 122
Paris 16, 59, 67, 105, 110n,
    129, 131-2, 137, 138, 155n
Parkhurst 69, 72
Payart, Jean 133
Payne, Stanley G 60-1n, 153n
Perelló, Josep 114, 121
Pérez Carballos, Francisco 186-7
Pérez Madrigal, Joaquín 192
Petrovic, Grujo 44n
Phipps, Sir Eric 59
Pingarrón Heights 75, 80
Pinochet, Augusto 15, 183
Plymouth, Lord 146, 202
Pollitt, Harry 33, 83-4, 91n,
    162, 166-7
Pons, Silvio 149
Poole-Burley, James (see Grant,
    Terry)
Powell, Margaret 81
Prague 137
Preston, Paul 9, 10, 11, 45, 49,
    120
Priaranza del Bierzo 182
Prieto, Indalecio 47, 185-6
Primo de Rivera, José Antonio
    51, 60n
Primo de Rivera, Miguel 48
Puente Genil 185
Pyrenees 106, 160, 161, 168

Queipo de Llano, Gonzalo 179, 185, 192
Quinto (battle) 36
Quisling, Vidkun 126n

Radosh, Ronald 152n, 153n
Renton, Donald 89n
Riccione 42
Richards, EC 96
Rimini 42
Ríos, Fernando de los 131-2
Roberts, Geoffrey 146
Rodríguez, Guillermo 40
Rogers, Byron 160
Rome 109n, 138, 153n, 194
Rosenberg, Marcel I 136, 138, 151, 154n
Ross, Rosaleen 123
Rubio Dalmati, Alejandro 178c
Rust, Bill 67, 89n, 161, 162, 163, 169, 170, 174n, 175n
Ryan, Frank 66c, 72, 78-9, 82, 88, 174n
Rybalkin, Yurii 131, 142, 152n

Sainz Rodríguez, Pedro 107
Salamanca 18, 170, 194
Salas Larrazábal, Jesús & Ramón 203
Salazar, Antonio de Oliveira 100
Salvador Merino, Gerardo 191
San Martín de la Vega 80
San Sebastián 194
Sanjurjo, José 49, 53
Sanmartí Falguera, Enrique 37-8, 40

Santander 35
Sartaguda 212c
Saxton, Reginald (Reggie) 9, 117, 123, 124
Saz, Ismael 49
Scannell, Vernon 164, 172
Scott-Ellis, Priscilla 34
Sender, Ramón 13, 16, 17
Sender, Ramón (Barayón) 13, 17, 21, 26
Serrano Suñer, Ramón 194
Seville 171, 177, 179, 185-6
Silva-Barrera, Emilio 182-3
Silva-Faba, Emilio 182
Simon, Lieutenant-Colonel 147
Skoutelsky, Rémi 203
Slad 159
Slutsky, Abram 139-40
Smyth, Denis 145
Sochi 137, 142, 146, 147, 149
Spender, Stephen 73
Springhall, Dave 66c, 69, 73
Stalin, Joseph 7, 47, 129, 133, 136-40, 142-51, 154n
Stern, Jan 42
Stratton, Harry 68, 75
Stroud 169
Suicide Hill 76, 77, 79
Sweeney, John 160
Swierczewski, Karol (see Walter, General)
Szurek, Aleksander 36

Tarazona de la Mancha 162, 165, 167, 168, 169, 171
Teruel (inc. battle) 162, 163,

165, 166, 167, 170-1, 174n, 181
Thomas, Fred 68, 69
Thomas, Hugh 79
Thomas, Sadie 172
Togliatti, Palmiro 149
Toledo 139, 142, 181, 189
Tolstoy, Leo 172
Tooting 42
Triana 185
Tunnah, John 85, 86
Tuñón de Lara, Manuel 47

University City (Madrid) 69, 189
Uritsky, Semyon Petrovich 135, 139
Urmston, Lillian 120
Utrera 185

Valencia 35, 67, 74, 75, 79, 89n, 94c, 133, 136
Valencia del Ventoso 179
Valladolid 181
Valle de Cuelgamuros 177
Valle de los Caídos (Valley of the Fallen) 122, 177, 189
Vallejo-Nájera, Antonio 187
Vansittart, Sir Robert 107

Varela, José Enrique 53, 74
Vidal, Cesár 60n, 195n
Videla Jorge Rafaél 15
Vienna 50, 164
Viñas, Ángel 9, 57, 203
Vorochilov, Marshall 135, 136, 140, 142, 143, 145, 148, 154n

Walter, General (Karol Swierczewski) 35-6, 39-40
West, Charles 89n
West, Frank 166, 174n
Wild, Sam 75-6, 86, 166, 174n
Williams, Bert 91n
Wintringham, Tom 66c, 69, 70, 71, 73, 77-8, 79, 90n, 166
Winzer (Vintser) I 135
Wolff, Milton 172

Yagoda, Genrikh 140, 148
Yezhov, Nikolai I 148
Yolk 135, 136

Zagier, David 122-3
Zamora 13, 15, 16-17, 181
Zaragoza 53, 190
Zinoviev, Grigory 147